Beyond Karel J Robot

A Gentle Introduction to the Art of Object-Oriented Programming in Java

Volume 2

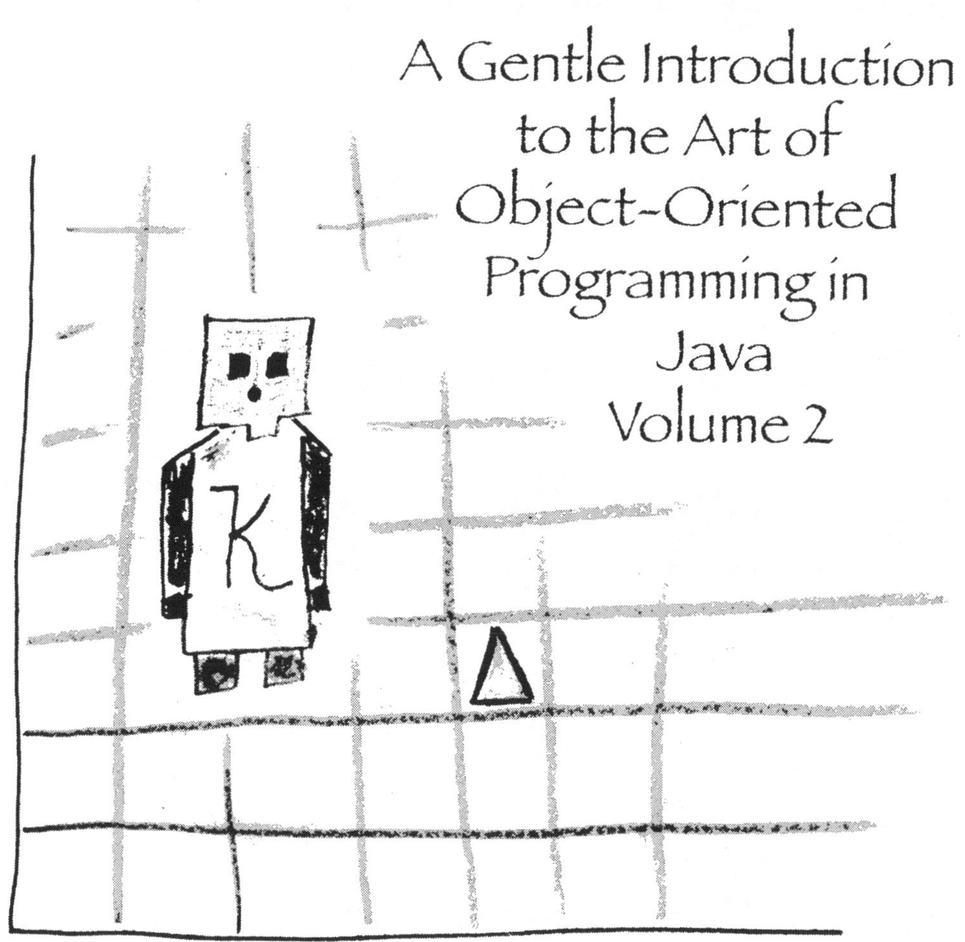

Joseph Bergin

Published by Joseph Bergin, Software Tools
February 1, 2008
Second Corrected Printing April 2013

ISBN: 978-0-9851543-0-1

Beyond Karel J Robot
A Gentle Introduction to the Art of Object-Oriented Programming in Java: Volume 2

Joseph Bergin

Preface

A number of users have asked for more material in the spirit of Karel J Robot. The original book is intended for only the beginning weeks of a course, which leaves some the dilemma of what to do for the rest of the term. This volume is an attempt to discuss some additional ideas as well as some more Java features. The chapter numbering begins where Karel J Robot leaves off and we will frequently make mention of what was learned there. However, we begin to leave the robot world here and will discuss many ideas from beyond that world.

The two volumes together should form the basis of a first college course in computing using Java. While I have generally followed the guidelines of the College Board recommendations for the APCS AB advanced placement course, I have not attempted to be encyclopedic. We will see int, double, char, etc., but no attempt was made to provide all the rules and caveats of such things. Many books that call themselves text-books seem to me to be, instead, reference works, with everything gathered together nicely to ease looking up information, rather than books to learn from. Instead, I have attempted to show, for the most part, how the features of Java are used to build real programs. This is a book about writing programs, including some quite interesting and difficult programs. You may struggle with some of this material, but the struggle will take you to a better place. I hope you agree that it is worth the work you will put in to it.

The Intermezzo sections are just examinations of long programs that use important techniques that the novice must master. Throughout we emphasize good Object-Oriented development, but also cover many other things as well. Chapter 14 is special. It is not intented to be used after the rest, but rather, along the way. It introduces a term-long project that will build something like the Karel J Robot simulator, though in a non-graphical form. In technical terms, it produces the model to which views can be added later. The sections of that chapter are keyed to the other chapters in the book, with many exercises that can be done as the student learns the material of those earlier chapters.

The appendix offers implementations of some collections classes that are similar to, but simpler than, the classes in the Java libraries. They are intended for reading and study, though we make use of them in the latter part of the book, starting with the Secondo Intermezzo.

For those who wish to use this as the basis of an AP course, note that the current case study (Grid World) is not discussed here. Materials exist elsewhere. The combination of these two volumes and study of Grid World should form a complete course of study for any novice.

Software to simulate Karel J. Robot is available on the Web.
http://csis.pace.edu/~bergin/KarelJava2ed/downloads.html

Joseph Bergin, Pace University
January 2008

Contents

9 The State of the Computation

What is your state of mind as you read this? As you read, does the state of your knowledge change? What is your state of health? This chapter makes explicit the notion of *state* in computer programs. There are three notions of state that we want to explore here: implicit state, execution position (program counter), and explicit state.

9.1 Implicit State

When programming in most languages, including the robot programming language, the programs are "stateful": they contain a lot of state. For example, when karel puts a beeper down, the "state" of the world changes, as it has an additional beeper at that corner. At the same time the state of the robot changes, as it has one less in its beeper bag. On the other hand, the number of beepers in the system as a whole has not changed: it is *invariant*. Most of your programming in the robot world up to this point has been moving the state of the computation forward in this sense. The world begins in some state, or configuration. Walls and beepers are in initial positions. Robots are placed initially at certain corners with beepers, directions, etc. Then the program begins to execute and the state begins to change with some things varying and some things remaining invariant. For example, the state of the robot nearly always changes when we execute an instruction, but the state of the walls never does.

This idea of an invariant is very important. On one hand it means that there is one less thing that the programmer needs to keep track of in writing the program. That permits you focus on the things that can change: on the sequence of state changes. We have also used the idea of an invariant to help us with the computation itself. For example, when a robot moves toward the Southeast, the sum of its street and avenue numbers is invariant. We used this idea effectively in Section 7.5.

Note also, that in most programs the state changes are locally predictable. You can look at any statement and predict what changes it will make to the state of the computation. That isn't always, the case, however. For example, if you introduce random elements into the program, such as multi-threaded execution, it may not be possible to predict precisely what will occur. That doesn't mean we have chaos, however. It just means that we have to rely on general, rather than specific, notions of state transition. So, for example, in the Dining Robots example, we can predict what will happen within each robot's execution, though our description is somewhat conditional: If a fork ever appears on this corner, the robot will pick it up… etc. The same is true in the real world, of course: If a bus ever appears on this corner, I'll be able to ride downtown to visit my friend.

There is another situation in which we are able to make only general statements about the state changes in a program. If we have employed dynamic polymorphism, then when we send a robot a message via a reference variable we may not be able to know, in principle, the precise type of the robot that will receive the message, so we don't know the precise method that will be executed in response to the message. All we know is that whichever robot receives the message will execute its own corresponding method, making some changes to the state that might not occur if some other robot received the message instead.

In fact, when any robot, or, more generally, any object, receives a message, the response of the robot will depend on both the type of that object and the current state of the object. For example if we send a putBeeper message to a robot it will execute its own version of that method, which may not be the one defined in UrRobot, but the response also depends on whether it has any beepers in its beeper bag at that moment as well. Its state "at that moment" depends on the sequence of state changes that have occurred up to then in the execution of the program. Again, the same is true in the real world. When you ask a friend to perform a service for you, the response of the friend will depend on what kind of friend he is, but also on his current state (of mind, of health, of your relationship, etc).

In many ways, your own ability to keep track of the state of a computation defines your true ability as a programmer. Of course you cannot maintain every detail in your head. There is just too much of it. In fact, much of the detail is hidden from you anyway. In the robot world, much of it is intentionally hidden within the simulator that executes your programs. You don't know, or care, for example, how the simulator's author decided to implement walls and beepers as long as you can make accurate assumptions about their behavior as your code executes. But at a different level, you need to do this yourself. Once we have written a new class and implemented methods within that class we can mostly forget the details, unless we learn that there is an error in the program.

Even deeper, if we have created a hierarchy of classes and built polymorphism into our programs then objects of each of our classes can behave differently when sent a given message. Can we forget the details in this case? That depends, of course. If we have used good names for the class, objects, and methods then we have made a good start. More important, though, is keeping discipline in making the actual actions we program within a method true to the idea of the method and the class. If our turnLeft method is changed so that the robot turns right instead, then we won't be able to keep general, abstract, notions of the result of a message. We need to guarantee that whenever an object executes an action that it "does the right thing" from the standpoint of the client that sends the message. It means that when we define a hierarchy of classes we need to be true to some concept that makes sense in *our* world, so that our mental ability helps us understand our own work, rather than hindering us, and overloading us with detail. We will return to this idea in Section 9.2.1.

We have tried, in creating the robot programming world, to set a consistent metaphor in which you can think about things. Sometimes it is a bit awkward, perhaps (helicopter pilots), but we needed a way to help you get started thinking about how it works in a way that seemed to us to be natural and not misleading. For example, in the real world physical robots naturally move in parallel. But as we saw in Chapter 8, it is harder to do here, so the helicopter metaphor was set simply to lead you to begin to think naturally about how the program would behave when you execute it.

But you need to do exactly the same thing when you write a program so that your natural innate thinking ability makes it easy to reason about the state of your program and the sequence of state changes you call for in its execution. This means good names, consistent implementation of concepts in hierarchies, metaphors for your objects, etc. Humans are good at abstraction. It is how we deal with complexity overload. We are good at metaphor. It is how we deal with ambiguity. So we need to use these tools to build programs that we ourselves can understand.

It must be pointed out, if it isn't yet obvious to you, that the purpose of writing a computer program is communication. The primary target of communication is not the computer, however. The characteristics of computer languages are designed (usually somewhat poorly) so as to help people organize their own thoughts and communicate them to other people. Most computer programs are built in teams. Most are built for other people than their creators. So good communication is essential. But the primary target of this communication is you, the programmer, yourself. Every program notation and statement is a note to yourself to remind yourself of your intent when you wrote it. That is why naming and consistency are so important. Computers have certain abilities that humans do not, primarily the ability to organize vast quantities of low-level detail. But they cannot "think" in any sense. You have to do the thinking to organize the appropriate series of state changes that will solve your computing problems. To do this effectively, rely on your abilities of abstraction and metaphor.

9.1.1 Assertions

One of the things that we humans do is to make assertions about the state of the world. "My computing course is hard." "My computing course is fun." An assertion is simply a statement that may be true or false: a predicate, actually. But by making an assertion we are claiming that it is true, in fact. Perhaps you have noticed that you cannot ask a robot which street it is on, or how many beepers it has in its beeper bag. This was intentional because we wanted you to learn to program at a deeper level. It is possible, however, within the robot world, to make assertions about the state of a robot, even though you can't query the robot about the state. The assertion methods are not implemented in the robots, however, but in special objects called TestCases. Perhaps you have already come across these.

There is a class in the robot world called KJRTest, discussed in detail in Chapter 12, that permits you to make assertions about robots. This is mostly used with the JUnit testing framework, by creating sub-classes of KJRTest and including test methods in your extension. But assertions can be used in other ways. An object of type KJRTest can make assertions about robots and about the world in which the robots operate. For example, if aTest is such an object, then

```
aTest.assertBeepersAt(5, 3);
```

is an assertion that there are one or more beepers in the world on fifth street and third avenue.

When an assertion "passes" (i.e. the statement of its truth is really true), nothing happens. The program that contains it just continues. But when it fails, it throws an exception. You have almost certainly seen exceptions by now if you have been executing programs using the simulator. Among the common exceptions that you will see is NullPointerException, thrown when you try to send a message using a reference that has not been made to point to any object. If you include these robot assertions in your regular programs, though they are not intended to be used that way, then your program will terminate whenever any assertion fails. The exception will be AssertionFailedError. However, if you use them in the JUnit framework, then the error will be caught by that framework and you will be given messages about which assertion failed. JUnit is discussed in detail in Chapter 12. We also note, for completeness, that Java has an assert statement that can be used, though it is less flexible than capturing such assertions in a class. Its discussion is also beyond the scope of this book.

However, even if you don't create executable assertions, it is good to get into the habit of making assertions about what you know to be true at each point in a program.

An example might help solidify the ideas here. Suppose we know that a robot has just executed the following instruction:

```
public void mysteryInstruction(){
   while( frontIsClear()){
      move();
      putBeeper();
   }
   turnLeft();
}[1]
```

[1] We will adopt the standard Java bracing convention in this text, in which the opening brace is at the end of a line and the closing brace is under the major element for which we have opened the block.

We can then assert with confidence (provided that we know that the instructions here have not been overridden to do strange, unexpected, things, that the robot has a wall to its right and to its left there is a sequence of beepers, perhaps of length 0, extending back to the corner just after its initial corner. We cannot assert, however, that there is a beeper on the current corner, just from this. Actually, it is a bit more complicated than this. We made an assumption that the above was executed without error shutoff as could happen if the robot runs out of beepers in the middle of executing it. So it would have been better to say that we can make the above assertion provided that the instruction was executed successfully.

We can also sometimes chain assertions together. Suppose prior to executing the above that we had been able to assert successfully that (a) the robot was facing West, and (b) that there were no walls in the world other than the boundary walls. Then we could additionally assert after successful execution of the above, that the robot was facing South at the West boundary wall.

There are two situations in programming when making assertions about programs and chaining them together in this fashion is especially useful. The first is when you are given an unfamiliar program and asked to determine what it does. The assertions about the state help you understand what is going on from statement to statement as you simulate its execution. We did this, actually, back in Chapter 3, to see how to develop new instructions. The second situation in which this is a useful thing to do is when you discover an error in your program and want to fix it. Before you can intelligently repair it, you need to know where, and probably why, it is broken.

We continue the discussion of state in the next section and what we have said above about assertions, etc., applies there as well.

9.2 The Program Counter

When you simulate the execution of a program, you probably use your finger or a pencil to point to the current instruction that you are examining, or perhaps write down the instruction number if you have numbered each one. When a computer actually executes your program it does essentially the same thing.

A program (the *compiler*) on your computer translates your Java programs into a simpler form that is more difficult for humans to read easily, but is more suitable for computers, since the instructions are extremely simple. One robot program statement may translate into hundreds of "machine language" instructions, in fact. Java often uses an intermediate form, called "byte codes," but they have much of the same characterization of this machine language: they are very simple and easy to execute for a machine that cannot think, but can only manipulate simple data using simple rules. Just as your program consists of a sequence of instructions, so does a machine language program, though the latter can be loaded into the memory of a computer, which you can think of as just a list of symbols encoded in numeric form. The important thing is that they are a *list* of symbols and so a single pointer, like your finger, can be used to tell where in the program is the next instruction to be executed. This place is called the *program counter*, since the value of it will normally advance by one position (counting) unless some logical instruction is executed to make it do otherwise (jump). But you can think of this very low level program counter as being just like what you do when you point at one instruction after another in tracing or simulating the execution of a program. We will look at the details of the pc and machine language in the Secondo Intermezzo.

The important concept of this section, however, is that knowing where the program counter is in a program gives you a lot of information about the state of a computation. Let's see an example or two. We will use our robot language here rather than try to go into the details of machine language, but the idea is exactly the same in each case, though the granularity is much finer in a machine language instruction: the individual machine language instruction does much less than the individual Java instruction.

Suppose we examine the following fragment of code in which we have numbered the instructions:

```
1  gil.putBeeper()
2  if(gil.frontIsClear()){
3     gil.move();
}
else {
4     gil.turnLeft();
5     gil.move();
}
```

Suppose that the program counter is at instruction number 3 and we are about to execute it. Then we can assert that gil is on a corner with a beeper and that its front is clear. However, if the program counter is at instruction 4 instead, then we can assert, instead, that gil's front is NOT clear, but that it is on a corner with a beeper.

In particular, note that when the program counter is within an IF or IF-ELSE statement that you have gained information depending on the test of that statement. You can think of this as "climbing information hill" since the level of information has increased. However, once you leave the IF structure you don't know anymore what the state is. The front could be blocked or clear. But the information is deeper than that. Recall that your program will only execute one clause of the IF statement. We write the THEN clause knowing that the front is clear (an assertion we can make) and the ELSE clause knowing that it is blocked. So the program has captured information, by executing the IF, that we make use of.

BUT, once we leave the IF statement, we not only don't know what the state is then, we no longer know what the state was previously, while the program was in the middle of the IF statement somewhere. We have lost the information that we had captured in the IF. We have "fallen down information hill." We will return to this idea in a moment.

If we have complex program structure, as was examined in Sections 5.5, 5.6, and 6.5, for example, we gain information as we move deeper into the structures. If we are in the THEN clause of an IF that itself was in the THEN clause of another IF, we know what both of the tests are true unless we have executed an instruction along the way that invalidated one or both of them. However, because of the nature of our thinking processes, it can get harder for us to remember what that information is. This is why we recommended earlier that deep nesting of structures not be employed in your programs.

One useful technique that is often employed successfully is this. Suppose you execute an IF statement and learn something in the process. Even more generally suppose you learn something in any way whatever about the execution of your program, just because you know what happened up to the point of the program counter. Suppose you need to know later in the program what was true back at this earlier moment and act on that knowledge at that later time. One way to do all of this is to create a new object that captures both the knowledge of what occurred at the early point as well as the behavior that will be appropriate later.

Here is an example of this that comes from a program outside the robot programming world. We are going to be moving outside the world of robots gradually in any case. Suppose you want to create a Dungeon Game that consists of Player objects, Place objects, and Thing objects. The players move through the places and may find, and carry things that they employ. One useful Thing is a transporter. The behavior of a transporter is as follows. If a player finds it somewhere the player may pick it up and carry it about. The first time that the transporter is "activated" it remembers the place in which the activation occurs. Then later, whenever it is "activated" again, it immediately transports the player back to the place in which it was first activated.

The transporter needs to remember if it has been activated or not. On the first activation, the program gains information and we don't want to lose it. In particular we climbed information hill to learn that it had been activated, and we don't want to fall down the other side and have to climb it again to regain the information we had earlier. Objects, especially Strategy objects, are very good at this. Suppose the transporter is given a strategy when it is created. The activation of the transporter is then delegated to the strategy object. The initial strategy, when executed, does two things. It tells the transporter to remember this place and it also tells the transporter to replace the "current" strategy (this initial strategy) with another: a transport strategy. This new strategy will then automatically be the one delegated to by the transporter if the transporter is again activated.

And what does this other strategy do? It causes the player carrying the transporter to go immediately back to the place that is being remembered by the transporter. Thus the information that the transporter was initially activated is captured in the second strategy object and is then itself executed when called for later in the program. In this way, knowledge gained at the site of the program counter can be preserved for later use.

Note that the two strategy objects capture different kinds of information. The first captures the fact that the transporter has NOT been activated and the second that it HAS. But the strategies also capture different behaviors. The first captures what to do if the transporter has not been previously activated, and the second the appropriate behavior if it has been.

When used this way, the strategy object can be though of as a *flag*. In American football, when a violation of the rules occurs, the referee will throw up a piece of cloth (the flag) to indicate the infraction. The play is usually allowed to continue, but the presence of the flag is an indication when it ends that the violation occurred. (Similar things occur in European Football (soccer) though play is normally stopped immediately.) The players can see the flag and know that something out of the normal order of play will happen. But here in our Dungeon Game, the flag itself also carries not just the information that something occurred, but also what must be done in the program later because of it. The behavior. Our flags have behavior. It is as if the referee had a whole bunch of flags, each with instructions about how to proceed after the infraction and was careful to throw the correct one when the infraction first occurred. That would be unwieldy in our world, but it is very useful in the computer world. That is because the referee is a thinking being and won't have to "climb information hill" to recover the knowledge of the nature of the rule breaking, but the computer, needs to record it specifically or else recreate it. But if we need to record a bit of information (the transporter was activated) we might as well record more (what to do).

From the standpoint of the strategy objects, each just implements its doIt method differently. So each is very simple. At the point at which the transporter is activated the transporter just sends the doIt message to whichever strategy it happens to have current at that moment, so the transporter is very simple as well. But we get polymorphic behavior just by having captured the information that was known at the point of the program counter.

9.3 Explicit State (Introduction)

Programs employ a third kind of state, and we have done this already, though sparingly. For example, a Choreographer kept references to the other robots it was directing. Likewise an Adder robot (Section 7.6) knew some helper robots and could send messages to them. Our most sophisticated use, however, has been Strategies. A Spy robot kept changing strategies as it moved through the world. The current strategy that it carries is part of its state. What it does depends on what kind of object it is (Spy) and also on its current state (the strategy it knows about). We have been able to do a great deal without depending too much on such explicit state, and now we will be able to do a bit more using it. It will make some of the things we have done much easier, in fact.

Explicit state wasn't introduced earlier so as not to get in the way of your learning of important techniques that might have been masked by these new ideas.

Instance variables, sometimes called *fields*, were introduced in Section 4.3. We saw there that an object of the Choreographer class could maintain references to other objects whose actions it directed. In our case the choreographer had two fields, one for each assistant robot. So creating a choreographer actually creates three robots. But note that if we create two choreographers we actually create six robots. Each of the choreographers knows its assistants by the names lisa and tony, by the way. Since the assistants were created within the choreographer object itself, we were using the *composition* technique to build a choreographer: A choreographer *has* two assistants. The assistants are unknown outside the choreographer in the sense that your program cannot send them messages directly. Only the choreographer can.

The situation was a bit different, though, with the StrategyLayer class in Section 4.6. There the initial strategy was given in the constructor invocation when we created a new strategy. Therefore, whatever code creates a StrategyLayer has access to the strategy that it used to create the new StrategyLayer and so can use that strategy itself, perhaps giving the same strategy object to different StrageyLayers. The StrategyLayer, then, doesn't *own* the strategy itself, though it uses it: *delegates* actions to it.

We are used to composition and delegation in the real world also. An automobile *has* pistons. It is built by composition of parts. A person *uses* the services of a doctor to recover from injury or illness. It delegates actions to the doctor. Composition and delegation are two of the most important techniques of the object-oriented programmer, and both are recognized by the presence of fields within the object. The difference between them is a bit more subtle, however and depends at least somewhat about how you think about your program, not just the code you write. It is pretty clear in a few situations, though. If one object, a Choreographer, say, creates an assistant and the program doesn't permit any other code to send messages to that assistant, then it is pretty clearly composition. But if other code can send messages, it may be delegation instead.

But how could other code access the fields within the choreographer if the choreographer creates them and makes them private? One way would be for the choreographer to have a method that returns a reference to one or the other of the assistants:

```
public UrRobot firstAssistant(){
   return lisa;
}
```

That would be poor idea here, since then the choreographer couldn't really determine what happens with this assistant. Other code could direct it as well. It is as if the audience could shout out instructions to the dancers on the stage and have them followed. It might be interesting to see, but the idea of a choreographer would be broken in this situation.

Encapsulation is the process of guaranteeing that things that should be private are really kept private. The purpose of encapsulation is to let the programmer guarantee that the object (choreographer) really can behave according to its specification. In particular it permits the programmer to guarantee invariant properties of the objects created. Here the invariant is that the assistants maintain the same locations and directions as the choreographer, relative to initial locations and positions. If we add the above method, we can no longer make such a guarantee.

There is another, also very important, reason for encapsulation. When you try to reason about a program you have a difficult task as it has so many parts. Encapsulation lets you consider the program piece by piece. As you move to bigger pieces, made up of smaller ones, you can ignore the details of the smaller pieces. For example, when you are driving an automobile, you can ignore the fact that it has pistons. Whether it has six or eight doesn't affect how you drive. At a lower level, repairing the car, it may matter, but you have specifically chosen, then, to look at this lower level. Suppose you needed to keep track of all the details of all the parts of an automobile just to drive it: whether each piston was on the up or the down-stroke, for example. We would find the task impossible. The same is true in programming and especially in reasoning about our programs. Therefore we encapsulate our objects and hide as much information as possible from the rest of our program about the inner workings of each object. Said another way, we give each object responsibility for its own inner workings and we specify these by thinking about their invariant properties as well as their variant properties (how they can change).

The StrategyLayer class has another property that is worth thinking about. Not only could we set its initial strategy in the constructor, it also has a setStrategy method by which any code with a reference to a StrategyLayer can change its strategy. We say that the StrategyLayer object is *mutable*: can be changed. We say that the setStrategy method is a *mutator* method for these objects. Thus, another object can change the state of a StrategyLayer by sending this message. So, even though the myStrategy field of a StrategyLayer is private, the object still isn't very well encapsulated. Therefore, encapsulation is about more than just making your fields private, though you should do that in nearly every situation. (The few cases in which you should use some other *visibility* marker for fields are outside the scope of this book.)

But since a StrategyLayer is not well encapsulated, it will be difficult to create invariant properties for it, and therefore to make assertions about its state without considering larger sections of the program than the class itself. This complicates our reasoning process, especially in the presence of errors in the program. By way of contrast, consider the situation of the BlockWalker in the same section. There, the current strategy was also changeable, but all changes were handled internally. The swapStrategies method, which is really a *mutator* for the myStrategy field is private and can, therefore, only be invoked from within the objects of the class themselves. So a BlockWalker object can change its own strategy, but other code cannot.

Actually, in Java, the visibility boundary is the class and not the object. Therefore, theoretically, one BlockWalker could actually send swapStrategies to another BlockWalker, assuming it maintains a reference to the other. We didn't do this, but this capability also complicates our reasoning about our programs if we take advantage of this flexibility. Notice, then, that flexibility in a programming language often leads to complications in its use. While it may be easier to do some things with the added flexibility it may be harder to reason about the effect, and it is this ability to reason about your programs that is your most powerful programming tool.

9.4 Primitive Data

In most object-oriented languages (Eiffel and Smalltalk are the main exceptions) not everything is an object. The language also defines more primitive things that can't be extended or receive messages, though they are encapsulated. Normally they can be manipulated in various ways, but using syntax other than message passing, since they have no methods. Even in the robot world, we have walls, which are not objects. They don't have behavior and they can't be manipulated, though the World can place and remove them. Java contains several different types of primitive data, most of which is numeric in nature. We have already used boolean values of course and our predicates return them and our IF and WHILE statements depend on booleans. The primitives types each form a *data type*. A data type is a set of values, a set of operations on the values, and a set of rules that define how the operations behave. For example, the boolean data type of Java consists of the set { true, false }. The operators are &&, || and !. The rules are given by the normal rules of logic (with short-circuit operations, of course). All the other primitives of Java are numeric and they are similar to numbers in arithmetic, though with some differences. Even the values of the *char* data type of java, which represents characters like 'a' and '%' are really numeric.

The simplest numeric data type of Java is *int*, and we have used it already, for initialization of the street and avenue of a robot when it is created, for example. Our constructors have all noted that the first parameter of the constructor has type int. The values of the integers of mathematics are infinite in extent, both in the positive and the negative directions of the number line. That is the first major difference with numbers in (nearly all) computer languages. In most languages the built in types form a finite range of values. In Java, an int is between the value -2^{31} and $+2^{31} - 1$. This gives exactly 2^{32} different values (a little bit over 4 billion values), which implies that an integer can be represented in 32 *bits* (base 2 digits) or four bytes, as a byte is 8 bits. An integer outside this range can't be represented in your java program as an int. There is another type called *long* that is similar, but is stored in 8 bytes (64 bits) so the range is much larger.

The representation in a fixed number of bits leaves us with the question of what happens when you do arithmetic on these values. The operators on int are + (addition), - (subtraction), * (multiplication), / (division), % (remainder), unary +, and unary -. If an addition or a multiplication (for example) would result in a value outside the allowed range of values, the result is "wrapped around" like arithmetic on a clock. If you add 5 hours to 11 (PM, say), you don't get 16, but rather 4. The same is true for Java int and for Java long. Note, however, that this is true of Java and will differ, perhaps, in other languages. Some make it an error to perform such operations. Thus, in Java you can add two large positive ints and get a negative one. You are encouraged to try this.

Java likewise has a short type, which is like an int, but is stored in only 16 bits, leaving its values between –65536 and 65535. (-2^{15} to $+2^{15} -1$). Note that there are just as many negative values as there are non-negative ones (including 0).

You can declare an int variable in Java with something like

```
int size;
```

This sets up an association between the name "size" and some int value. If you don't initialize such a value or otherwise assign it, Java will usually assume it is zero, or else make you give a value to it. Better, is to do an initialization when you declare it, giving the initial value of your variable:

```
int size = 0;
```

Note that such variables can vary (hence the name *variable*). At a given instant of execution, however, a variable is associated with a single value. At the next instant, it could be changed by the programmer's code. But objects use variables to remember things.

Note that the declaration introduces the name and since languages like Java need to know the type of every variable, we include the type in the declaration. Once we introduce the name, however, we don't repeat the type when we use the name, or *identifier*, later.

Changing an int variable by incrementing it (giving it a value one larger than the value it currently has), which you can write

```
size = size + 1;
```

is very common. So common, in fact that there is a shorthand for it:

```
size++;
```

In either case the value size + 1 is computed and the variable size is then given this new value. Think of a variable as an association between a name and a value. You do this. Your name may be Mary, but YOU are not Mary. Mary is just a name (identifier) that people use to designate you. You are YOU. There is an association between the word Mary and the person you. Note that the name can actually refer to different people at different times and in different contexts. There are lots of "Marys" in the world. The same is true of variables. We have seen this before with reference variables that refer to robots. All variables have this property. A variable is associated with a single value at any time, but it can be changed.

Conversely, several variables can denote or be associated with the same value, and at the same time in this case. You could also have the name "dear," as your parents might denote you. Multiple names for the same value. The same is true with variables in Java and most computer languages as well. Associations size = 6; and age = 6; can be simultaneously in effect. Likewise different reference variables can refer to the same objects simultaneously, as we have seen before.

Operators: Java has a number of numeric operators that can be used to modify values. We have just seen the increment operator ++, such as:

a++; which adds one to a.

There is a similar decrement operator that subtracts one from a variable, changing its value. In fact, there are four such operators. Suppose y has value 5. If you write

x = y++; then x gets value 5, but y is changed to 6. If you write
x = ++y; then both x and y end up with value 6. The value of y is changed before it is used. Similar

things will happen with the decrement operators --y and y--. Java also has operators that combine assignment with arithmetic. These are just shorthand, but you often see them.

x += 3; adds 3 to x. It is shorthand for x = x + 3
y *= 5; multiplies y by 5, shorthand for y = y * 5.

The division and even boolean operators have similar combinations.

So far we have used only references to robots and strategies as fields of our classes. We can actually use any types that we like.

For example, a robot could be made to remember the location at which it was delivered to the world, like this:

```
class Rememberer extends UrRobot{

   public Rememberer(int street, int avenue, Direction direction,
         int beepers){
      super(street, avenue, direction, beepers);
      initialStreet = street;
      initialAvenue = avenue;
   }

   private final int initialStreet;
   private final int initialAvenue;
}
```

We made the instance variables *final* as well as private since we don't want the program to ever change them. Once they are set in the constructor, they cannot be modified. Of course, we would want to take advantage of this new knowledge. Such a class could provide an *accessor* for the information. For example:

```
public int initialStreet(){
   return initialStreet;
}
```

Then a client of this code could know where the robot was created. Note that we can have both fields (instance variables) and methods with the same name. Java has no trouble with this, and it lets us associate a single name with a concept, which can be very helpful.

9.5 Making Use of Arithmetic on int Values

What we say here will also apply to short and long values, actually, but we will use int as a sort of standard primitive value. Later we shall see some primitives with very different characteristics, though.

Lets suppose for a while that we are putting robots into a world without walls other than the boundary walls. Having created a robot somewhere, we can make it move to the origin by having it execute the following sequence of instructions. Note that we shall assume a few simple instructions exist in the class of this robot. We have built these in the past, so it won't be difficult to provide them if you want to execute this code.

```
faceWest()
while(frontIsClear()){
   move();
}
turnLeft();
while(frontIsClear()){
   move();
}
```

Let's illustrate simple arithmetic with robots, though we will use a technique that is too simple for general use since it will only work once for a given robot.

Suppose we have the Rememberer class from the previous section, but we also give it two additional fields:

```
private int westDistanceWalked = 0;
private int southDistanceWalked = 0;
```

The intention is that the robot will record the distance it walks toward the west in the first of these and the distance it walks toward the south in the other.

We can take advantage of these by overriding the move method of this class as follows:

```
public void move(){
    if(facingWest()){
        westDistanceWalked++;
    }
    else if (facingSouth()){
        southDistanceWalked++;
    }
    super.move();
}
```

Then, every time the robot steps west, it increments that variable. We will ignore here the problem of what gets recorded if there is an error shutoff, but you can think about that on your own.

Given this framework, we can have the robot go to the origin (but only once) with this instruction:

```
public void goToOrigin(){
    faceWest();
    while(initialAvenue - westDistanceWalked > 1){
        move();
    }
    turnLeft();
    while(initialStreet - southDistanceWalked > 1){
        move();
    }
}
```

Note that the overall structure is like what we have done before, but instead of using external sensors (frontIsClear()), the robot uses internal counters. It depends on the fact that when it is created its current corner is (initialStreet, initialAvenue). The reason it only works once (and even then, only if it hasn't moved previously) is that the current corner changes and this only works from the initial corner. Still, it illustrates the counting principle. The westDistanceWalked is initially zero. Each time the robot walks toward the west this is incremented by one. The expression `initialAvenue - westDistanceWalked` is its current avenue number and when this reaches 1 (first avenue) we must stop.

You may like to know that hidden inside the Karel J Robot simulator that you have probably been using, there is a more sophisticated version of the above so that the program can keep track of where all the robots are as the execution of your program progresses.

Of course it is possible to make errors in this sort of programming as in any other. Suppose we replace the > (greater than) operator with >= (greater than or equal to)? The program will break and the robot will experience an error shutoff. An error in counting in which the result differs by one from the desired result is called an *off by one error*. It is very common in programming. The same thing happens when you use the wrong stopping condition in a FOR-LOOP.

Note the six numeric binary comparison operators (==, !=, <, <=, >, and >=) require numeric arguments[2] and produce boolean results. Java is pretty forgiving, actually, if you use numeric arguments of different types in these operators. You can add an int and a long (getting a long). You can compare a short and an int, etc. This is not the case in all computer languages, however, so be careful as you move on.

Not everything you can do has so little value, however. You can give a robot a method that will ask it to move any distance you like, rather than just one block. Here we use two additional features of Java, int valued parameters and int valued *local variables* within a method. Each of these has a lifetime only that of a single message execution. Fields (instance variables) on the other hand, live as long as the object does.

```
public void move(int howMany){
    for(int count = 0; count < howMany; count++){
        move();
    }
}
```

Note that we again called the method *move*, but it has a different *signature* so Java won't confuse it with the UrRobot move instruction. Here *howMany* is a parameter to the instruction and *count* is a local variable. Actually count is only visible within the FOR statement, not even throughout the method. We could have made it visible throughout with a very slight variation. Note the two changes here.

```
public void move(int howMany){
    int count;
    for(count = 0; count < howMany; count++){
        move();
    }
}
```

If jonny is a robot of this type, then `jonny.move(8)` is like our earlier moveMile instruction. But be careful with such instructions. If you try to execute them when there are walls in front of the robot you are subject to error shutoff.

We can turn this idea around also. Suppose a robot named paat is facing west and we want to know how many steps paat is from the first wall it is facing, perhaps the boundary wall. Then patt can execute this functional method:

```
public int howManySteps(){
    int result = 0;
    while (frontIsClear()){
        move();
        result++;
    }
    return result;
}
```

This sort of loop is called a counting loop. Note that since you have the count, it isn't hard to make the robot return to its original location if that is required as well.

---

[2] Actually == and != can be used with any arguments of the same type, but we only focus on numeric uses here.

9.6 A Program Using Numeric Data and Built by Composition

In this section we will see the core of an implementation of a simple calculator. The program will be both simple and sophisticated. It will, however, not involve robots at all, so this is our first attempt to build a program not in the robot world. It won't even be graphical. There is a reason for this that you should understand. When you build a sophisticated program it is important to divide it up into independent parts as much as possible. This lets you focus your attention at any time on a more limited number of concerns. In particular, programs that *are* graphical should have a clean separation between the graphical part and the underlying algorithms that do the work. You have been doing this all along, actually, since the authors provided the graphical parts of the robot world in the simulator without regard to the algorithms you would write, and you wrote algorithms for this world without concern about how the graphics is implemented. The underlying algorithmic part of an application is called the *model*, and the graphical part is the *view*. Another reason for the separation is that a given model can have multiple views. If you have ever used a spreadsheet program, be aware that the normal rows and columns view, is just that, a view. There is an underlying, but invisible, set of structures of data as well as algorithms. If you have seen a graph of a set of cells in a spreadsheet, then that is just another view, but the model isn't changed in any way to show this view.

Here we shall build just the model and shall do it in stages. The calculator will have only integer (int) data. It will have only a few keys, and will have a general algebraic structure, though we won't worry about the precedence of operators here. Such calculators used to be sold for a few dollars, but are now likely obsolete as more sophisticated ones can be manufactured for the same money as this simple model we shall build.

To get started, our goal is to make a sequence of key "presses" like "5 5 + 3 =" produce a 58 for the result at the end. Initially we will build only the four keys needed for this, but others can be added easily once we work out the details. In Chapter 12 we will see a set of steps that might have led to this design. It was not, however, developed in the order it is presented here.

9.6.1 A Calculator Model with a Display

The very first thing we want to do is: Create a calculator that will give you its display. A new calculator should have a display of 0.

If we want to test this as we go we have some options. Here we will just build a main function somewhere that will exercise the calculator. So the above says that if we write the following main and execute it, we should see a 0.

```
public static void main(String [] args){
   CalculatorModel calculator = new CalculatorModel();
   int value = calculator.getDisplay();
   System.out.println("The display is: " + value);
}
```

Our basic framework then is a class called CalculatorModel and it needs at least a getDisplay method.

```
package calculator;

public class CalculatorModel{

   public int getDisplay(){
      return display;
   }

   private int display = 0;
}
```

We have put the code into package calculator. All Java code should be in packages as it aids us in reusing the code in other programs. We don't need any imports here. We called the class *CalculatorModel* to emphasize that it is just the model. If we give it a graphical part later we can call that part the *Calculator*. The display field is an int and is private. We have a method to retrieve the value of this variable. A bit of explanation of this print method is in order.

System is a class defined within Java. It knows a lot of things about your computer. One of the objects in class System is called *out* and it is an *OutputStream* object that is connected to your system console or other command window if you run the program from such a window. The *println* method of the out object prints a single Java *String* object: its argument. However, Java Strings are very sophisticated. They form a data type in the sense we defined above and + is one of the operators on this data type. It means string catenation (pasting together) here. To indicate a fixed Java String (a constant), put the characters of the string in double quotes: "Karel J Robot". But note that "", adjacent double quotes is just a string with no characters: the empty string. Now it gets interesting. After this opening *label* string we have written the string catenation operator, +, so Java is expecting another String object. It doesn't find one, but it finds an int instead. But Java is really good about being able to translate things into String objects, so an automatic transformation is applied from the int value (now 0, but it might be 53 later) into a string (sequence of char values). The resulting string is catenated to the label string resulting in just the characters that go to make up the int. Without the initial label String, however, Java sees that we are trying to println an int, when it wants a String so it complains about the type error. We have provided a String with the same characters that go to make up the int, so Java is happy.

In our getDisplay method

```
   public int getDisplay(){
      return display;
   }
```

note that the return value's type must match the type specified in the method protocol as usual: an int.

9.6.2 Numeric Keys

Next we want to achieve this: Give the calculator keys like 5 and 3. When you hit a single key the value of the key should "show" in the display.

So far what we have done has been extremely simple. There is only one class and one object. However, we said we wanted to do this using composition so now we will start to build some objects. Actually the display itself could have been an object rather than an int, but it seems a little simple for that. Objects have behavior and the display has none yet. Later, perhaps we will decide to change the code (*refactor* is the technical term) and make an object of it also. We are going to build parts of the calculator. These parts will be objects, therefore defined by classes. These parts will be internal to the calculator itself. Therefore the classes that define the parts will also be inside the CalculatorModel class. We discussed inner classes briefly in the exercises of Chapter 4 and here we need them extensively.

First let's note that we shall have several kinds of keys and the action we want to do to all of them is to press them. Therefore lets start out by building a unifying framework for keys using an interface. We will define this inside the CalculatorModel class as a private inner interface.

```
private interface CalculatorKey{
   public void press();
}
```

Making it private means that having a reference to a CalculatorModel still gives us no access to this. Had it been public, then CalculatorModel.CalculatorKey would have been visible throughout the program. This way it is just an implementation detail for building calculators, like the design of a Piston in an automobile.

Next we need a class that we can use to define the number keys like 3 and 5. Here we can use one class and give its constructor a value saying which value we want the key to have. The key will remember this value

```
private class NumberKey implements CalculatorKey{
   public NumberKey(int value){
      this.value = value;
   }

   public void press(){
      display = value;
   }

   private final int value;
}
```

As usual the field of these objects (value) is private. We implement the CalculatorKey interface here so we need to include the press method. The implementation we have given of this method is very naïve, however. If we create a five key and a three key as fields of the CalculatorModel with:

```
private final CalculatorKey five = new NumberKey(5);
private final CalculatorKey three = new NumberKey(3);
```

then pressing the five key (five.press()) will change the display to 5, but following this with a three.press() will change the display to 3, not 53. Still it is all the above "development story" called for, so let's delay the more sophisticated thing for a bit.

However, the keys are private (as well as *final*, since we don't want the five to suddenly produce a 4). Final fields cannot be changed. They are constant. But if they are mutable objects, they can still receive messages that change their state. Constant (final) applies to the reference, not to the object itself. Here, however, the NumberKey objects have no methods to change their state.

But, since they are private, code that "sees" a calculator still needs to have some way to get these keys pressed. We can provide methods of the CalculatorModel itself for this:

```
    public void pressThree(){
        three.press();
    }

    public void pressFive(){
        five.press();
    }
```

Since we have developed this in pieces, perhaps it would be good to see it all together.

```
public class CalculatorModel{

    public int getDisplay(){
        return display;
    }

    public void pressThree(){
        three.press();
    }

    public void pressFive(){
        five.press();
    }

    private interface CalculatorKey{
        public void press();
    }

    private class NumberKey implements CalculatorKey{
        public NumberKey(int value){
            this.value = value;
        }

        public void press(){
            display = value;
        }

        private final int value;
    }

    private int display = 0;
    private final CalculatorKey five = new NumberKey(5);
    private final CalculatorKey three = new NumberKey(3);
}
```

Now let's update main a bit:

```
public static void main(String [] args){
   CalculatorModel calculator = new CalculatorModel();
   int value = calculator.getDisplay();
   System.out.println("" + value);
   calculator.pressFive();
   value = calculator. getDisplay ();
   System.out.println("" + value);
   calculator.pressThree();
   value = calculator. getDisplay ();
   System.out.println("" + value);
}
```

This will show 0, 5, and 3 on separate lines, of course.

9.6.3 Accumulation

Next we want the numeric keys to behave better: If you press a sequence of number keys, the results should accumulate in the display. A 5 followed by a 3 should display 53.

When we enter digits into a calculator we enter them from the right end of the accumulating value. When we press the 5 key, 5 becomes the rightmost digit. When we then press 3, the 5 moves to the left and the 3 becomes rightmost. But shifting a value to the left, in numeric base 10, is the same as multiplying by 10. So if we multiply the current display by 10 it will shift left, permitting us to simply add the new digit, which is one of 0…9 and so only occupies one "space" in the value. Thus we can change (refactor) the press method for the NumberKey class, which now becomes:

```
private class NumberKey implements CalculatorKey{
   public NumberKey(int value){
      this.value = value;
   }

   public void press(){
      display = display * 10 + value;
   }

   private final int value;
}
```

Notice that in a numeric assignment like this, we evaluate the right side first, before we can do the actual assignment. So we take the current value of display, multiply it by 10, thereby shifting it to the left, and then adding the value of this key. If the display was previously 52 and this is the 3 key, the value should now be 523 = 52 * 10 + 3.

Let's back up a bit and think about our design. Note that we are capturing the numeric keys as objects (private final objects, actually) and it is up to us to decide how many of them to create. We can therefore assure that we create keys for numbers 0…9, but no others. On the other hand, if we had instead just given the CalculatorModel a pressNumber method with an int parameter such as this:

```
public void pressNumber(int value){
   . . .
}
```

then it would be more difficult to guarantee that the value is a legal digit, though we could certainly do this with an IF structure. But eventually someone would possibly try pressNumber(10) even though there is no 10 key on a calculator. We have made that impossible with this design, though at a cost of requiring many methods, one for each key to be pressed.

With the above change, the main of the previous sub-section will now produce, 0, 5, 53 on successive lines of the output since we show the display after each key press. Like counting, this process of accumulation is very common in computing. It simply means that a value is changed, usually repeatedly by somehow using its old value to help compute its new value. Counting is a special case of accumulation, of course as we just modify the old value by adding one each time we *accumulate*. Another common form of accumulation is to repeatedly add a series of numeric values to a current value as the new ones become available using some process, such as pressing keys in a graphical interface or reading in values from the keyboard (which we have not seen yet here). For example if we execute:

```
int currentValue = 0;
```

once and then repeatedly execute:

```
currentValue = currentValue + newValue;
```

as the newValue values become available, then currentValue will hold the sum of all of the values that have been obtained. Perhaps this latter *accumulation* step appears in a WHILE structure.

9.6.4 Operators

Next, let's add an operator key: Give the calculator a + key that adds the results of two operands. Other operator keys will be added later (-, *, /). Sum isn't done till you hit equals, though.

Note that when you press the + key there is only one value (operand), but addition is a binary operation. So we need to also accumulate the second operand and then perform the addition later, when we press the = key. This means that we will need to save the current value we have been accumulating, of course. Another small detail is that pressing + doesn't clear the display. You can still "see" the accumulated value. It isn't until you press another number key that the display seems to change its behavior. Therefore pressing a numeric key has two different possible behaviors, depending on what has recently happened. If we just hit a numeric key, keep accumulating. If we jut pressed an operator, start over on a new value. This is a perfect place for strategies and pressing the = key is a perfect place to switch from one strategy, accumulating, to the other, saving. Before we write these strategies, however, it might be good to look at the transitions that can occur in the internal state of the calculator as the user presses keys. Figure 9.1 is a simplified *state transition diagram* that shows what we have discovered up to now.

The calculator starts out in the Accumulate "state," and as long as we keep seeing digit keys pressed, it stays in that state. The strategy in effect is also an instance of AccumulateStrategy. However, once we see an operator key, such as + we go to the Save state and get a new Strategy. But if in that state another digit appears, we go back to accumulating, but for the second value. Later, when the "user" presses the = key we perform the operation of the operator key. Thus we need to save that operation somehow. We will have strategies to represent both the accumulate state and the save state, as we shall see.

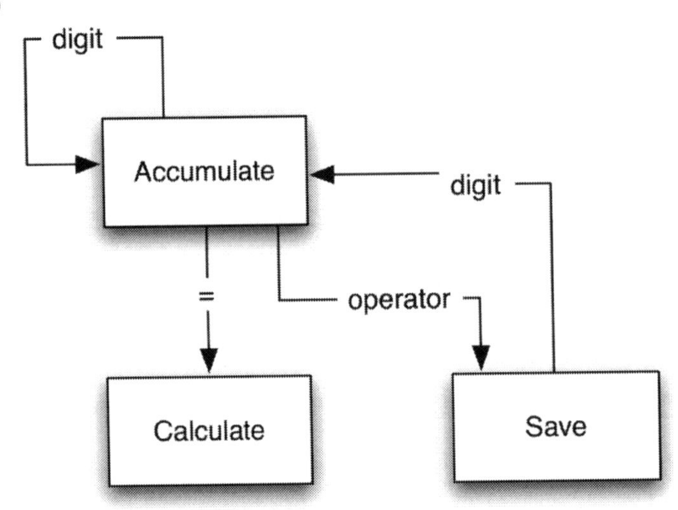

Figure 9.1. State Transition Diagram (simple version)

To get started building this we need to define the NumberStrategy interface that gives the framework of our strategies. The number keys will delegate the press method to one of these each time.

```
private interface NumberStrategy{
   public void execute(int value);
}
```

Inner classes and Nested classes: Sometimes we need to define a class whose objects only make sense to use within another. It is therefore useful to be able to put one class definition inside another. There are two ways to do this and they have different meanings. A *static inner class* is more properly called a nested class and it is used simply to keep the use of the class encapsulated inside the containing class. The two classes otherwise have no relationship to one another

```
class Outer {

   private static class Inner {
   . . .
   }
. . .
}
```

It is sometimes useful to do this, just to hide it's definition. However, without the static keyword, the meaning changes drastically. In that case, objects of the inner class are, in a real sense, contained automatically within objects of the outer class. If the inner class object is created within an ordinary method of the class this association between the objects is automatic. Otherwise it needs to be specifically set up. In either case, objects of the inner class type can see even private fields of the outer class, and conversely. They are not private from one another. This is often a convenient way to strongly link objects of two different types together, especially when the outer class is being built by composition of parts. Therefore the *display* field is visible within AccumulateStrategy

The AccumulateStrategy must implement this interface:

```
private class AccumulateStrategy implements NumberStrategy{
   public void execute(int value){
      display = 10 * display + value;
   }
}
```

Next we need to create one of these and connect the NumberKeys to it. Note that this class defines objects without any state at all. There are no fields and the only data they use is in a parameter to the method. Therefore we never need more than one of them. So we will let the CalculatorModel create one of these and we will use it as needed. On the other hand, we need to switch strategies as we discovered above. Therefore we also need a currents strategy field in the CalculatorModel that knows which strategy the keys of the model are using at that instant.

```
private final NumberStrategy accumulate = new AccumulateStrategy();
private NumberStrategy currentNumberStrategy = accumulate;
```

Then we need to change the press method of NumberKey so that it delegates to the current strategy. We repeat the entire class definition, since it is short:

```
private class NumberKey implements CalculatorKey{
   public NumberKey(int value){
      this.value = value;
   }

   public void press(){
      currentNumberStrategy.execute(value);
   }

   private final int value;
}
```

Note that so far we have changed no behavior, but just refactored the code: it has the same behavior, but a different structure. If you run it at this time it will produce exactly the same results as before as well as having the same limitations.

Now we need to see the operator keys, like + and the new strategy that will be substituted for the accumulate strategy when we push +.

Next, let's note, again, that the actual operation of the + key will be delayed until we later press the = key. Since we can't execute it immediately we need to capture the operation somehow. The operator key itself seems like the best place to capture this, since with different operators we can capture the explicit operation of each right there. Suppose, then, that we extend the CalculatorKey interface to add another method. We won't modify the CalculatorKey interface, since NumberKeys don't need the new operation but operator keys need both press and operate.

```
private interface OperatorKey extends CalculatorKey{
   public void operate();
}
```

Then the plus key can implement this interface. Note that an interface *extends* another, not *implements* in Java. The PlusKey class will be used to implement just this one key here, though we might be able to generalize it later. Note that it needs both press and operate. Here we show just the structure and will fill in the method bodies after we examine the situation a bit more.

```
private class PlusKey implements OperatorKey{
    public void operate(){
        // TODO
    }

    public void press(){
        //TODO
    }
}
```

The calculator itself needs to remember some additional things. When the plus key is pressed we need to assure that the current display is saved somewhere so that we can start to accumulate the next value.

```
private int savedValue = 0;   // field of CalculatorModel
```

The display will be moved to this location with an assignment at the right moment.

The body of PlusKey.operate can then use this value and the display to update the display.

```
public void operate(){
    display = savedValue + display;
}
```

Note that in a MinusKey the only difference would be the subtract operation instead of the addition above.

Next, we need to remember a most recent operation so that we know what operator key was pressed as we accumulate the second value, so that we can apply its operate when the = key is pressed:

```
private OperatorKey lastOperation; // field of CalculatorModel
```

And then, the press method of PlusKey looks like the following:

```
public void press(){
    lastOperation = this;
    currentNumberStrategy = save;
}
```

A *press* has the calculator remember that this key is the most recent operator and it changes the current strategy to one we have not yet developed or even discussed. But relating this to the state transition diagram is useful. When we press the plus key we want to move (in the diagram) to the Save state from the Accumulate state. When we do this we replace the accumulate strategy with a save strategy. Anticipating what we are about to see below, if we then press another number key we want to go back to the Accumulate state and put the accumulate strategy back in place. Think about what else needs to happen as we go from the Accumulate state to the Save state on pressing the plus key. It is the save strategy that will be responsible for these *state* changes.

Recall that it is the number keys that actually send messages to the strategy objects: the execute message. The accumulate strategy makes that key accumulate its saved value into the display. The save strategy on the other hand has to copy the display to the saved value. It then has to put the current number key's value into the display because that key has just been pressed and we are starting a new accumulation. Finally it has to set the current strategy back to the accumulate strategy. Figure 9.2 shows a sequence diagram with the sequence of operatons. Things farther down the diagram happen after things above. The arrow indicates which object sends a message to or otherwise operates on which other object.

Here is the code that carries this out:

```
private class SaveStrategy implements NumberStrategy{
   public void execute(int value){
      savedValue = display;
      display = value;
      currentNumberStrategy = accumulate;
   }
}
```

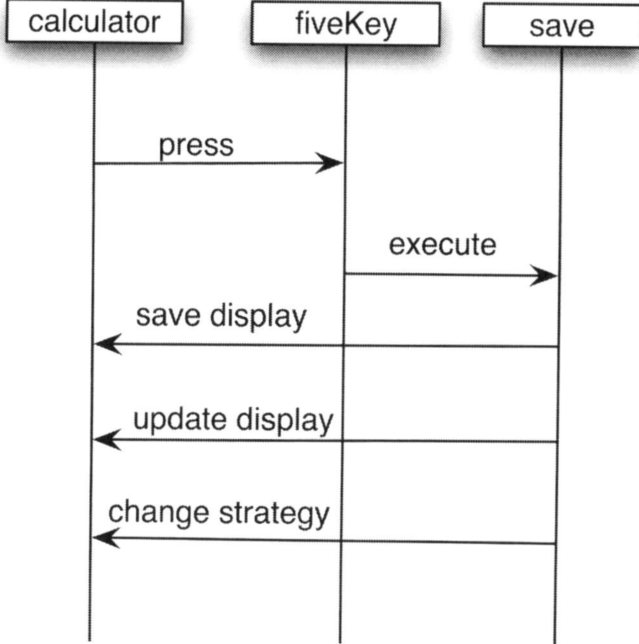

Figure 9.2 Sequence Diagram for a Number Key press.

Then, the calculator model must create one of these strategies and save it in the field *save* since the PlusKey class refers to this field.

```
private final NumberStrategy save = new SaveStrategy();
```

We aren't done yet, but it is time to see everything together again. We now have a lot of interacting parts here, so be sure you can connect them all together in your mind. We have also added pressPlus to the model. It may help to go through the explanations above once more and find the code here that we refer to. Notice especially that the public interface of the calculator model is quite simple, that we have quite a lot of objects, and that we have both composition (to build the model) and delegation (to build the number keys) going on here. Also, it would be useful to step through pressing a few keys in a legal sequence watching what happens in the code and also in the state transition diagram.

```
public class CalculatorModel{

   public int getDisplay(){
      return display;
   }

   public void pressThree(){
      three.press();
   }

   public void pressFive(){
      five.press();
   }

   public void pressPlus(){
      plus.press();
   }

   private interface CalculatorKey{
      public void press();
   }

   private class NumberKey implements CalculatorKey{
      public NumberKey(int value){
         this.value = value;
      }

      public void press(){
         currentNumberStrategy.execute(value);
      }

      private final int value;
   }

   private interface NumberStrategy{
      public void execute(int value);
   }

   private class AccumulateStrategy implements NumberStrategy{
      public void execute(int value){
         display = 10 * display + value;
      }
   }

   private interface OperatorKey extends CalculatorKey{
      public void operate();
   }
```

```
    private class PlusKey implements OperatorKey{
        public void operate(){
            display = savedValue + display;
        }

        public void press(){
            lastOperation = this;
            currentNumberStrategy = save;
        }
    }

    private class SaveStrategy implements NumberStrategy{
        public void execute(int value){
            savedValue = display;
            display = value;
            currentNumberStrategy = accumulate;
        }
    }

    private final NumberStrategy accumulate = new AccumulateStrategy();
    private final NumberStrategy save = new SaveStrategy();

    private int display = 0;
    private int savedValue = 0;
    private OperatorKey lastOperation;

    private NumberStrategy currentNumberStrategy = accumulate;
    private final CalculatorKey five = new NumberKey(5);
    private final CalculatorKey three = new NumberKey(3);
    private final OperatorKey plus = new PlusKey();
}
```

Now let's update main once more:

```
public static void main(String [] args) {
    CalculatorModel calculator = new CalculatorModel();
    int value = calculator. getDisplay();
    System.out.println("" + value);
    calculator.pressFive();
    calculator.pressThree();
    value = calculator. getDisplay();
    System.out.println("" + value);
    calculator.pressPlus();
    value = calculator. getDisplay();
    System.out.println("" + value);
    calculator.pressThree();
    value = calculator. getDisplay();
    System.out.println("" + value);
}
```

The last line of this should just be a 3 and we expect that 53 is in the savedValue field, but have no way to test it here. But just before and just after pressing the plus key, the display prints as 53 at least.

What we have done here is simpler than you might think. We have added two strategies, one to capture each possible behavior of the number keys. We organized the switching between them using a state transition diagram. That is the core of what has happened in this section.

A few things might be subtle, though. Note that the strategies are properties of the calculator, not the number keys themselves. This is for a number of reasons, but primarily because we have ten number keys (only two created so far), and they must all behave alike and the changes in behavior are the same for all. Changing this in the number keys themselves, if that were necessary, would be a messy solution that we might like to avoid. Conceptually, the current strategy *of* the number keys is a property of the calculator as a whole, of course, so we don't do damage to our guiding metaphor here by doing this. Java helps us here since the encapsulation boundary is the class: the containing class, CalculatorModel, so the number keys have access to these strategy fields even though they are private.

9.6.5 The Equals Key

It is the = key that actually gets the work done: Give the calculator an = key that performs any outstanding operation and clears for a new calculation.

After the previous section we will see that not much is left to be done. The equals key must perform the previously saved operation, stored in the operator key and make sure that we can use the calculator for a new calculation.

```
private class EqualsKey implements CalculatorKey{
    public void press(){
        lastOperation.operate();
        savedValue = 0;
        currentNumberStrategy = save;
    }
}
```

With this, the calculator works as far as it goes, but it has a couple of flaws. The main one is that adding three numbers is a bit awkward. This is because the calculator only performs any operation when you press =. So to add 5, 3, 5 you need the key sequence 5 + 3 = + 5 = and you will then see 13 properly. But the = in the middle is kind of superfluous and easy for a user to forget. We can correct for this quite easily, but also having the operator key perform the previous operation along with saving itself for future use. PlusKey.press then becomes:

```
public void press(){
    lastOperation.operate();
    lastOperation = this;
    currentNumberStrategy = save;
}
```

Alas, this breaks something else. If you now try to do two independent operations back to back, you find that the second just continues the first. The correction for this is also quite easy and corrects another flaw we haven't mentioned yet. Notice that the lastOperation field of the calculator was not initialized when it was declared and didn't get any value until we press an operator key. But if the user presses the equal key before any operator key the program will fail (try it) with a null pointer exception since the equals key tries to send a message through this reference. But what *is* the lastOperation when you start up the calculator? There isn't one, of course, but null will give us exactly the same difficulty. We could use an IF structure to check for null but once you let null fly around in your program you seem to have to check for it everywhere. Better if we avoid that by initializing the reference to an object that will "do the right thing" in this context, which is nothing. This suggests we create a NullKey operator class and object that has completely empty behavior for both of its methods. We can then initialize lastOperation to this nullKey object and set lastOperation to it at the end of EqualsKey.press as well.

```
private class NullKey implements OperatorKey{
   public void operate(){
      // nothing
   }

   public void press(){
      // nothing
   }
}

private final OperatorKey nullKey = new NullKey();
private OperatorKey lastOperation = nullKey;
```

and:

```
private class EqualsKey implements CalculatorKey{
   public void press(){
      lastOperation.operate();
      savedValue = 0;
      currentNumberStrategy = save;
      lastOperation = new NullKey();
   }
}
```

Note that if we press an operator immediately after = we continue a calculation, but pressing a number key instead starts a new one. This implies that there are additional state transitions here that we have not discussed yet. With the above changes Figure 9.3 shows our state transitions.

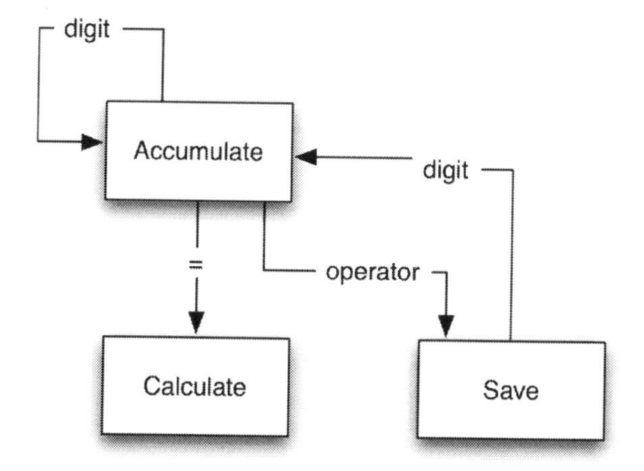

Figure 9.3. State Transition Diagram (complete)

9.7 Other Primitive Types in Java

Java has a number of other built-in types that you might need from time to time. Some programs use them extensively and some very little or not at all. We have mentioned short, int, and long so far. The other discrete number types are byte and char. The *byte* type requires 8 bits of storage and holds only small values (-128 ... 127). It is mostly intended for capturing data as you read it from an input stream as we shall discuss in another chapter. The *short* type requires 16 bits and normally represents character data, but is actually numeric. Note that char is the same size as a short. But char is special in that it knows how to translate from character encodings that are human readable. The encoding used is called UNICODE, which is an international standard for encoding. It covers most of the world's languages completely. It has a subset, Latin-1, that is frequently used in the U.S. to encode keyboards and such. Character values can be numeric, in which case they are interpreted as Unicode values, OR you can singly quote a single character. So 'a' is a char, as is '='. Note that if you use double quotes you have a String value instead, which is not the same.

Note that what we are describing is specific to Java. Other languages use different types and different rules for types that might use the same names. So *int* in C++ means something similar, but not exactly the same.

The numeric types mentioned so far are called *discrete* since they model subsets of the integers of mathematics. The opposite of discrete is continuous and the *floating* (sometimes called *real*) types are an attempt to model the real numbers of mathematics. That is very difficult (though not impossible) since the digital nature of computers makes them discrete not continuous. There were once analog computers (even the slide rule is a simple example) that better model continuous mathematics. The floating point types of Java are float (32 bits) and double (64 bits). The encoding uses a binary fraction and an exponent, much like the scientific form of numbers, though in base 2 instead of 10. Double values have more range as well as generally more precision than float values.

Floating numbers trade range for precision. A 32 bit *int* type in Java covers a range from about –2 billion to + 2 billion. Its values are all of the integer values in between, represented precisely. But it isn't possible to represent 2.7 with an int other than very approximately as either 2 or 3. Floating values do a little better with this.

A 32 bit float value in Java represents a value somewhere in the range beyond -2^{127} to $+2^{127}$. That is beyond 1.7 x 10^{38} which is vastly bigger than 2 billion. Float values are also good for representing values between the integers, but only approximately. 2.7 can be represented approximately and 2.7 is a valid float value. However, it is not precisely represented. Think about it for a minute. There are still only a bit over 4 billion different values that you can represent in 32 bits. So if we are covering a much wider range, we must not be covering it as well as the integers. And since we can represent many values between integer values, it must also be true that successive floating values at some point of the range must be a lot farther apart than the integers are.

One of the most disconcerting things for novices about float values is that arithmetic is not precise. If you add up .1 (point 1) a thousand times you don't get 100. You get something approximating 100, but that is because the float value .1 only approximates the real number one-tenth. There are some programs that do so much floating arithmetic in a naïve way that the answers are completely meaningless. It is even true that if you add up a long string of float values from smallest to largest and again from largest to smallest you are extremely likely to get different results. So even though we can represent values with decimal points using float values, they aren't very good for representing things like money. In fact money is a very sophisticated concept since the money value of a number depends on where you are. 100 (dollars) is very different from 100 (yen). Conversely two different numbers can therefore represent the same *money*. By the way, calendar dates are similarly sophisticated, since people use different calendars around the world and calendar systems have changed over time.

Java also has wrapper classes for all of the built-in primitive types. For example Float is a class that wraps and encapsulates a single float value. The Float class has many methods for translating between internal (binary) and external (human readable) forms. If you want to put a float into a Vector, you must wrap it in a Float object first. In recent versions of Java this wrapping, called *boxing*, has become automatic.

We won't try to give all the rules here (there are a *lot* of rules), but it is possible to translate from one type to another. Sometimes it is seamless and invisible, and other times you need to specify better what you might mean. For example, something like

```
float x = 7;
```

is permitted, even though 7 is an int. This is considered a *widening* conversion and it is the closest float to 7 that will be stored in x. By the way, if you want 7 to be considered as a long, write 7L, instead. And there is one disconcerting thing about int values. If you use zero as the leftmost character, the value will be treated as if you want octal (base 8) encoding, not the normal base 10, so 0377 is really the same as 255.

If you want to make a *narrowing* conversion, where information might be lost, you need to specify it with a *cast*. For example the following is illegal:

```
int y = 7.2;
```

Instead you need to be specific, thereby indicating that you realize you are losing information and want it to happen.

```
int y = (int) 7.2;
```

The decimal part is lost. Here for simplicity of example we have used constant values, but the same will be true if you try to assign a variable of one numeric type to that of a different type. Narrowing conversions must be specified. By the way there are many helpful methods for rounding, etc., in java.lang.Math. And don't be surprised if something like:

```
int z = (int) 7.0;
```

turns out to be 6 instead of 7. Remember that float values are approximate, and you are calling for truncation here, not rounding.

There are no casts between numeric types and boolean.

Finally, if you put a sequence of characters in double quotes, like "Karel J Robot", it is a String, but String is a class type and strings are objects.

9.8 Scope of Variables

How and where you create a variable determines what part of the program it is associated with. This is related to, but slightly different from visibility, which also affects where the variable can be used.

We have defined fields in our classes in this Chapter and earlier. Ordinary fields belong to the objects that we create. If we create two CalculatorModels, for example, we have two fiveKeys as well, one for each.

It is also possible to create variables that are not part of the objects of the class, but part of the class itself. These variables are defined within the class, just as fields are, but are marked *static* by the programmer. These are sometimes called *shared* variables because all of the objects in the class have access to the same variable, and if any one changes it, it is changed for all to see. If it is public then other places in the program can see and alter it as well. It is sometimes permissible for a *static final* field to be public, since, being final, the value associated with the variable can't be changed. However, if the variable is a reference variable and the value is mutable, then any code that can see the variable can pass it a message causing a state change. Had we made the keys in the CalculatorModel static, then all calculators would share the same keys. That wouldn't match our metaphor of a physical calculator very well, and then pushing the five key in one calculator would push it for all. Note that System.out is a public static object defined within the System class. Static variables are prefixed with the class name to access them. Within the class the prefix is not needed.

One possible use for a static counter variable in a robot program might occur if you had a lot of robots of a given class wandering around the world putting down beepers. You might want to know the total number of beepers placed by all the robots. You could have a static variable totalBeepers, initially 0, to keep track of this. The putBeeper method could be overridden to increment this variable. You would also probably provide a static method in the class to get the current value of it. Static methods are discussed below.

We can also define variables within methods. The scope of the variable is that method itself and the variable is visible nowhere else. These *local variables* are never marked public, private… or static. That is meaningless for local variables. You can, for example, declare and create a helper robot within a single method and it can be used only there.

It is also possible to define new variables whenever you open and close braces, for example for the body of a while. One particular instance of this is when you define the control variable of a FOR loop in the for statement itself. In all such cases the variable is only visible in the braced *block*.

In general, it is a good idea to define variables with the smallest scope that makes sense: class, object, method, block. This limits the places at which the variable can be modified and that helps you with your thinking process since it means there is a smaller part of the program over which you need to keep track of it mentally.

By the way, methods can also be static, and this just means, again, that the method belongs to the class and not to individual objects of the class. There is no polymorphism possible with static methods (or with constructors). They don't have access to any "this" variable, nor to any ordinary fields. They can manipulate static variables, however. The ubiquitous *main* function is such a static function. Static "methods" aren't really methods at all. They are just like the more primitive functions of languages like C and Pascal. You don't send messages to invoke them. You just *call* static methods. The implication is that the invocation of a static method explicitly names the precise method to be invoked. With a true (non-static) method, the message is interpreted by the receiving object, which then uses its own version of the method to complete the message. This can only be done while the program is running, since it is only then that objects exist.

Methods can even be final, in which case they cannot be overridden in a subclass. One use of a final method is to do some initialization for use in a constructor. Constructors should only call final methods if any. This is because an object executing a constructor is only partially created and a method that has been overridden may well fail if called from a constructor. Other uses have to do with the logic of a program. Programs might break if especially important control methods are overridden.

9.9 Introduction to Arrays

Often a program will need to manipulate more information than we can conveniently provide individual names for. With three or four robots it is not a problem, but if the program needed to manipulate 3000 robots it would be a big problem. While we could incorporate numbers into the names (karel_1, karel_2,...) it would still be difficult to make all of them move, for example. We therefore need a more flexible way to handle large amounts of data. For this we need some sort of *data structure*. Data structures are various ways of organizing data with associated operations for manipulating the data or the structure itself.

One of the oldest mechanisms for this, and still supported by most programming languages, is the *array*. An array is a linear (one after the other) structure that is compactly and efficiently stored in computer memory. An array consists of a fixed number of cells, each of which can hold one item, perhaps an int, perhaps a reference to an object. Anything you like, actually; even other arrays! Arrays are homogeneous; they hold one kind of thing, either primitive data or objects. Arrays are *indexed*, meaning that you retrieve items by knowing their relative locations in the array. In Java, indexing starts at zero, so the first item is in cell 0, the second in cell 1, etc. The reason-to-be for arrays, is that it is very efficient for the computer to retrieve an item knowing its index. If we have an array of Harvester robots named *crew*, then crew[5] is a reference to the sixth Harvester, provided that the array has at least six *elements*. In fact, crew[5] is a variable, so we can assign a new value to it as well as retrieve the reference it holds. To create an array of 1000 Harvester robots you would start by writing:

```
Harvester [] crew = new Harvester[1000];
```

There are two things to note here. The first is that an array is an object with fields and methods. One of its fields is *length* and it is public, though it is also constant. Once we create an array its length never changes. So crew.length will be 1000. The second important fact is that the above creates the array, but not the robots. It is really an empty array of 1000 null references, so not yet very useful. We create the robots with a for loop.

```
for (int street = 0; street < 1000; ++street){
   crew[street] = new Harvester(street + 1, 1, East, 0);
}
```

We would then have 1000 Harvester robots "arrayed" along first avenue. And note that the array cell numbers start at zero, but our streets in the world begin at 1, so we needed to make an adjustment in our delivery specifications here: the robot referenced in cell k is standing on street k + 1. It is easy to make errors, of course, when you need to do this kind of adjustment. It is just one more thing you need to keep track of as you program. In fact, using the name *street* in the above might be misleading, as there is no street 0.

Note that in the assignment within the for loop above, we are giving a new value to each element in the array. What was null, will now be a reference to a new robot. So the syntax *array[cellNumber]* is valid in any context in which a variable of the same type could be used. In particular, since our array crew holds references to robots, we can send messages to them as we see next.

Now with a thousand robot crew, we could harvest a huge field of beepers, by having each one harvest one row. To do this, however, we would want to use another for loop (or perhaps a while loop). For loops and arrays are sort of made for each other, of course.

```
for (int street = 0; street < 1000; ++street){
   crew[street].harvestOneRow();
}
```

Recall, that crew[k] is a reference to the k+1st cell, which is a reference to a Harvester, so the above works, though writing an extra statement might make it more clear initially:

```
for (int street = 0; street < 1000; ++street){
   Harvester harvester = crew[street];
   harvester.harvestOneRow();
}
```

But these are really the same thing, and there is no need for the intermediate local variable named *harvester*.

It is easy to make errors in you array indexing, especially when you notice that the index, also called the *subscript*, can be any integer expression. So we could make every other robot harvest one row with this for loop:

```
for (int street = 0; street < 500; ++street){
   crew[2*street].harvestOneRow();
}
```

This references cells 0, 2, 4, etc, up to … what, exactly? The last value of street is 499, and so the last cell referenced is cell 998 and this is the robot on street 999, so all is well here, but you'd need to be a bit more careful with every seventh robot. If you index an array cell outside the range 0..length-1 you will get an `IndexOutOfBoundsException` and will need to fix your error.

If the size (length) of the array isn't too large, and especially if the values stored in it won't change, there is a nice way to create and initialize the array. For example, back in Chapter 4, the Chorographer had two helper robots named lisa and tony. There was really no need for them to have individual names, however. We could have done this instead, using an array to hold the two helpers:

```
public class Choreographer extends UrRobot {

   private UrRobot [] helpers = {
      new UrRobot(4,2,East,0),
      new UrRobot(6,2,East,0)
   };
   . . .

   public void move(){
      super.move();
      for(int i = 0; i < helpers.length; ++i){
         helpers[i].move();
      }
   }
   ...
}
```

We replace the declarations of lisa and tony with the declaration of an array of UrRobots (references to UrRobots, of course) and immediately initialize it with two values we get using the *new* operator to create the robots immediately. The list of values is enclosed in braces, separated by commas and the entire construct is ended with a semicolon, since it is a declaration. This is a new use of braces, by the way. The move instruction then just sends move to each helper, but using a for loop bounded by the length of the array. If we add another robot to the array declaration, this for loop will still send the move message to each helper, since we didn't assume here that there would be just two. Had we *hard coded* the 2 into the loop bound an update would have been more error prone. An array initialized this way is just like any other and its elements can be changed as usual, though this is most often used for fixed arrays - even quite large ones.

In Chapter 11 we shall see other, slightly less efficient, but much more flexible, collections of data. In old computer languages, such as Fortran, arrays were the only collections provided, so programmers got very good at manipulating them. We shall see an application of arrays in the next chapter and will use them extensively in the Primo Intermezzo.

9.10 Important Ideas From This Chapter

implicit state
program counter
explicit state
instance variable (field)
local variable
static variable
inner class (static and not)
invariant
variable
primitive
int
array
counter
counting loop
off by one error
accumulator
String
System.out
accessor
mutator
encapsulation
information hiding
composition
delegation
refactor
numeric types (float, double, byte, short, char, int, long)
cast
final

9.11 Problem Set

1. What changes to the state occur when:
    a. A robot moves?
    b. A robot turnsLeft?
    c. A robot putsBeeper?
    d. A robot is created with the new operator?
    e. The simulator for the robot world executes World.readWorld(...)?

f. An int variable is incremented?
g. The program executes any statement?

2. Build a simple Robot class in which a robot keeps count of how many moves it has made and will report return that value (as an int) from the method distanceTraveled. Would there be any reason to use a long for this?

3. Build a Robot class in which the robot keeps track of the number of beepers in its beeper bag and can report it if asked.

4. Write a robot program in which a robot has a method to count and return the number of beepers on its current corner.

5. Build a Robot class in which the robots can keep track of their current street and avenue and return the int value when asked. To do a good job of this, you must consider error shutoff situations as well.

6. Exercise 5 normally requires a lot of IF statements. Can you think of a way to employ strategies instead? A North facing strategy, for example. How (when) will you switch between strategies? This has a simple state change diagram that you might explore.

7. Extend the CalculatorModel class with one more feature. Make it possible to toggle between two states. The first is the normal state in which it does just exactly the same as above. The other state is such that whenever the display changes, it is automatically printed to System.out. This is easy to do with an IF statement and a simple boolean flag. It might be more interesting if you employ two more simple strategies. In either case, it will be helpful to find all of the places in the program in which the display changes and replace them all with an invocation of a simple (private) message: setDisplay(value).

8. Suppose a robot needed to employ a different strategy depending on which street it was on. Suppose that we could also be sure that it would never go north of 12th street. Would an array be a good way to store the strategies? Why or why not? What else might we need in order for this to work? Write a program to test your ideas.

9. The distance from a robot to the origin is simply the sum of its street number and its avenue number minus two, but only in a world without walls other than the boundary walls. Write a class with a method to compute this.

10. If the world has walls, the distance to the origin is harder to compute. It might not even be possible to do so, as the robot might not be able to reach the origin at all. Write a class with a method to find the length of the shortest path to the origin if one exists and to signal that it can't reach the origin if that is the nature of the world. This is a hard problem. One solution involves *recursive backtracking*, which you would need to explore. Problem 2 of Chapter 7 actually gives some insight into this problem. If the robot starts out with an infinite number of beepers and is willing to put down a lot of beepers, another solution might be devised.

11. When we have given delivery specifications for robots we have so far always used constants for all arguments in the constructor, but that isn't necessary. Here is an idea to explore. Suppose that a Choreographer-like robot doesn't know how many dancers it will need, but there is a pile of beepers at the origin that holds the right number – one dancer per beeper. The dancers should be arrayed out along first avenue starting with 2nd avenue. The Choreographer picks up the beepers in the pile, and for each one creates a dancer one block farther north, with the first on 2nd aveune, the second beeper causing creation of a dancer on 3rd, etc. After all of the

robots are created all should move one block to the East. Implement this. We note that any of the parameters of creation of robots can be set with variables. You might want to explore this creatively.

12. A robot named karel is going to go for a stroll round and round a square four blocks on a side. Karel won't know how many steps to take until sent the *meander* message which has this prototype

```
public void meander(int steps)
```

Karel should move exactly *steps* times while walking around the square. But karel needs to turn after every fourth step, of course. At the end, we would like to know how many steps karel took along the final side, which may be 0 to 3 steps. This number should be printed to System.out.

Hint, you many want separate counters for steps on a side and total steps. Can you do this with local variables in the meander method or do you need fields?

13. A robot named countula is in a completely enclosed room that contains zero or more beepers. Give countula a method that will return the number of beepers in the room.

14. Give countula another method that will return true if and only if the number of beepers in the room is an even number. Can you use the method of problem 13 to help you do this?

15. There is an associate of countula named reportula that is outside the room. (See the two previous exercises.) Devise a way for coutula to tell reportula how many beepers are in the room. The robot named reportula will then put that many beepers on its current corner. The two robots may be in different classes, of course, since they have different behaviors. Test this thoroughly.

10 Input, Output, and Exception Handling

In this Chapter we discuss getting information into and out of the computer. Input and output in Java is handled by classes in the Java libraries. The package that contains these classes is java.io. You need to import the classes we mention here into your programs when you want to use them.

```
import java.io.FileWriter;
```

There are separate classes for input and for output and separate classes for producing and reading human readable files (character files) and machine-only readable files (data files). There are also classes for simple things and classes for more complicated things. In general the classes for simple things can be thought of as strategies and those for more complex things decorate these strategies. We have seen exactly this same concept before, starting in Chapter 4.

10.1 File Output

We have seen how to send character information encoded in Strings to System.out so that it can be seen by the user. But suppose that we want to keep a permanent record in a file. A file is a named collection of data somewhere in your computer; usually on your disk drive. Files are managed by your computer's operating system, so your Java program needs to be able to communicate with the operating system when using files. First, we will need to give the file a name so that the operating system knows where to save our information, and we need to connect our program to the file.

Before we do this however, we need to make a decision. Is the information going to be read by a person or are we just saving it so that another program can read it back in? Java provides different classes for these purposes. In Java, *Writers* are used to store information in the form of readable characters, and *OutputStreams* are used when the data needn't be read by people. Information written by a Writer can later be read by a *Reader*. Information written by an OutputStream will usually later be read by an *InputStream*.

A *FileWriter*, defined in the java.io package, will connect you to an external file.

```
FileWriter writer = new FileWriter("data.txt");
```

We can now write characters (char) to the file named *writer*. There are two things to note about this, however. First is that the operating system may not be able to provide the file for us. If this happens we have an error and the Java system will *throw* an exception. More specifically, it will throw an *IOException*, also defined in java.io. Exceptions, throwing, and catching, are explained in the next section. In general, errors can occur with most forms of input and output. And, in general, you must deal with these errors in your programs.

The second thing to note is that a FileWriter isn't very convenient. We can write characters to it, but not much else. The integer 68 is internally encoded not as two characters, but as an int. If we try to write 68 to a FileWriter (writer.write(68);) something unexpected will occur. The character "D" will be written since 68 is the internal character code (Unicode) for a "D".

In Java, the input/output classes are each designed to do one job well and several classes are used together to do sophisticated things. The way in which the Java I/O classes work follows a general pattern called *Decorator*. Many of the I/O classes are used to decorate objects of another I/O class by providing some "fancy packaging." A decorator for a Writer will itself be a writer and will provide some additional services that the object it decorates does not provide. Here, we would like to use a PrintWriter, which knows how to write most of the things known to a Java program, not just char. A print writer doesn't actually print, however. It just knows how to format the things you give it (like ints) and pass them to the writer it decorates. We must layer up a PrintWriter onto a FileWriter to get output to a file. This is quite easily done also, though it too may throw an exception.

```
PrintWriter output = new PrintWriter(new FileWriter("data.txt"));
```

Notice that we have created two objects here. First we create a FileWriter for the file "data.txt", but we don't give that object a name. Instead we pass this as a parameter to the PrintWriter constructor. Therefore the PrintWriter will decorate the FileWriter. We can pass ints to the PrintWriter, which will translate them into characters and then pass them to the FileWriter, which will itself put them into the file.

```
output.print(68);
```

A PrintWriter can print ints, doubles, Strings, etc. It can also *println* any of these things, in which case an end of line mark will be added after the value is printed.

One important thing to note is that when you open a Writer or an OutputStream in a program, you need to close it before the program exits if you want the contents of the stream to be preserved.

```
output.close();
```

If you forget this, you won't find the file when the program exits.

A PrintWriter can decorate either another Writer or an OutputStream. This means that you can write ints and doubles, for example, to data files as well as character files though the data will be stored as characters if you do this.

Another output decorator is *BufferedWriter*. This class might be used if you only wanted to write Strings to a Writer, such as a FileWriter. It provides internal buffering that makes the output more efficient by holding on to the information we write until there is quite a bit of it and then writing it all at once. Since the physical write process to a file takes a long time compared to the internal speed of the computer, this can speed up a program simply due to the fact that it executes fewer write instructions if it writes more in each one. The last output decorator we will discuss here is the *OutputStreamWriter* which decorates an OutputStream, turning it into a Writer.

Sometimes you need to layer more than one decorator onto another object. Here we seldom use more than two decorators and one object that is not a decorator. The outermost decorator is the one you wish to actually use. The innermost Writer gives the final destination for the characters you produce. For us the innermost has been a FileWriter, but Java is very flexible. You can use the same ideas to send information from one program to another while they both execute, for example.

10.2 Exceptions

Errors occur in Java programs as in most human activity. When an error occurs in a Java program we say than an exception (small e) has occurred. When this happens an Exception object (capital e) is created and "thrown". This can be caught or not, depending on the kind of Exception it is and on the program. Here is the result of an uncaught exception that occurred when a robot tried to walk through a wall.

```
Exception in thread "main" com.jbergin.robot.RobotException:
      Robot tried to walk through a wall.
   at com.jbergin.robot.SimpleRobot.move(SimpleRobot.java:205)
   at com.jbergin.robot.Driver.findPut(Driver.java:15)
   at com.jbergin.robot.Driver.findPut(Driver.java:16)
      at com.jbergin.robot.Driver.main(Driver.java:32)
```

The code that was executing when this was thrown was the move method of a class called SimpleRobot on line 205 of the file that defines this class. That move instruction was invoked most recently from a class called Driver, in its findPut method on line 15 of the file.

It is easy to generate an exception. Simply declare a new Robot variable and send it a message without actually creating any robot.

```
Robot john = null;
john.move();
```

This will generate a NullPointerException which will be thrown, but not caught. The program will terminate and we will get a message informing us of the fact, perhaps even telling us which line in our program contained the error. (Actually, it is just the thread that executes the error that terminates, not necessarily the entire program.).

We can *catch* this exception and therefore prevent the program from terminating. To catch an exception if it arises you include the statements that might throw the exception in a try block. Here is a program fragment with no purpose but to demonstrate the idea.

```
try{
   Robot john = null;
   john.move();
}
catch(NullPointerException e){
   System.out.println(" A null pointer exception occurred: "  + e);
}
```

When we catch an exception we name the class of the exception we are interested in and give a variable that will have that type. Within the body of the catch clause we can send the Exception object messages, or print it out as here. You can do anything you like in the catch clause, including trying to recover from the error.

When an exception is thrown in a try block, the execution of the try is abandoned immediately and the system searches for a handler (a catch clause) of the type of the exception that was thrown.

If the code can throw more than one kind of exception, then you can have several catch clauses with a single try. These are written one after the other following the closing braced of the try clause. The most specific ones should be listed first, and the more general ones later. Exceptions are objects from classes. Here, more general means a super class, and more specific means a sub class.

There are two basic kinds of exceptions in a Java program: Exception and RuntimeException. A null pointer exception is of the latter kind and these need not be caught. In fact, a correct program should never have any of these, so if you have one, you need to fix your program. In the above we need to make john refer to some robot before we send it any messages.

The other kind, Exception, is one that can occur even in a correct program. For example, when we try to create a file, the operating system may not permit it, perhaps because the disk is locked, or there is no space available. These kinds of problems are beyond the control of the programmer. Therefore, even a correct program can generate them. For this reason such exceptions must be caught by the programmer. The IOExceptions discussed in Section 10.1 are like this so all the code there must be taught to handle exceptions. They must be caught or passed on for handling elsewhere.

```
PrintWriter output = null;
try{
   output = new PrintWriter(new FileWriter("data.txt"));
   . . .
}
catch(IOException e){
   System.out.println(" File could not be created: "  + e);
System.exit(1);
}
```

Here we have indicated with ellipsis that some things have been left out. The question arises as to how big a try block should be. This depends on whether you can recover from the exception or not. If you can't create a file, then you can't write to it, and perhaps your program can't continue. In this case, any statement that writes to the file should also be in the same try block, though you can make the program terminate as we have done here. If the statement writing the file were outside the try block, then we might be trying to write to a file that we haven't created. Here the variable called *output* would still be null if the exception is thrown.

Another possibility, not applicable here, is to provide some default value for the information that was being created when the exception was thrown. If this can be reasonably done, then the program can continue, and the try block can be relatively short. This might be possible if ArithmeticException is thrown because we divide by zero.

In some circumstances, an exception must be caught, but it doesn't make sense to catch it at the point at which it was thrown. In this case we need to *propagate* it. For example, suppose we want to create a method to open an output file for us. It might make sense for the client of this function to handle any exception thrown when it executes.

```
public PrintWriter openFile(String filename) throws IOException{
   return new PrintWriter(new FileWriter(filename));
}
```

We declare that the method itself may throw IOException whenever it is called. Then, invocations should be enclosed in try blocks or the exception propagated farther. So we propagate the exception to the location of the client code.

Exception objects have quite a lot of state themselves. In particular, when a program fails, the exception object that is thrown captures information about all the methods that have begun execution but not yet finished execution in that thread. If a method sends a message, some other method starts but the current one suspends until the new one completes. This is the runtime stack structure that the java runtime uses to manage the execution. If you don't catch the exception, the standard procedure is for the system to send the *printStackTrace* message to this exception object. Usually this stacktrace (most recent message at the top) includes the program line number at which the program failed. This is very useful in finding program errors during development.

It is possible for the programmer to create new Exception classes using inheritance. It is often useful to do this to indicate special program specific errors that might occur. When the program finds that the error has occurred it throws an exception by creating a new object and "throwing" it:

```
throw new ExplodingRobotException();
```

The exception can be caught or not in the usual way. The typical superclass of your own exception classes is *Exception*. With this superclass the programmer is forced to catch the exception or propagate it, or the compiler will complain. If you use *RuntimeException* then the exceptions don't need to be caught and will propagate automatically to the main program. The philosophy, however, is that a RuntimeException is appropriate when it represents an error in the program that should be corrected as it should never appear in a correct program, while an Exception indicates one that might occur even in a correct program, so the program must watch out for it explicitly. If you try to create a file on a disk drive, for example, but someone has locked the drive so that you can't write on it, then you would get a runtime exception because it is impossible in your program to control what humans do.

10.3 Input

Input is the opposite of output. We are trying to obtain information from somewhere for the program. The principles of use via decorators are the same as for output, but more exceptions may be thrown. In fact, nearly every input statement might throw an exception since the source of the data might have become unavailable.

We can read from a file using a *FileReader* or *FileInputStream*, the former if the file contains character data. We can layer on a *BufferedReader* to read Strings from the file using the *readLine* method of BufferedReader. This will read an entire line of input, where it is assumed that the file is broken up into lines, perhaps because it was written using the println methods of a PrintWriter.

So far, so good, but what if we want to read other things besides Strings. As it turns out, there is no exact input analogue of a *PrintWriter*. Instead we use a BufferedReader and its readLine method, and a special object called a *StringTokenizer* from the java.util package.

A *StringTokenizer* is an object that can break up a String into pieces separated by characters of our choice. To create a StringTokenizer initialized with information from a file, we might do something like the following.

```
try{
   BufferedReader input = new BufferedReader (
      new FileReader("data.txt"));
   String oneLine
   while((oneLine = input.readLine()) != null){
      StringTokenizer tokens = new StringTokenizer(oneLine);
   . . .
}
}
catch(IOException e){
   System.out.println(" File could not be opened: "  + e);
   System.exit(1);
}
```

Note that a readLine will return null at the end of the file. We use this fact to exit the loop. Notice that the while test contains an assignment to oneLine as well as a test of the result. This seems like very strange practice, but it is a standard Java *idiom*, so you need to become familiar with it. It works because an assignment *statement* is also an *expression*. It has a value the same as that set into the variable on the left hand side. By enclosing this expression in parentheses we can give a test of its value. A BufferedReader returns null at the end of the file.[3]

If we are inside the while loop body, we have a non empty string, so we wrap a StringTokenizer around it to give us access to its parts. This isn't a decorator, however, since StringTokenizer has a different interface than String. It is an *Adapter*, which adapts the interface to a more useful form.

Once we have the tokenizer, we operate on it to get access to its string. We do this by writing a while loop controlled by calls to the tokenizer's *hasMoreTokens* method. We get access to an individual "word" or "token" in the string with the tokenizer's *nextToken* method. Continuing the above, and repeating part of it:

```
while((oneLine = input.readLine()) != null){
   StringTokenizer tokens = new StringTokenizer(oneLine);
   while (tokens.hasMoreTokens()){
      String word = tokens.nextToken();
      . . .
   }
}
```

Now, we can do anything we like with the String named Word. If we know that it encodes an int, for example, we can get that int with

```
int ivalue = Integer.parseInt(word);
```

though this latter message may throw a NumberFormatException if the String doesn't actually contain an int value. Integer is a class in java.lang that is usually used to turn ints into objects, though it also provides this static method *parseInt* to translate Strings.

Notice that to do the above effectively, we need to know what to anticipate at each "word" in the file.

---

[3] The fact that assignment is an expression explains why cascading assignment works: x = y = 3.0; This works from the right, with y getting a value and then x taking its value from y. (y = 3.0) is an expression.

There is another variation on the StringTokenizer constructor in which we give it a string as the second parameter. The individual characters in this string will be taken as the ones that are used to break up the String. For example, we could have a String of words separated with slashes and tokenize this with a tokenizer whose second parameter was just "/". If we don't give this parameter, the default value is used with consists of the so-called white space characters: space, tab, and newline. The delimiters are not part of the tokens, by the way.

Let's look at an example of how this might all fit together. Suppose we want to examine one of the karel world files and write a simple function that returns how many beepers it specifies for the world. Here is an example: the *stairworld.kwld* file:

```
KarelWorld
streets 5
avenues 10
beepers 4 4 1
beepers 3 3 1
beepers 2 2 1
eastwestwalls 3 4 4
eastwestwalls 2 3 3
eastwestwalls 1 2 2
northsouthwalls 4 1 1
northsouthwalls 4 2 2
northsouthwalls 4 3 3
northsouthwalls 3 3 3
northsouthwalls 2 2 2
northsouthwalls 1 1 1
```

Among other things, this file says that on street 4 and at avenue 4 there is one beeper. The total beepers in the file is three here. The lines of the file don't have to come in any specific order, however.

The following uses what we have learned so far:

```
public static int countBeepers(String filename) throws IOException {
   int result = 0;
   BufferedReader input =
      new BufferedReader(new FileReader(filename));
   String oneLine;
   while ((oneLine = input.readLine()) != null) {
      StringTokenizer tokens = new StringTokenizer(oneLine);
      if (tokens.nextToken().equalsIgnoreCase("beepers")) {
         String street = tokens.nextToken();
         String avenue = tokens.nextToken();
         String beepers = tokens.nextToken();
         result += Integer.parseInt(beepers);
      }
   }
   return result;
}
```

We simply look for lines that begin with the word "beepers", spelled in any case and then only look at the last token on the line, which is the number of beepers. We accumulate this into the *result* local variable, which we eventually return. The tokens are String objects, however, so we need to parse the final token to extract the int encoding that it contains. The string "1" and the int 1 are not nearly the same thing in Java or most languages.

10.4 File At A Time Input

In some ways the most efficient way to read a file, assuming that it isn't absolutely HUGE, is to read it all at once into a buffer. The FileInputStream class lets us ask how big a file is with its *available* method. So we base this technique on that class, but we layer an InputStreamReader on top of it. This class will let us read a buffer (char array) of any size, so we create one of the size of the file. We then read the entire file into the buffer and then put the characters in the buffer into a new String. This we can wrap with a StringTokenizer.

```
    try{
       FileInputStream f = new FileInputStream("republicOfPlato.txt");
       InputStreamReader read = new InputStreamReader(f);
       int bufsize = f.available();
       char [] text = new char [bufsize];
       read.read(text, 0, bufsize);
          // You have the entire file in this array.
       System.out.print(text); // Show the file.

       String s = new String(text); // Now the array is in a string
       StringTokenizer t = new StringTokenizer(s, "\r\n");
          // break up on return and newline characters.
       while(t.hasMoreTokens()){
          System.out.println(t.nextToken());
          // show the file one line per line.
       }
    }
    catch(IOException e){
       System.out.println("Failed");
}
```

Here we set up the tokenizer to break into lines by using the newline and return characters as token separators: "\r\n".[4] If we use a standard initialization of StringTokenizer, without the parameter, we would get the tokens broken on whitespace characters (space, tab, and new line) and so we would have one word per line in the output,

10.5 Character At a Time Input

Sometimes you really do need to process a file one character at a time. There are a couple of standard tricks for doing this. Here we will use a buffered reader for efficiency only, not to get access to its readLine method.

---

[4] The backslash character '\', called the escape character, has a special purpose in Strings. When followed by r it means a return character. Also \n is a newline, \t is a tab. To actually see a backslash, use \\.

```
try { // reading a byte at a time
   BufferedReader b =
      new BufferedReader(new FileReader("republicOfPlato.txt "));
   int ch; // YES int;
   while((ch = b.read()) >= 0) {
      // YES assignment. Note: the parens are required.
      char c = (char)ch; // cast to char
      . . . // Do whatever you like with c.
   }
}
catch(IOException e){
   System.out.println("Reading failed");
}
```

When we read the file b, we read an int, not a char. This is because an int (32 bits) is bigger than a char (16 bits) so the system can signal end of file with a negative value. We do the read in the control part of a while loop in which we again have an assignment to the int variable and a test for non negative. Char values themselves are never interpreted as negative values, so storing the char in an int lets the system use this trick. Note that when reading Strings with a BufferedReader it is *null* that signifies end of file, while here, reading chars, it is a negative value.

Inside the loop, we know the read succeeded, but we must cast the int to a char to use the value that was read. This does seem tricky, but it is the standard way to read a character at a time from a file.

This technique of reading a file, one character at a time, is a Java *idiom*. It won't be the same in another language and there is little in the Java language definition that will lead you to think of this trick as obvious. In fact it is rather ugly: an assignment as part of the test. It is, however, the *right* way to do it and you need to learn a certain number of idioms when you learn any new language. This one depends on the fact that an assignment is really an expression as well, whose value is the value given to the left hand side (which may be different from the right side value, because of automatic conversions that might be applied).

10.6 Reading From the Console

Some programs want to take information from the user typing into a command window. Graphical windows for input are actually much more common today, but in the past command entry from the console was just about the only way a program could take data from a user.

The console has three parts from the Java standpoint. System.out, System.err, and System.in. The first two are for output with the err stream intended for messages indicating errors in the program or system errors discovered as the program runs. On large computers (mainframes) the err stream might go to the system operator's console, not your workstation. For historical reasons, System.out and System.err are PrintStreams. PrintStream is a class that isn't used much anymore as it proved awkward in practice. The Writer classes were added to Java later and proved more satisfactory. However, the out and err objects were left as they were so that older programs still run. It is at least useful enough that we can write Strings upon it.

System.in is an InputStream (java.io.InputStream) and this too is only marginally useful: in fact, it is an abstract class. However, the ability to layer one i/o class upon another (decorator, again) helps us here and can provide a more useful interface to System.in. The major flaw in InputStreams for this use, however is that stream objects are not intended to produce human readable data. An input stream reads bytes, not chars.

Therefore it doesn't do any translation to a user readable form. But we can always layer a Reader on it: specifically an InputStreamReader, which will do the translation for us.

However, an input stream reader layered on System.in still reads just one character at a time, which is not very efficient, so a BufferedReader is usually layered on the other two. A buffered reader has a readLine method that produces a String object from a line of input.

```
BufferedReader inData =
   new BufferedReader(new InputStreamReader(System.in));

String aLine = inData.readLine();
```

Now we can use a StringTokenizer to split this into tokens. An alternative class, called Scanner, is discussed in the Primo Intermezzo.

10.7 A Simple I/O Illustration

Here we will illustrate a few ideas about input and output in a simple program. It might be the very beginning of the development of a program to manage your growing library. It will be overly simplified, since all we want to do here is to show how to put the I/O classes together to do some simple work.

First we want a simple class to represent a Book object, though we won't really do anything with these here.

```
package books;

public class Book{
   public Book(String title, String author){
      this.title = title;
      this.author = author;
   }

   public String title(){
      return  title;
   }

   public String author(){
      return  author;
   }

   private String title;
   private String author;
}
```

Books have a title and an author, and can report these values when asked. A more realistic class would include publisher, etc, and perhaps the date we purchased it, and our cost.

Somehow or other, though, we would need to find a way to start to build up the information in our "library" and to save it in files. Here for example is a simple example of a file of books, with just two books.

```
Tom Sawyer
Twain

Huckleberry Finn
Twain
```

Let's see how this file might have been created by reading information from a user at a keyboard, creating objects for each book and saving the results in the file we see here. The file happens to be called books.txt on the disk drive of my computer system.

Before we get started, though we need to think about how the user will interact with this program. It is a difficult and error-prone task to enter data into a computer. At a minimum, the computer needs to prompt the user for what is needed at each stage. Here is the minimum needed and it is what we shall build here.

```
Name of the output file: books.txt
Input books. Answer no to end.
More? [YES/no]
Title:  Tom Sawyer
Author: Twain
More? [YES/no] y
Title:  Huckleberry Finn
Author: Twain
More? [YES/no] no
```

The first line of the above is called a *prompt* and it was output by the program up to the space following the colon. The user then typed *books.txt* followed by the return/enter key. The next line is another prompt giving a simple instruction about how to proceed.

The third line is another prompt also showing the options [YES/no]. The intent of capitalizing the YES is to indicate that this is the default response and that unless you type no it will assume yes, more books. The user has responded with just the enter key so you don't see anything but the computer will assume there is to be another book because of this.

The computer then prints another prompt "Title: " and the user has responded with Tom Sawyer and a return. Then the computer asks for the author. The user responds Twain. The computer then asks again if there is more input and this time the user responded *y* and a return. And so it goes until the user specifically types *no*.

This is really inadequate for a real program, since it gives the user no chance to correct errors or even confirm that what was entered is correct. People make typing mistakes all the time doing this, so it is critical to make this as safe as possible. But it is enough to illustrate input and output processing. The first program we will see manages this dialog with the user and captures (reads) the users responses. Note that it goes back and forth between output (prompting) and input (user's response captured). When the program has a title and author it creates a book object and also writes a notation about the book to the output file that the user specified after the first prompt.

We will just show a simple program all done in a main, though in a more realistic example we would capture this instead in a class method. The class is called WriteMain and it is in the same package as the Books class.

```
package books;

import java.io.BufferedReader;
import java.io.BufferedWriter;
import java.io.FileWriter;
import java.io.IOException;
import java.io.InputStreamReader;

public class WriteMain{
   public static void main(String[] args){
      try{
         BufferedReader inFile =
            new BufferedReader(new InputStreamReader(System.in));
         System.out.print("Name of the output file: ");
         String filename = inFile.readLine();
         BufferedWriter outFile =
            new BufferedWriter(new FileWriter(filename));

         System.out.println("Input books. Answer no to end.");
         String response = "";
         System.out.print("More? [YES/no]");
         response = inFile.readLine();
         while(!response.equalsIgnoreCase("no")){
            System.out.print("Title:  ");
            String bookTitle = inFile.readLine();
            System.out.print("Author: ");
            String bookAuthor = inFile.readLine();
            Book book = new Book(bookTitle, bookAuthor);
            // Should do something with the Book object here. . .
            outFile.write(book.title());
            outFile.newLine();
            outFile.write(book.author());
            outFile.newLine();
            outFile.newLine();
            System.out.print("More? [YES/no] ");
            response = inFile.readLine();
         }
         outFile.close();
      }
      catch (IOException ioe){
         System.out.println("File error, cannot proceed.");
      }
   }
}
```

First we import all of the classes that we will use from java.io. The main method starts by first wrapping System.in in an InputStreamReader and then again in a BufferedReader. Only this latter object needs a name, *inFile*. The InputStreamReader is a real object, but we don't need to send it messages directly so it doesn't need a name. The inFile will send it messages, of course, since this is a decorator. The BufferedReader decorates the InputStreamReader which itself decorates System.in. Working the other way, System.in knows how to listen to the console, the InputStreamReader knows how to translate those bytes into characters that a human can understand, and the BufferedReader manages lines of input at a time instead of just bytes.

Next the program prints a prompt, but uses *print* instead of *println* so that the users console cursor stays on the same line as the prompt. The system waits (forever if necessary) for the user to type in something. The program then reads a line from the input file and stores the result in a String called *filename*. All of this is wrapped in a try block because this readLine might fail. There might not be a console, for example. If an IOException is thrown here or by any other statement, it will be caught and we will see a message and the program will halt. Let's assume this doesn't happen and continue.

Then it creates an output file by wrapping a FileWriter on this filename with a BufferedWriter so that we can write Strings (lines), not just characters.

Next, two more prompts are printed out and the program reads a response string from the user. The response is compared with "no" but ignoring any case changes, so that "NO" is the same as "no", etc. If the response is anything else the program enters the loop in which it gets a title and author, again prompting for each. The "more" prompt is output again at the bottom of the loop so that the program knows whether to loop again or quit.

For each title-author pair, the program creates a Book object (which isn't actually used here in any way, though it could be; see Chapter 11), and writes two lines into the output file by asking the just-created book for its title and author. Actually we already have those, but this is just an illustration. Another blank line is written as well to separate the books in the file. Notice the messages sent to the *outFile*. A buffered writer can *write* a string (not print). But to make it go to the next line you need to send it the *newLine* message as well.

Next we show another main that can read such a file (and re-create the book objects, though, again, we won't use them). There is one additional complication, however, in that the name that the user gives for the file to be read may not exist. In this case we will print a message and exit. The last thing you need to know to understand this is that a BufferedReader will return null if you try to read a line after you have reached the end of the file. We test for this to know we are done.

```
package books;

import java.io.BufferedReader;
import java.io.File;
import java.io.FileReader;
import java.io.IOException;
import java.io.InputStreamReader;

public class ReadMain{

   public static void main(String[] args){
      try{
         BufferedReader inFile =
            new BufferedReader(new InputStreamReader(System.in));
         System.out.print("Name of the input file: ");
         String filename = inFile.readLine();
         File theFile = new File(filename);
         if(!theFile.exists()){
            System.out.println("There is no file named: " + filename);
            System.out.println("Exiting.");
            System.exit(1);
         }
```

```
            BufferedReader bookFile =
               new BufferedReader(new FileReader(theFile));
            String sentinel = "";
            while(sentinel != null && sentinel.equals("")) {
               String title = bookFile.readLine();
               if(title == null){
                  break;
               }
               String author = bookFile.readLine();
               Book aBook = new Book (title,author);
               sentinel = bookFile.readLine();
               System.out.println(
                  "Book: " +title + " by: " + author);
            }
         }
         catch(IOException ioe){
            System.out.println("File Error. Can't proceed. " + ioe);
         }
   }
}
```

A File object is nothing more than an association between a filename and a file on the system. It may also include system path information so that there is flexibility in where the file is placed on the computer.

By convention, if you make a program exit with System.exit(n), the value determines whether it is a normal exit (use value 0) or an error termination (use something other than 0). There is nothing magic about this, but some operating system programs can read these codes after the program terminates and take various actions depending. This is especially helpful if a series of programs are run from a script and starting the next one depends on successful termination of a previous one.

In the above programs we were processing String data. This made things easier, since BufferedReaders, especially, make this really easy. If we wanted numeric data, on the other hand we would still get strings, but would then have to extract the numeric data from the strings. We shall see some hints in the next section about how to do this. It is the numeric wrapper classes, like Integer and Long that do this for us.

break and continue: When a loop is executing it occasionally happens that you learn either that the loop should exit prematurely or that this pass around the loop is done and the remaining statements in the body need not be executed. We see a case of the former in the above. If the book's title is null there is nothing more to do in this read loop, so we execute a *break* statement. This takes us out of the closest containing loop, though there are other forms.

If instead, you still need to stay in the loop, but are finished with this one iteration, you can execute the *continue* statement instead. It too has more complex forms.

These statements are fairly rare, but occasionally they represent the clearest way to code a solution to the problem at hand.

We note that break is also used in another kind of statement called a switch that we will see later in the book. It has a similar meaning there, but the double usage has occasionally caused problems in programs. Make sure you know which statement is being exited when you use these statements.

10.8 Introduction to Graphical User Interface Programming: Dialogs

The other way to get information from the user (as well as to display limited amounts of information) is to use a Dialog box. This is a window that you pop up onto the screen that has controls that the user can manipulate. The typical controls are labels, buttons, and fields. Labels simply present simple information. Fields permit user input, and buttons let the user control the dialog. Here we shall build a simple dialog, a Prompter, that will accept either a long or a double from the user, depending on the needs of the program. Dialogs are built by composition of parts and there are a lot of parts. This is also an introduction to general Graphical User Interface (GUI) programming. It is a topic that isn't intellectually very deep, but has a lot of complexity because of the large number of options and the large number of parts required to get even simple things done.

The World Builder dialog of the Karel J Robot simulator is an example of such a dialog. It has fields in which to enter the number of streets and avenues, Buttons so that you can "pick up" the various tools, such as the beeper tool. More buttons so that you can read or save a world, etc.

Once we have created the Prompter class, using it is very simple. Here is an example:

```
Prompter prompt = new Prompter();
long longVal = prompt.getLong("How old is it?");
System.out.println("Age: " + longVal);
double doubleVal = prompt.getDouble("What is its width?");
System.out.println("Width: " + doubleVal);
```

The dialog will be shown twice. In Figure 10.1 we see it the first time after we send the getLong message. It is waiting for the user to enter a long value into the Reply field and then press the Long button. This is being run on a Macintosh, by the way. On another computer it will look more like your own system dialog boxes. If you enter a value that can't be interpreted as a long, the dialog won't disappear. That "verification" of data is much more difficult in the command window version above. It usually requires testing the input value and then looping until the program gets a value it will accept. The same thing happens here, but it is easier to program, though other things are more detailed.

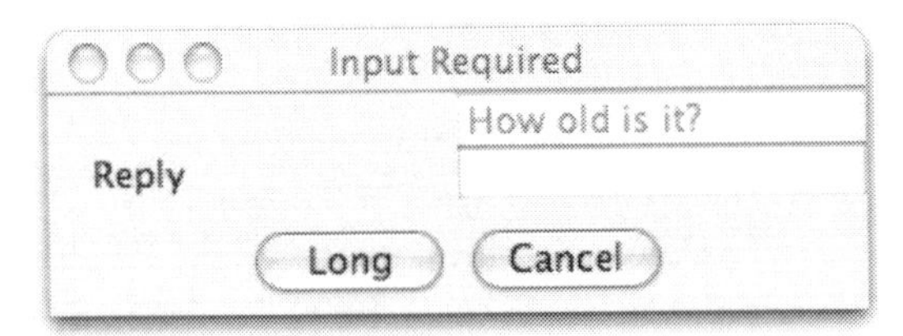

Figure 10.1 A Dialog Input

The getLong method of a Prompter is also not difficult:

```
public long getLong(String prompt){
    InputDialog longDialog = new InputDialog(prompt, "Long");
    longDialog.setVisible(true);
    long value = longValue;
    longValue = 0;
    return value;
}
```

First we create the dialog itself giving it the code "Long" that will become the label in the left button as well as determine what kind of data is desired. Once we set it visible the user is in control until he or she hits either the Long or Cancel button. The value entered into the reply field needs to be saved in a Prompter field called *longValue* so that the *getLong* method can pick it up to return it. There is a similar method, *getDouble*, that will do about the same thing, using exactly the same InputDialog class for its display. It's look will be a bit different, as the button will say Double instead and it will get a double value, of course.

Note that keeping both long and double values in the Prompter is a bit awkward, but we have the advantage of having a single dialog class, rather than one for each kind of data. So changes to it affect what the user sees both for a long request and a double request. We don't have to maintain two different, but nearly identical, dialog classes and keep their changes consistent as the program grows and changes. This is the *Say It Once* principle.

Now let's look at how the dialog window itself is built.

Graphical windows like this are built up in layers using a process also called composition. It is made up of objects called *Components*, but one kind of Component is a JPanel that can hold other components. This permits the layering. It IS a component and it CONTAINS other components, including perhaps other panels. This is called the *Composite* design pattern, by the way. We now have two uses of the word "composition," the general sense introduced in Chapter 9, and this more specific use when we apply the Composite pattern. The general sense of the word doesn't imply that the parts have the same type (Component, in this case) as the container. We will use the word in both senses below.

The overall structure of the dialog is controlled by a (javax.swing) JFrame, which has the look of a window on your computer. That includes the top title bar label ("Input Required") and the close, minimize, and grow buttons at the left or right, depending on your operating system. The above is from Mac OS X. Inside the frame are two panels. Panels have layout objects that determine how the components inside them are arranged. There are two panels in this frame. The upper one has a 2 by 2 grid layout with the upper left cell empty and the lower left cell a JLabel with value "Reply." The two right cells are JTextFields that can be used to display information like the prompt in the upper one or accept information from the user, as in the lower text field. The lower panel here contains two JButtons. No boundaries are shown between the panels, so they seem to be invisible, but they control the overall layout of this dialog.

These components are all defined in the javax.swing package in the Java libraries. Buttons work by delegation, by the way. When you push a button, what happens is delegated to a special object called an ActionListener. Listeners register with the buttons whose events (pushing the button) they want to handle. This is the *Observer* design pattern that was introduced in Section 4.9. Each button can have several listeners, though it usually only has one. But each button can (and should) have a different listener. The listeners implement the dynamic part of dialogs. Everything else is really just layout. An action listener attached to a button is an observer of the button just like the observers that were discussed back in Chapter 4. Each listener registers with the button and is informed when the button is pressed.

We shall use another level of indirection, in fact. A prompter won't be a dialog, but it will know how to create them: a dialog *factory*. A Prompter creates dialogs as required. When we ask the prompter for a long value, it will show us a new dialog tailored for long values. After the dialog is successfully dismissed, the prompter gives us the value. If we cancel the dialog, either by pressing the Cancel button or closing the window, the value returned will be 0.

We will again build by composition (general sense), so that the InputDialog class will be inside the Prompter class and the ActionListener classes (one for each button) will be inside the InputDialog class. This is complex enough that perhaps we show it in Figure 10.2.

We will depend on some knowledge below about how inner classes work. Normally, an object can refer to itself with the keyword *this*. We have seen this before. Within a method of a robot class, `move()` is the same as `this.move()`. Sometimes an object of an inner class type needs to refer to the object of the outer class of which it is a part. The way to do this is to *qualify* the keyword *this* with the name of the containing class. So, within a CancelListener, we can refer to the InputDialog object as `InputDialog.this`, and to the Prompter object with `Prompter.this`. Recall that these objects are all linked to one another, which makes this possible, and which also enables each to see and use the private information of one another.

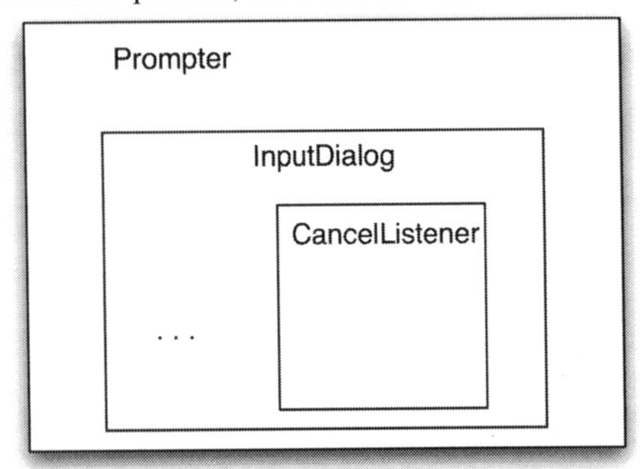

Figure 10.2 The Inner Class structure of a Prompter.

InputDialog extends JDialog, one of the Java library classes specialized for this kind of window. And the listeners, like CancelListener extend ActionListener.

There is usually very little to a GUI class other than its constructor and the listeners of its components. The layout is set in the constructor and all the parts are connected. Once you send it the setVisible(true) message the dialog is displayed on your screen and it just sits there waiting for you to interact with it and eventually activate one of the controls (such as a button) that will dismiss it. Here is the constructor for the inner InputDialog class:

```
1         public InputDialog(String prompt, String typeTag)
2         {
3               super(new JFrame(), "Input Required", true);
4               setLayout(new BorderLayout());
5
6               JPanel centralPanel = new JPanel();
7               centralPanel.setLayout(new GridLayout(2,2));
8               centralPanel.add(new JLabel(""));
9               JTextField promptField =
10                    new JTextField(prompt, prompt.length());
11              promptField.setEnabled(false);
12              centralPanel.add(promptField);
13              centralPanel.add(new JLabel("    Reply"));
```

```
14              response = new JTextField("");
15              centralPanel.add(response);
16
17              add(centralPanel, BorderLayout.CENTER);
18
19              JPanel buttonPanel = new JPanel();
20              JButton aButton = new JButton(typeTag);
21              buttonPanel.add(aButton);
22              ActionListener itsListener = new GotItListener();
23              aButton.addActionListener(itsListener);
24              response.addActionListener(itsListener);
25
26              aButton = new JButton("Cancel");
27              buttonPanel.add(aButton);
28              aButton.addActionListener(new CancelListener());
29
30              add(buttonPanel, BorderLayout.SOUTH);
31              setSize(300, 100);
32              setLocation(100,100);
33              if(typeTag.equalsIgnoreCase("double")){
34                    wantlong = false;
35              }
36              setResizable(false);
37        }
```

We create an InputDialog by telling it what prompt should appear in the upper right text field, and what kind of data we want: Long or Double. This latter will just determine the label of the left button. (line 1)

The super message (line 3) is from JDialog and creates the containing frame, the window label ("Input Required") and defines the dialog as *modal*. This means that the program must wait until the dialog is dismissed before it can continue. The Karel J Robot World Builder is not modal and it can sit visible on your screen while you do other things. It doesn't require that you dismiss it before you can continue. Here we need to supply a value to the program before we go on, so modal is the right choice.

Next we give the dialog an overall BorderLayout (line 4). It will therefore have a large central section (containing the first panel) and smaller regions surrounding it for other components. We put the button panel to the South of the central panel as we shall see (line 30). Next we create the central panel and give it a 2 by 2 grid layout (lines 6-7). When we add things to the panel they will be inserted into this grid by rows. First we

add a new label containing an empty string, then a text field containing our prompt (lines 8-12). In the example the prompt was "How old is it?", but it is a parameter of this constructor, of course. We disable this text field so that it can't be edited by the user (line 11). Then we add the *Reply* label and finally the field into which the user is expected to type (lines 13-15). The text field is called *response*. Note that we didn't give variable names to all of the components. Sometimes we just use the *new* operator in an argument position of a message. This is fine unless our code needs to also send messages to that object created with new. Often we don't and the manipulation will be entirely inside the method we invoke with the message. Now that the *centralPanel* object is complete we add it to the dialog (line 17). This is a step easy to forget and you sometimes wonder where your components are when you first run the program. Sometimes you have done a bad layout (tried to add five components to a 2 by 2 layout) and sometimes you just forget to add the component to the layer below it.

Then (lines 19-28) we create the buttonPanel, add two buttons to it, give each of them listeners (discussed below) and add the buttonPanel to the dialog (line 30). We then (lines 31-36) set the size of the dialog (in pixels), set its location on the screen (near the upper left), and indicate that it has a fixed size that the user cannot alter. Finally we remember in a field of the dialog whether we want a long (or a double). This field isn't shown here as we just see the constructor.

That is the whole GUI except for the listeners for the buttons. These add the dynamic aspects. There are several kinds of listeners and some are more complicated, but ActionListeners are used for buttons and text fields. Note that we also added an action listener to the response field; the same one we added to the main button (other than the Cancel button).

The *CancelListener* class is itself inner to the InputDialog class. It is mostly simple, but with one new Java feature. ActionListener is an interface with one required method: actionPerformed. This will be executed whenever a component for which this listener is registered (with addActionListener) is activated, such as by pushing a button.

```
private class CancelListener implements ActionListener{

   public void actionPerformed(ActionEvent e){
      InputDialog.this.setVisible(false);
      InputDialog.this.dispose();
      Prompter.this.resetValues(0, 0.0);
   }

}
```

When we create a CancelListener it knows which Prompter it is associated with via the name *Prompter.this*. All inner class objects know which container object they are associated with in this way. We haven't looked at the Prompter class yet, actually. All we need to know about it here is that it has a method (resetValues) that sets both a long value and a double. Likewise, the listener here knows that it is nested inside a particular InputDialog object and can refer to it as *InputDialog.this*. As we see it can send messages to them as above.

When the cancel button is pushed, then, the input dialog itself is made invisible, it is disposed, and the prompter remembered by the listener is reset to zeros. It will then return zero values whether asked for a long or a double. Disposing of a window (like a Dialog) releases certain system resources for use elsewhere in the program. Some operating systems manage windows themselves and the data structures to do this are large and complex. When we don't need a window any more, we usually dispose of it.

Every object can refer to itself as "this." But inside the CancelListener *this* refers to the cancel listener object itself. We don't want to make the listener invisible, or dispose of it, but rather the object of the InputDialog class that controls this object. Every object of an inner class (other than a static inner class, which we have not considered) is linked to an associated object of the outer class. This is how the inner and outer objects refer to each other's fields, by the way. The outer object can be refereed to by prefixing "this" with its class name; here `InputDialog.this`. By the way, if the inner class were static, it could only refer to static variables of the outer class, which wouldn't help us here.

Finally we can see the action listener for the main button. It is labeled Long in our example, but would be labeled Double if we had asked to prompter for a double instead. The *wantLong* field of the Prompter determines which is wanted and note that it is visible all the way down in the action listener.

```
 1        private class GotItListener implements ActionListener{
 2
 3           public void actionPerformed(ActionEvent e){
 4              String raw = response.getText().trim();
 5              if(wantlong){
 6                 try{
 7                    Prompter.this.resetValues(
 8                       Long.parseLong(raw), 0.0);
 9                    InputDialog.this.setVisible(false);
10                    InputDialog.this.dispose();
11                 }
12                 catch(NumberFormatException ex){
13                    return;
14                 }
15              }
16              else{
17                 try{
18                    Prompter.this.resetValues(
19                       0, Double.valueOf(raw).doubleValue());
20                    InputDialog.this.setVisible(false);
21                    InputDialog.this.dispose();
22                    }
23                 catch(NumberFormatException ex){
24                    return;
25                 }
26              }
27           }
28
29        }
```

The Prompter object has two values, one long and the other double. But when the dialog is presented, only one of them will be used, depending on our initial parameter. This listener also knows the prompter and will also reset one of the values of the prompter, but not both, to zero. It will, however, set the one we want, in each case, to the value extracted from the text field named *response*. Note that *response* is a field of the input dialog that contains *this*. When the Long (for example) button is pressed, the action listener's actionPerformed method is called as usual. First we extract the field's value (line 4), strip away any space and tab characters with *trim*, and call the result *raw*. It is a string, not a number. Next, what happens depends on whether we want a long or a double from this dialog and that was determined and set at the end of the constructor. Let's assume a Long. The idea is the same for a Double, but the message structure there is not quite the same. The first thing we do is ask the Long class to give us a long value from the string raw (lines 7-8). This can succeed or fail. If raw contained something like "karel" there is no *long* value to retrieve and the static *parseLong* method of Long will throw a *NumberFormatException*. If that happens the actionPerformed method returns but without dismissing the dialog (line 12-13). It is still on the screen. If Long.parseLong can successfully extract a long value no exception is thrown, so it just continues execution which hides and disposes of the dialog but not until the value that was parsed is sent to the *resetValues* method of the prompter as its first (long) argument (lines 7-8, again). The *else* clause (lines 16ff) here is the same, except the means of extracting a double from a String. Here we ask *Double.valueOf(raw).doubleValue()*. There are two messages sent here (lines 18-19). First *valueOf* produces a Double object and then *doubleValue* produces a double primitive equivalent to it. Why the difference in structure between Long and Double is a question I'd like to ask the developers of the Java libraries.

Perhaps you are worrying about the message:

```
Prompter.this.resetValues(Long.parseLong(raw), 0.0);
```

in the above. We are sending a message to the prompter that requires two arguments. The first of these we obtain by executing a static method of the Long class. The static method will be executed first even though it appears to the right in the text above. Of course it is in parentheses, but more importantly, the principle of message passing is that the arguments are all evaluated before the message is sent. This is called *eager evaluation* of arguments and Java uses it exclusively, though a few languages use the alternative, called lazy evaluation. Therefore, the *parseLong* message returns a *long* value (unless an exception is thrown) and then the *resetValues* message can be sent.

We give each button a separate listener object. This makes it easier to change and grow the program, since the different actions of the buttons are in different objects, so that changing the action of one can't affect that of another. These objects often come from different classes, if the behavior is truly different, but can sometimes come from the same class. For example, if we were building a GUI for our CalculatorModel of Chapter 9, we would have ten buttons for the numeric keys. We wouldn't need ten classes, though, since we can parameterize them with the digit (int) value that each button represents. You will likely see code, when reading programs of others, that have a single listener for all of the buttons, using an IF structure to distinguish which button was pressed. This is not object-oriented programming and has disadvantages as a program grows. If you separate your actions into different objects it is easier to read the smaller methods, of course, but also much more natural to add additional listeners to a button when needed (not very often) and also add the same listener to different components as we did here.

Since we left out a few of the minor details, here is the entire Prompter class.

```
package utilities;

import java.awt.BorderLayout;
import java.awt.GridLayout;
import java.awt.event.ActionEvent;
import java.awt.event.ActionListener;

import javax.swing.JButton;
import javax.swing.JDialog;
import javax.swing.JFrame;
import javax.swing.JLabel;
import javax.swing.JPanel;
import javax.swing.JTextField;

public class Prompter{

   public long getLong(String prompt){
      InputDialog longDialog = new InputDialog(prompt, "Long");
      longDialog.setVisible(true);
      long value = longValue;
      longValue = 0;
      return value;
   }
```

```
public double getDouble(String prompt){
   InputDialog doubleDialog = new InputDialog(prompt,
      "Double");
   doubleDialog.setVisible(true);
   double value = doubleValue;
   doubleValue = 0.0;
   return value;
}

private void resetValues(long v, double fv){
   longValue = v;
   doubleValue = fv;
}

private long longValue = 0;
private double doubleValue = 0.0;
private boolean wantlong = true;
private JTextField response;

// inner
private class InputDialog extends JDialog{
   public InputDialog(String prompt, String typeTag){
      super(new JFrame(), "Input Required", true);
      setLayout(new BorderLayout());

      JPanel centralPanel = new JPanel();
      centralPanel.setLayout(new GridLayout(2,2));
      centralPanel.add(new JLabel(""));
      JTextField promptField = new JTextField(prompt,prompt.length());
      promptField.setEnabled(false);
      centralPanel.add(promptField);
      centralPanel.add(new JLabel("    Reply"));
      response = new JTextField("");
      centralPanel.add(response);

      add(centralPanel, BorderLayout.CENTER);

      JPanel buttonPanel = new JPanel();
      JButton aButton = new JButton(typeTag);
      buttonPanel.add(aButton);
      ActionListener itsListener = new GotItListener();
      aButton.addActionListener(itsListener);
      response.addActionListener(itsListener);

      aButton = new JButton("Cancel");
      buttonPanel.add(aButton);
      aButton.addActionListener(new CancelListener());

      add(buttonPanel, BorderLayout.SOUTH);
      setSize(300, 100);
      setLocation(100,100);
```

```
         if( typeTag.equalsIgnoreCase("double")){
            wantlong = false;
         }
         setResizable(false);
      }

      private class GotItListener implements ActionListener{

         public void actionPerformed(ActionEvent e){
            String raw = response.getText().trim();
            if(wantlong){
               try {
                  Prompter.this.resetValues( Long.parseLong(raw), 0.0);
                  InputDialog.this.setVisible(false);
                  InputDialog.this.dispose();
               }
               catch(NumberFormatException ex){
                  return;
               }
            }
            else{
               try{
                     Prompter.this.resetValues(0,
                        Double.valueOf(raw).doubleValue());
                     InputDialog.this.setVisible(false);
                     InputDialog.this.dispose();
               }
               catch(NumberFormatException ex) {
                  return;
               }
            }
         }

      }



      private class CancelListener implements ActionListener{

         public void actionPerformed(ActionEvent e){
            InputDialog.this.setVisible(false);
            InputDialog.this.dispose();
            Prompter.this.resetValues(0, 0.0);
         }

      }
   }
}
```

The GUI libraries of Java have many classes and many options. Some are more complex than this, but in general, the ideas are about the same throughout the libraries. Layouts in particular are messy and it takes some experimentation to get used to them. The Karel J Robot simulator, by the way, consists in large part of a Canvas object within a frame. The program can draw on the canvas and does so to make the walls, beepers, and robots visible to the programmer. It also has a few dialogs, such as the World Builder dialog. The Karel Universe editing system is much more sophisticated. Not counting the simulator that it is integrated with, the editor has about 140 classes spread over about 60 files. Some of these are for presentation, similar to what we see here, and some are for managing the flow of information as the user manipulates the interface.

10.9 Important Ideas From This Chapter

Reader
Writer
InputStream
OutputStream
Decorator Design Pattern
StringTokenizer
Exception
Try … catch
GUI
ActionListener
Composite Design Pattern
Observer Design Pattern
Say It Once

10.10 Problem Set

1. Write and test a subclass of Robot that will print a trace of all robot actions to a file that the user can name when he or she creates the robot to be traced. The trace should consist of lines with commands like the following:

```
move
turnLeft
turnLeft
move
turnOff
```

2. Investigate the following classes in the reference literature: Integer, Double, PrintWriter, BufferedReader, FileReader, FileWriter, StringTokenizer. What constructors and public methods do they provide? The documentation is available to browse or download at http://java.sun.com.

3. Extract the knowledge about how to retrieve a long from a String that we saw in the GUI example and apply it to the console input example. Suppose we want to ask the user for the number of pages in a book, as well as its title and author and add this to the information we save and later retrieve.

4. Build a GUI dialog that will prompt the user for the street and avenue number on which to create a robot and creates a North-facing robot there with no beepers. Note that the street and avenue numbers must be positive for this to be sensible, but you can ignore that for an initial version and then add the checking.

5 A robot named wcfields is going to take a random walk of 100 steps. At each step, wc will roll a four sided die (with faces 0, 1, 2, and 3) and will then make that many left turns. Wc will the step and roll again, repeating this 100 times. At each step, wc will put down a beeper. Random walks introduce interesting properties of random numbers. If you run the program a large number of times, recording your results in a file, do you notice anything about the paths taken? The Die class is shown below.

6 Our robot wcfields is going to go on a random walk in a room that is completely enclosed and 10 blocks on a side. If wc finds its front is blocked it will roll again (and again...) until it can actually move in the direction indicated by the die roll. Wc still needs to take 100 steps, not just 100 tries. If you run this program 100 times, what is the average number of different squares visited by wc per walk? Note that you can automate the counting of the squares a beeper counting robot. Record your results in a file.

```
import java.util.Random;
import java.lang.Math;

public class Die {
	private int value;
	private Random generator = new Random();

	/** Create a die with faces in range 1..faces inclusive
	* @param faces the number of faces for this die
	*/
	public Die(int faces) {
		value = faces;
	}

	/** roll a die obtaining a uniformly distributed integer value
	* @return the value of the roll of one die
	*/
	public int roll(){
		return Math.abs( generator.nextInt()) % value + 1;
	}

	public int faces(){
		return value;
	}
}
```

Primo Intermezzo – The French Military Game

Let's take time out from the main topic sequence to consolidate some of the things we have learned. We will develop an interesting game using object decomposition and (especially) arrays, with a bit of input and output, both from the console and from files. Overall, it will require about 400 lines of Java code.

1 The Game

The French Military Game (FMG) is a moderately small game, bigger than Tic-Tac-Toe, but smaller than Checkers. It is small enough that a complete analysis of it is possible. The person will play one side and the computer the other. Initially the computer plays badly, but it will learn from its mistakes. This is possible since there are not too many possibilities, so it can record everything about every game it has ever played. It can also save these results in a file, so that when it returns to a game it "remembers" what it learned when run previously. It represents the simplest kind of *artificial intelligence* by having and improving its memory.

The version we will work on will only use the console for input, output, and display, but a graphical version might look like this:

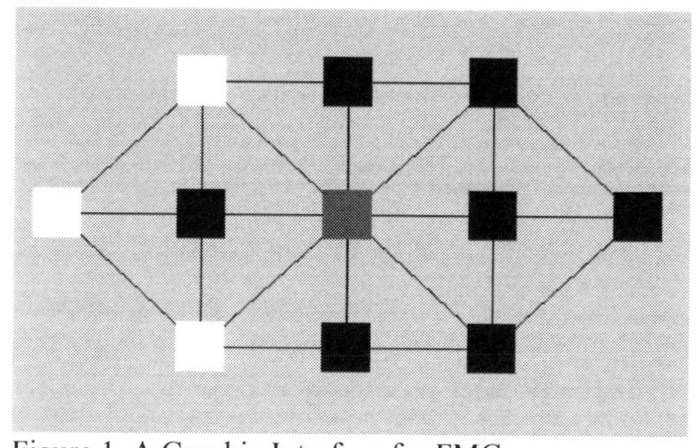

Figure 1. A Graphic Interface for FMG

There are eleven cells, connected by pathways. The white player, called The Police, has three pieces and the red player (shown here in medium grey), called The Fox, has one. The person plays the police and tries to trap the fox so that it has no legal move. Moves are along the pathways and the police can only move vertically and to the right. The fox moves in any direction and has the goal of reaching the leftmost cell. If the fox can evade the police for twenty moves it also wins the game. The board looks like this:

```
     1--4--7
    /|\ | /|\
   / | \|/ | \
  0--2--F--8--10
   \ | /|\ | /
    \|/ | \|/
     3--6--9
Police at 0, 1, 3
Fox at 5
```

In this form, the fox starts at 5, the police at 0, 1, and 3 and the fox wants to get to cell 0. The police can perhaps trap the fox at 6 if they occupy cells 3, 5, and 9.

The player will make a move by typing the from and to squares for one of his or her police pieces, separated by a space. If you want to move the piece at 0 to cell 2, type "0 2" (without the quotes). A graphical version might play by using mouse clicks or drags. Here is a transcript of the beginning of a game:

```
      1--4--7
     /|\ | /|\
    / | \|/ | \
   0--2--F--8--10
    \ | /|\ | /
     \|/ | \|/
      3--6--9
Police at 0, 1, 3
Fox at 5
Your move: from to   ( 0 0 to resign)
0 2
Police at 2, 1, 3
Fox at 4
      1--F--7
     /|\ | /|\
    / | \|/ | \
   0--2--5--8--10
    \ | /|\ | /
     \|/ | \|/
      3--6--9
Police at 2, 1, 3
Fox at 4
Your move: from to   ( 0 0 to resign)
2 5
Police at 5, 1, 3
Fox at 7
      1--4--F
     /|\ | /|\
    / | \|/ | \
   0--2--5--8--10
    \ | /|\ | /
     \|/ | \|/
      3--6--9
Police at 5, 1, 3
Fox at 7
Your move: from to   ( 0 0 to resign)
```

The computer program has control of the fox and will try to make the best move it can. After it has played for a while it becomes very difficult to beat it. The graphic we have used here is an example of something often called *ASCII graphics*, named for a character encoding (American Standard Code for Information Interchange) that was standard in the early days of computing. We now use a more sophisticated code called UNICODE that permits the representation of all of the world's languages, but in only simplified form for Chinese, which as so many symbols. It was once quite common for students to create sophisticated artwork

with just ASCII graphics. Some email signatures still use this, and "smileys" are another example ;-). Something like ASCII is a subset of UNICODE, by the way, but it is called Latin-1 there.
We will build a number of classes and they are dependent on each other. Here is a class diagram to show the structure. An arrow from A to B says that class A needs to know something about class B.

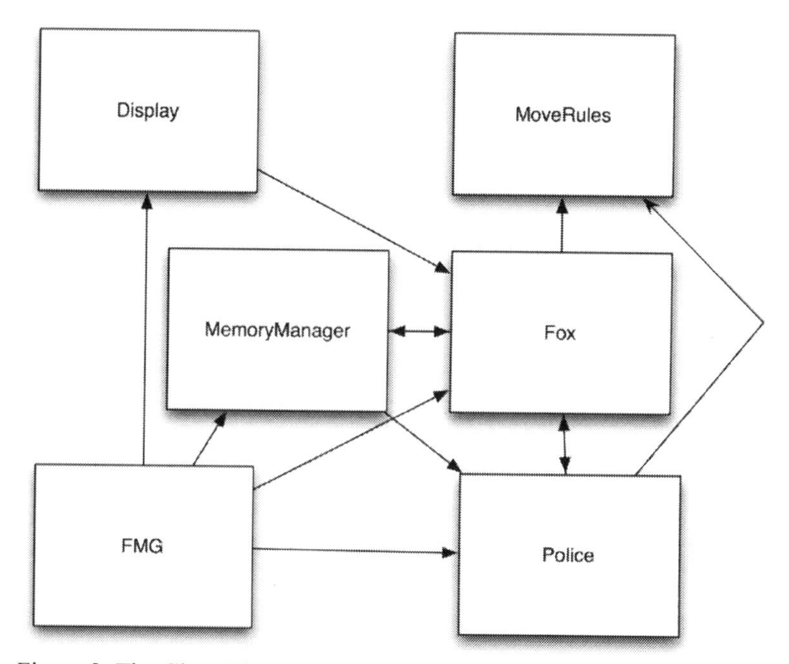

Figure 2. The Class Diagram

2 Move Rules

The MoveRules class keeps track of legal moves for all players. The Fox and Police classes manage information about each player, such as the current position. Display is just the ASCII graphic figure we've shown above, but encapsulated so as to make it easy to use and less error prone. The MemoryManager keeps track of everything having to do with the game remembering an individual game, a sequence of games, and the file that stores the information between plays. The FMG class is the game itself and carries on a dialog with the user, via the console.

As is usually the case, the classes that don't depend on others are the easiest to understand, so we start with the MoveRules class. We need a way to indicate the board and what constitutes a legal move upon it for both the fix and for the police. Since there are only 11 board positions, a square table or *matrix* (array of arrays) can be used for this, with a non zero entry at row x and column y could indicate a legal move from cell x (say 5) to cell y (say 3). We have two players, so we could use two such matrices, or we could encode the moves in a single one. Here is the definition of such a matrix. Note that it is a two-dimensional array or an array of arrays:

```
private static final int[][] LAYOUT = {
   { 0, 2, 2, 2, 0, 0, 0, 0, 0, 0, 0 },
   { 1, 0, 2, 0, 2, 2, 0, 0, 0, 0, 0 },
   { 1, 2, 0, 2, 0, 2, 0, 0, 0, 0, 0 },
   { 1, 0, 2, 0, 0, 2, 2, 0, 0, 0, 0 },
   { 0, 1, 0, 0, 0, 2, 0, 2, 0, 0, 0 },
   { 0, 1, 1, 1, 2, 0, 2, 2, 2, 2, 0 },
   { 0, 0, 0, 1, 0, 2, 0, 0, 0, 2, 0 },
   { 0, 0, 0, 0, 1, 1, 0, 0, 2, 0, 2 },
   { 0, 0, 0, 0, 0, 1, 0, 2, 0, 2, 2 },
   { 0, 0, 0, 0, 0, 1, 1, 0, 2, 0, 2 },
   { 0, 0, 0, 0, 0, 0, 0, 1, 1, 1, 0 }
};
```

This is a field of the MoveRules class. It will never be changed. Note that it is a pre-initialized array, so we don't need to say the size of the array anywhere, but if you count rows and columns you see that it is 11 by 11. The outermost braces indicate we are initializing an array and the inner braced lines are the elements of that array, and are themselves arrays of integers. We have capitalized LAYOUT to indicate it is a constant, and have made it *final*, but it is still an array and any code with access to it can change it. So we make it private within its class and provide no way in that class to modify it. Here a 2 represents a legal move for the police, say from cell 1 to cell 2, and any non-zero entry is legal for the fox: 3 to 0, say. Recall that the police can only move to the right. There isn't much else to the MoveRules class so here it is, entire:

```
class MoveRules{
   private static final int[][] LAYOUT = {
         // fixed array: 11 by 11, rectangular
         { 0, 2, 2, 2, 0, 0, 0, 0, 0, 0, 0 },
         { 1, 0, 2, 0, 2, 2, 0, 0, 0, 0, 0 },
         { 1, 2, 0, 2, 0, 2, 0, 0, 0, 0, 0 },
         { 1, 0, 2, 0, 0, 2, 2, 0, 0, 0, 0 },
         { 0, 1, 0, 0, 0, 2, 0, 2, 0, 0, 0 },
         { 0, 1, 1, 1, 2, 0, 2, 2, 2, 2, 0 },
         { 0, 0, 0, 1, 0, 2, 0, 0, 0, 2, 0 },
         { 0, 0, 0, 0, 1, 1, 0, 0, 2, 0, 2 },
         { 0, 0, 0, 0, 0, 1, 0, 2, 0, 2, 2 },
         { 0, 0, 0, 0, 0, 1, 1, 0, 2, 0, 2 },
         { 0, 0, 0, 0, 0, 0, 0, 1, 1, 1, 0 }
   };

   public static boolean legalPoliceMove(int from, int to){
      return LAYOUT[from][to] == 2;
   }

   public static boolean legalFoxMove(int from, int to){
      return LAYOUT[from][to] > 0;
   }
}
```

Note, however, that a two dimensional array isn't necessarily rectangular. It is just an array of arrays, and the inner arrays can have different lengths. This makes it important to keep track of things to avoid a IndexOutOfBoundsException.

Since MoveRules is immutable and is only queried for the basic game rules, it is encoded with static methods. No object of MoveRules is ever created. The static methods here are just ordinary functions, invoked via the class name: `MoveRules.legalPoliceMove(f, t);` for example.

3 The Display

The Display class is conceptually simple, but very messy. It also uses a two dimensional array to do the graphics, but in this case it isn't rectangular. Notice that the lines in the board display are all of different lengths. We also want to be able to display an F at the position of the fox, so Display needs to know about the fox, though only as a parameter to a method. The display won't send any messages to the fox other than to ask it for its location.

The display itself is held in a two dimensional array of Strings. We would use characters, except that cell 10 needs two characters for its name. We could use two array cells for that, but this works as well if a bit less efficiently. The array itself took a long time to get exactly right so we want to encapsulate it to make sure that we can perform only legal operations on it.

```
private String[][] display = { // a list of lists. It will be modified
   // during a game to show the Fox. Warning: NOT rectangular
   { " ", " ", " ", " ", " ", "1", "-", "-", "4", "-", "-", "7"},
   { " ", " ", " ", " ", "/", "|", "\\", " ", "|", " ", "/", "|",
            "\\"},
   { " ", " ", " ", "/", " ", "|", " ", "\\", "|", "/", " ", "|", " ",
            "\\"},
   { " ", " ", "0", "-", "-", "2", "-", "-", "5", "-", "-", "8", "-",
            "-", "10" },
   { " ", " ", " ", "\\", " ", "|", " ", "/", "|", "\\", " ", "|",
            " ", "/" },
   { " ", " ", " ", " ", "\\", "|", "/", " ", "|", " ", "\\", "|",
            "/" },
   { " ", " ", " ", " ", " ", "3", "-", "-", "6", "-", "-", "9"}
}; // seven rows and various length columns
```

This is what it looks like if we print out each internal array on a single line:

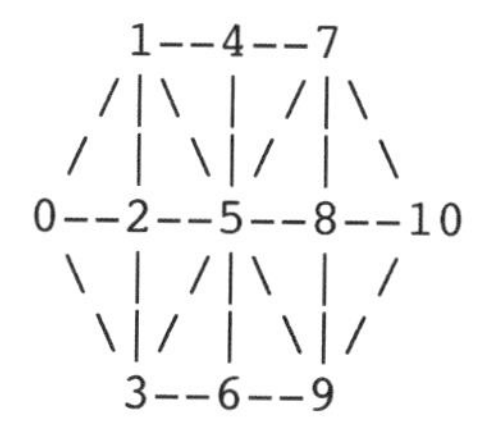

We need to be careful in doing this, of course, since each row has a different length. The fact that any array knows its own length helps us here. The method to show this is like this:

```
public void show() {
   for (int i = 0; i < display.length; ++i) {
      for (int j = 0; j < display[i].length; ++j) {
         System.out.print(display[i][j]);
      }
      System.out.println();
   }
}
```

There are seven rows in display and display[i].length is the length of row i. If we had to keep track of this ourselves it would be very painful. Note that we use print to print a one or two character item (only the 10 requires two characters). After printing out a row we issue a println to move to the next line.

The double backslashes in some cells is just a way to show a single backslash. The \ character has a special use in Strings and characters. It is used to *escape* or *quote* other characters to get special effects. For example '\n' represents a newline character and '\t' is a tab. This means to get backslash itself we need to also escape it, so '\\' is a single backslash.

However, when we actually display this during a game, we want to overlay the fox position on it. We will do so, by changing the cell in the array that represents the fox position to the character 'F'. The rest of the game knows the fox's position just by a game cell number, so we want a mapping that will translate that into an array cell in this display. For example, the fox is initially at cell 5, but that is on row 3 in column 8 of the display array. We use an array to do this mapping and initialize it as follows:

```
private Point[] mapper = {
      new Point(3, 2), // 0
      new Point(0, 5), // 1
      new Point(3, 5), // 2
      new Point(6, 5), // 3
      new Point(0, 8), // 4
      new Point(3, 8), // 5
      new Point(6, 8), // 6
      new Point(0, 11), // 7
      new Point(3, 11), // 8
      new Point(6, 11), // 9
      new Point(3, 14), // 10
      //Maps the game cell numbers to display array locations
};
```

Point is a class defined in java.awt and it is mostly used for graphic applications, but we can use it here just as well. It isn't encapsulated and so has public fields x and y, but it does have a constructor by which we can create a point and initialize x and y. We have used comments in the above to show the mapping. Cell 5 of array mapper contains a reference to a point with x = 3 (row 3 for us) and y = 8 (column 8).

The Display object remembers the old position of the fox (in variable *theFox*), so to change it to a new position we can use the following method:

```
   public void moveFox(Fox fox){
      Point where = mapper[theFox];
      display[where.x][where.y] = "" + theFox;
      theFox = fox.position();
      where = mapper[theFox];
      display[where.x][where.y] = "F";
   }
```

Suppose the fox is currently at cell 5. The display object remembers that in its *theFox* field. The cell to move to is held in the Fox object passed as a parameter. Perhaps the *position* method of this object will return 7. We first use the mapper array to get a point that represents a row and column that needs to be restored to its previous numeric value (here 5). The display at that location is then reset to its numeric value, which is the remembered location of theFox. We then remember the new position for the future and again use the mapper to find the new cell to be changed and put the 'F' there. We have seen everything in the Display class except the field declarations, but here it is in its entirety.

```
class Display{

   private int theFox = 5;

   public Display(int theFox){
      this.theFox  = theFox;
      Point where = mapper[theFox];
      display[where.x][where.y] = "F";
   }

   private String[][] display = { // a list of lists. It will be modified
      // during a game to show the Fox. Warning: NOT rectangular
      { " ", " ", " ", " ", " ", "1", "-", "-", "4", "-", "-", "7"},
      { " ", " ", " ", " ", "/", "|", "\\", " ", "|", " ", "/", "|",
            "\\"},
      { " ", " ", " ", "/", " ", "|", " ", "\\", "|", "/", " ", "|", " ",
            "\\"},
      { " ", " ", "0", "-", "-", "2", "-", "-", "5", "-", "-", "8", "-",
            "-", "10" },
      { " ", " ", " ", "\\", " ", "|", " ", "/", "|", "\\", " ", "|",
            " ", "/" },
      { " ", " ", " ", " ", "\\", "|", "/", " ", "|", " ", "\\", "|",
            "/" },
      { " ", " ", " ", " ", " ", "3", "-", "-", "6", "-", "-", "9"}
   }; // seven rows and various length columns

   private Point[] mapper = {
         new Point(3, 2), // 0
         new Point(0, 5), // 1
         new Point(3, 5), // 2
         new Point(6, 5), // 3
         new Point(0, 8), // 4
         new Point(3, 8), // 5
         new Point(6, 8), // 6
         new Point(0, 11), // 7
         new Point(3, 11), // 8
```

```
        new Point(6, 11), // 9
        new Point(3, 14), // 10
           //Maps the game cell numbers to display array locations
  };

  public void show() {
     for (int i = 0; i < display.length; ++i) {
        for (int j = 0; j < display[i].length; ++j) {
           // handles various length columns
           System.out.print(display[i][j]);
        }
        System.out.println();
     }
  }

  public void moveFox(Fox fox){
     Point where = mapper[theFox];
     display[where.x][where.y] = "" + theFox;
     theFox = fox.position();
     where = mapper[theFox];
     display[where.x][where.y] = "F";
  }
}
```

Let's step back a moment and consider the larger picture. It would be possible to put all of the game into a single class. Dividing it up like this, however, lets us put distinct concerns in different places: What are the rules of the game; How shall we show it, etc. This makes it easier to develop and to understand, easier to find errors, and easier to bring a team of programmers together in its solution. All of these are valuable, but you need to do the division sensibly. You want minimal interactions between the parts if possible. So the Display class doesn't know much about the Fox, other than that the fox can tell it its own location on the grid. As you program, you should continuously ask yourself "Which object should be responsible for that?". So the fox should know its own location and how to compute its next move, etc.

4 The Police

Let's look at the Police class next as it is fundamental in understanding how this program can be "smart." There are exactly 165 different positions for the Police pieces. That is, there are 11 cells for the first piece. For each of those, 10 for the second, since they can't occupy the same location. And for each of those 110 combinations, 9 for the third. But that 990 must be divided by 6 = 3 * 2, since which piece is "first" doesn't matter and so, imagining them colored, the green one on 0 and the blue one on 2 is the same as the opposite. But since there are 6 ways to order the three pieces before assignment, we get 990/6 = 165 possible positions. We want a way to encode these so that we can record them. We could use a three dimension array (or several other possibilities, but we shall use a bit of a trick. First an excursion into binary numbers.

Binary numbers are just like decimal numbers, only the base is two, rather than 10. There are two symbols (0, and 1) rather than 10 (0 through 9) and the position of a symbol in a multi *bit* (= binary digit) number represents multiples of powers of 2 not multiples of 10. For example in base 10, 132 represents 1 times ten squared plus 3 times ten (to the first) + 2 times 1 (ten to the 0). Likewise in base 2, 1101 represents 1 times 2 to the 3rd, plus 1 times 2 to the 2nd + 1 times 2 to the 0. This is the number 13, of course back in good ol' decimal.

Our board has 11 positions, so let us consider 11 bit binary numbers. If the police have a piece on square x let's put a 1 in the x'th bit position, counting from 0 and from the right. So the initial position of the police (0, 1, and 3) is represented in 11 bits as 00000001011. Back in decimal, this is number 11. The smallest such value is 7 = 00000000111 and the largest is 1792 = 11100000000. And, of course, there are exactly 165 such values, but these are not all of the 11 bit values of which there are 2048 = 2 to the 11th. The actual values of these are: 7, 11, 13, 14, 19, 21, 22, ...1568, 1600, 1664, and 1792. If the police occupy squares 3, 5, and 9, then we can encode it as 2 to the 3rd plus 2 to the 5th plus 2 to the 9th = 8 + 32 + 512 = 552.

The game wants to remember the outcome of every game. More than that it wants to weight each position held in the game more or less, depending on how many times the game was in that position and the fox turned out to be the winner in the end. Being conservative about it there are 165 police positions and for each of these the fox could be in any of 11 positions. Well, not exactly, because the fox can't hold a square held by the police, but it will be easiest if we just assume all of these are possible. That means 165 times 11 positions. We could conceivably hold these in a two dimension array with 165 rows and 11 columns where each row represents a police position and each column one for the fox, so the intersection is a full game position. If this cell holds a large positive number it means the fox was in this position often and later won. If it is a large negative number it lost from this position often.

The problem with this analysis, however, is that we only have 165 values from 2048 possible values, since the police "values" aren't the numbers from 0 to 164, but some of the numbers from 7 to 1792. What to do. Here is the trick we will use, but there are many others. Some of the others will become easy after we have seen the next chapter, in fact. Suppose that we store the 165 possible police values in an array, ignoring their order. We will store them, in fact, in an order in which it is easy to generate them using nested for loops. Then, to find a "value" for the police, we will compute the sum of powers of two as above for the locations of the three pieces and then search for this number in the array. We have to find it, since we store all such three bit numbers. If we find it in cell k then we shall use k as the value instead of the sum of powers. The disadvantage of this is that we have to do the search, but the advantage is that the resulting value k is a number in the range of 0..164 and so serves as a subscript into the 165 by 11 array of total game positions. We can call this trick *reverse lookup* since we are using the value in an array to give us a subscript, rather than the other way about which is the usual usage. If we sort the array we could make this search go faster, but we won't since there are *only* 165 values. Instead we shall just use a *linear* search, examining the items one after the other until we find the cell we want. After studying Chapter 11 you might want to consider a HashMap for this, as well.

The Police class has a field

```
private int[] allMoves = new int[165];
```

to hold all of these moves. When we create a Police object it is initialized, as well as initializing the three pieces.

```
public Police(){
   init();
   // Compute all police position values and save them.
   // Never changed again.
   int i = 0;
   for (int L = 0; L < 9; ++L) {
      for (int M = L + 1; M < 10; ++M) {
         for (int R = M + 1; R < 11; R++)
            allMoves[i++] = (int) (pwr(L) + pwr(M) + pwr(R));
      }
   }
}

public final void init(){ // for a new game
   policePosition[0] = 0;
   policePosition[1] = 1;
   policePosition[2] = 3;
}
```

We factored out the init method because we want to be able to reset the position for a new game, but don't need to re compute the array again. The three pieces for the police are held in an array with three cells. The *init* method is final so that we can safely call it from the constructor.

The loop control limits in the constructor are chosen as follows. L represents the police piece with the lowest game cell number. It can only be 0 through 8 if the others have to be higher. The middle loop then only starts at L + 1 but goes to 9. The final piece must have a cell number higher yet, so that loop starts at M + 1 but runs to 10. Again, there are 165 ways to do this. Each computes a value stored in the *next available* cell of allMoves.

The pwr method computes powers of two.

```
private long pwr(int x){ // Computes 2 to the (x).
   long result = 1;
   for (int i = 0; i < x; i++){
      result *= 2;
   }
   return result;
}
```

The method (of Police) pwr computes a long, since powers grow fast, but we won't need any power bigger than 10, of course. We could actually store the 11 powers (0 through 10) in an array and just look them up as well. It would be much faster, actually, but not enough to notice in a program like this. Most of the time is spent when the person plans his or her next move.

Once allMoves is initialized, we can compute a *value* (i.e. the subscript discussed above), like this using reverse lookup:

```
public int computeValue() {
   // actually the array cell number that contains the value
   int a = (int) (pwr(policePosition[0])
            + pwr(policePosition[1]) + pwr(policePosition[2]));
   for (int s = 0; s < allMoves.length; ++s)
      if (allMoves[s] == a)
         return s;
   return 0; // Should never be returned, in fact.
}
```

The **for loop** examines each element in the allMoves array, one after the other, until a match is found. This is called sequential (or linear) search. For a small array this is ok, but in a larger array sequential search can be very slow, especially if the examination of each element also takes more time. This is a simplified form of sequential search, actually, since we are guaranteed to find the item in the array. That isn't always the case.

The other interesting method of the Police class is its move method. Actually this does two things. It makes a legal move if possible from values supplied by the human player, and signals the client program (an instance of FMG) as to whether it was able to move successfully. Of course a person can give incorrect inputs, so we need to check the legality. The user has said to move the piece at location *from* to square *to*. If that is legal we shall do it, other wise do nothing but signal false.

```
public boolean legalMove(int from, int to, Fox fox) {
   if (! MoveRules.legalPoliceMove(from, to)) {
      return false; // No such move for the police.
   }
   if (fox.position() == to){
      return false; // Already occupied by theFox.
   }
   int here = -1; //Try to find one police piece at location from
   for (int i = 0; i < policePosition.length; ++i) {
      if (policePosition[i] == from) {
         here = i;
         break; // found one
      }
   }
   if (here < 0) {
      return false; // Police not at from location now.
   }
   for (int i = 0; i < policePosition.length; ++i) {
      if (policePosition[i] == to) {
         return false; // Location to is already occupied by Police.
      }
   }
   policePosition[here] = to;
   return true;
}
```

The logic of the above is this. First we ask MoveRules if this is ok. Next we ask if the fox is already on the to square. If either is a problem, we can't do the move. Next we look to see if the Police actually have a piece on the *from* square and if so which one. If not, we signal. false again. Finally we need to be sure that the Police doesn't already have another piece on the *to* square. If we pass all the tests we make the move and signal true.

The game will also want to know if the Police hold a given square so the final method of Police provides this information:

```
public boolean holding(int position){
   for(int i = 0; i < policePosition.length; ++i){
      if(policePosition[i] == position)
         return true;
   }
   return false;
```

Aside from the declaration of the policePosition array and a simple method to print the positions of the three pieces, there is nothing else in the class. Note, however, that whenever we wrote a for loop to process an array, we used the length of the array as the upper bound, rather than a hard-coded constant like 3 or 165. It is much harder to make a mistake this way, and much easier to correct them when you do. Assuming you want them to *stay* corrected, of course, as the program might change.

5 The Fox

In many ways the Fox class is simpler, but it does have the interesting feature that it computes an optimal move, based on past experience. It maintains its own piece position, of course, and can return and display it. It also provides an *init* to reset the piece for a new game, but the only interesting method of this class follows. This is invoked just after the police have moved, so we need to know the new position of the police. The memory manager object keeps the history of the game and will give us information about relative value of potential moves. Note when we start that there may not be any legal move at all. The police may have just trapped the fox. That will be signaled by setting the position to –1. Otherwise it will be a new "best" square on the board.

```
public void optimalMove(Police police, MemoryManager memory) {
   int policeEntry = police.computeValue();
   int best = -1; // will signal that fox is trapped unless replaced
   for (int trial = 0; trial < 11; ++trial){ // Check each position.
      if (MoveRules.legalFoxMove(position, trial)
            && !police.holding(trial)) { // Legal  move.
         if (best < 0) {
            best = trial;
            // Prime the search. There is at least one legal move.
         } else {
            if (memory.smaller(policeEntry, best, trial)) {
               // search for biggest value = best move
               best = trial;// New best move is at location trial.
            }
         }
      }
   }
   position = best;
}
```

The for loop checks every possible square, first looking for some square that it is legal to move to. If it can't find any, it is trapped. Otherwise, it sets the first one found as its current best and looks for more. From that point, every time it finds a legal move it asks the memory to compare the new trial move with its current best. If the trial is bigger (better) the best becomes trial. We haven't seen yet, how the memory manager maintains the information and updates it, but we soon shall. It is similar to the analysis we did on the police positions. Notice here that our nesting of logic structures is pretty deep. Too deep? Can you understand it without the explanatory material? Without the comments? Perhaps this should be refactored so that helper methods handle some of the inner structures.

6 Playing the Game

Let's look at the game itself next and then look at how information is remembered. The game is managed by the FMG class.

The *play* method will interact with the user, playing several games as desired. Each game is managed by the *oneGame* method. It also interacts with the user through the console. We looked at console input in Chapter 10, but will use an even easier method here. A *Scanner* object (from java.util) combines a BufferedReader and a StringTokenizer to make input very easy, and not just from System.in. We can point a Scanner at a file or a String, etc, and it will break it up into tokens for us, similar to what a StringTokenizer does. However it is smarter about knowing how to extract things other than Strings. It has a *nextInt* method, for example, to get an int. The user here will be typing integer cell numbers so that will be what we use in onGame. In *play*, however, Strings are enough, since the user just needs to respond yes or no when asked if a new game is wanted. Note that *play* uses an infinite loop, with break statements to end the loop. If break is executed it will exit the closest containing loop. The program prints a prompt and then awaits input. If the loop ever exits, the execution of the program terminates, but not until the memory object saves the game information for all games played in this session.

```
public void play() {// many games
   while (true) {
      oneGame();
      System.out.println("Play again?[no]");
      Scanner in = new Scanner(System.in);
      if (!in.hasNext()) { // Guard against —no- input.
         break;
      }
      String raw = in.next();
      char reply = raw.charAt(0);
      if (reply != 'y' && reply != 'Y') {
         break;
      }
   }
   memory.saveMemory();
}
```

The raw input has its first character extracted as the basis of making the decision. Any answer to the prompt that begins with 'y' or 'Y' is interpreted as a desire for a new game, but anything else will result in termination. This is not very *robust*. In a more important situation you would need to do more to make sure the game correctly understood the user's intention. But notice how easy the scanner was to use. Since we used a simple form, it is breaking up whatever the user types into chunks separated by whitespace: space, tab, and newline. You can make it break the input very flexibly by giving additional options. A Scanner is also used in FMG to get a move from the user. Here the response is a pair of integers, so we will encode them in a Point object. The prompt precedes the input, as usual.

```
private Point getMove() {
    showPositions();
    System.out.println("Your move: from to  ( 0 0 to resign)");
    Scanner in = new Scanner(System.in);
    return new Point(in.nextInt(), in.nextInt());
}
```

Again, this is not very robust. It will fail if the user types something other than an int. One way to solve this problem is to put everything in a try – catch block inside a loop, so that if the scanner fails, we get to try again after some explanation to the user.

One thing is important about the above. We assume here that Java will process the arguments of the Point constructor from left to right so that the first invocation of in.nextInt() is the one in the left position, rather than the other. This is, in fact, how Java is defined, Other languages, however, for perfectly good reasons, process arguments right to left rather than left to right. Then the first invocation would pick up the *from* location of the user and assign it to the *y* component of the point. This would certainly lead to an error in the program since we expect it to be the other way. Java gets it right, however. Other languages get it wrong, partly because they don't define precisely what should happen in this situation, so the programmer who writes the language translator (the *compiler*) is free to do it in any convenient way. And one convenient way for a compiler to work is to capture an entire statement and then process it backwards. For the reason, you will need to wait for an advanced course, or do some exploration. But the operative word here is the *Stack* data-structure.

The actual play of a game is managed by the *oneGame* method. It is also an infinite loop with breaks. Each time around the loop we handle one play by both players. First the police, then the response from the fox. As soon as we know the game result we break. The outcome variable records +1 (WON) or –1 (LOST) depending on whether the fox wins or not. And recall that the fox wins if we go 20 moves. Note that if the person gives an illegal move we just ignore it and go around the loop again. Once more, not very robust, but this is a simple game. Perhaps you want to improve it.

```
public void oneGame() {
    init();
    int moves = 0;
    int outcome = 0;
    while (true) {
        if (moves >= MAX_MOVES) {
            System.out.println("Fox wins = timeout");
            outcome = WON;
            break;
        }
        display.show();
        Point move = getMove();
        int from = move.x;
        int to = move.y;
        if (from == 0 && to == 0) {
            System.out.println("Fox wins = resign");
            outcome = WON;
```

```
            break;
        }
        if (police.legalMove(from, to, fox)) { // police move if legal
            fox.optimalMove(police, memory); // fox responds
            int position = fox.position();
            if (position > 0) {
                memory.record(moves, fox, police);
                moves++;
            } else if (position == 0) {
                System.out.println("Fox wins - home");
                outcome = WON;
                break;
            } else if (position < 0) { // no legal move
                System.out.println("Fox loses - trapped");
                outcome = LOST;
                break;
            }
            display.moveFox(fox);
            showPositions();
        } // else ignored
    }
    memory.summarize(moves - 1, outcome);
}
```

7 The Memory Manager

So that is everything except how the game learns. All of that is encapsulated in the MemoryManager class. But note that in the above, we ask the memory to record each successful move by the fox, and we ask it again to summarize the game at the end when we know the outcome. The task of managing the game's memory has three parts. It must remember each move in a single game. It must transfer the game information to an overall history data structure and it must be able to read such a structure at the beginning of play and save it again at the end. We will look at these in turn. There are two main data structures used by the MemoryManager and we will use two dimensional rectangular arrays here for both.

```
private int[][] thisGame;
private int[][] history = new int[165][11];
```

The *thisGame* field is initialized in the constructor when we know the maximum moves allowed (usually 20). It will have maximumMoves rows and two columns, one for the police and one for the fox. Each time a successful move is made memory.rexord is invoked. We can see the message above in oneGame. here is the method itself in MemoryManager:

```
public void record(int moves, Fox fox, Police police){
    thisGame[moves][0] = police.computeValue();
    thisGame[moves][1] = fox.position();
}
```

This data structure is treated like a simple list, since each time it is invoked, the oneGame method will increment the moves variable so that the next invocation will insert the new data in the next row. So, when the game ends we have the complete record of that game in the thisGame array. Column 0 holds the police positions as the "magic" array subscripts defined by the allMoves structure we discussed above. Column 1 holds the corresponding fox location at that point in the game.

At the end of the game, the oneGame method sends the message `memory.summarize(…)` , which transfers the game information into the history array. That array has a row for each possible police position and a column for each fox position. It's contents are integers that are incremented if a position (row, column) results in a fox win, and are decremented if the fox loses:

```
public void summarize(int moves, int outcome) {
   for (int i = 0; i < moves; ++i) {
      int police = thisGame[i][0];
      int fox = thisGame[i][1];
      history[police][fox] += outcome;
   }
}
```

Recall that the outcome can be either +1 or –1 and the last statement uses the += operator to add the right hand side value (outcome) to the left side variable. a += b is a shorthand for a = a + b. There are similar operators for all of the usual arithmetic operators; +=, -=, *=, /=, %=. There are even more, in fact, but those you can look for yourself.

One possible flaw in our design is this. The MemoryManager doesn't encapsulate the moves variable. It depends on the client (oneGame) to send consistent values of moves when it invokes both record and summarize. The information should be held in one place, not two, and here it is also needed in oneMove to determine whether a game should end, but we could have held it in MemoryManager instead with an accessor. You can explore a refactoring that implements it that way and then analyze the two for (a) ease of use, and (b) maintainability and safety.

Recall that the fox uses the MemoryManager object as a service to help it find an optimal move. The memory knows the history so it can tell us which trial move is better:

```
public boolean smaller(int row, int current, int trial){
   return history[row][current] < history[row][trial];
}
```

The question asked here is whether on row "row", which represents a police position, the current fox position is smaller than some trial (but legal) move. If so, the trial is a better choice so the fox will remember it as its current best choice. This is the basis of "intelligence" of the fox; nothing more. Really, it just remembers not to make the same mistakes repeatedly, but to repeat its successes. Not a bad strategy for most life situations, actually.

All that remains is the file processing methods. When the MemoryManager is created it is given a filename of the memory file, as well as the maximum moves in a game. This file is initially read and is later written. Things can go wrong, of course. The filename might not point to a file when it is read, or some other IOException might occur. Writing is a bit more definite, but it is possible that the disk we want to write to is locked or offline. So, as is typical, in i/o we need to deal with at least IOException, either by handling it or by propagating it. We will see both here. First, let's look at how we save the history array into a file at the end of play.

```
public void saveMemory() {
   String all = "";
   for (int i = 0; i < history.length; ++i) {
      for (int j = 0; j < history[i].length; ++j) {
         all += history[i][j] + " ";
      }
   }
   try {
      BufferedWriter out =
         new BufferedWriter(new FileWriter(filename));
      out.write(all);
      out.close();
   }
   catch (IOException e) {
      System.out.println("Could not write the memory file.");
      e.printStackTrace();
   }
}
```

We wrote earlier about making i/o more efficient by doing less of it. Here we employ that idea. The first thing that this method does is stream the entire history array into a String with spaces separating the numbers. The array is read by rows; the outer for loop runs 165 times and the inner one 11, We don't hard-code those numbers, of course, but use the array lengths to control the loops. Note that we can use the += operator here, but this time it represents string catenation, since that is the meaning of + for String objects. Note, however, that we create a large number of Strings here, since catenation always produces a new String, rather than modifying an old one. The innermost statement runs 165 times 11 times. However, we hope to get back the time this takes, by doing only one write to the file. We only need to write the String named *all* to the file as one chunk.

We do the write in a try block so that we can catch the IOException if it should occur. First we create a FileWriter pointed at the filename given earlier (in the constructor) and then wrap the FileWriter in a BufferedWriter so that we can write a String. We must also remember to close the file when done writing so that it is preserved by the operating system. But if something goes wrong we will wind up in the catch block instead. Here we just write out a message as well as the system's usual stack trace, and exit. We don't try to actually recover from this. In a more important application it might be essential to do a recovery as valuable information could be lost. It might be possible to arrange a re-try, perhaps with a different filename. The coding for this can be quite complex and we won't attempt it here.

At the beginning of play we need to read the file back in. The MemoryManager uses two methods for this. The getMemory method is the one the client (FMG) calls. The *smart* parameter determines whether we want the file read at all. If it is false (or if the file can't be found), the history will be initialized to all zeros. If smart is true we invoke readFile to try and load the history array from the file. Note that the MemoryManager already knows the filename, from its constructor, so we don't need to pass it here. We need to catch IOException here, since readFile might throw it via propagation.

```
public void getMemory(boolean smart){
   try{
      readFile(smart);
   }
   catch(IOException e){
      for (int i = 0; i < history.length; ++i) {
         for (int j = 0; j < history[i].length; ++j) {
            history[i][j] = 0;
         }
      }
   }
}
```

Finally, the method to actually attempt to read the file uses the smart parameter to determine whether to initialize the history from the file or simply to set zeros. If opening or reading the file throws an exception, we simply propagate it back to the client (getMemory). We again use a simple Scanner object pointed at a File with the given filename.

```
private void readFile(boolean smart) throws IOException {
   Scanner memoryFile = null;
   if(smart){
      memoryFile = new Scanner(new File(filename));
   }
   for (int i = 0; i < history.length; ++i) {
      for (int j = 0; j < history[i].length; ++j) {
         if (smart) {
            history[i][j] = memoryFile.nextInt();
         } else {
            history[i][j] = 0;
         }
      }
   }
}
```

There is the possibility for another exception here, of course. If the memory file gets corrupted and there isn't an int where it is expected then an InputMismatchException will be thrown and this is not an IOException. Also, if the file gets truncated somehow, then the Scanner will throw a NoSuchElementException. We could guard against all of these by simply propagating Exception instead, and also catching that in getMemory. In this situation, that would probably be an improvement.

That is it; an interesting game that is quite challenging for the human player. More important, it exercises your knowledge of arrays quite thoroughly. Most of our arrays have held ints here, but one held Point objects. Actually our two dimensional arrays can best be thought of as simple arrays that hold arrays as data, with those arrays being available for any legal array operations. We emphasize that arrays themselves are objects, created with *new* and whose contents need to be created/set separately.

Before we end, however, you, the reader, must understand that this program was not developed in the order in which it was presented here. It is very valuable to read and understand such programs, but the development order and the presentation order are utterly different. The development did not start with the class diagram we showed at the beginning. It began, in fact, with a few ideas that were tried out, with some successful and some failing. The ideas had to do mostly with *features* that someone thought the program should have, and the features were added one at a time. Adding a feature takes "a little of this (data structure development, say) and a little of that (writing methods or classes)." Along with frequent testing as the program emerges. The first thing done (most likely – it was done by others, not this author, and has been in the literature for a long time) was to get the actual program flow right. Interacting with the computer, printing prompts and getting inputs. The ASCII art likely came much later and the saving to files among the last things to be done. The current form was refactored into the classes we present from a more monolithic version that the author once found in the language BASIC. In Chapter 12 we will look at a way that such a program might be developed from scratch.

We will examine some alternate data structures that might be used to organize this game in the next chapter and you will get a chance to refactor it again.

8 Important Ideas From This Intermezzo

Scanner
two dimensional arrays
ASCII
reverse lookup
linear search
binary numbers
bit (binary digit)
array initialization

9 Problem Set

1. Verify that the following Display structure has the same effect as what we saw above. Then explain why the *show* and *moveFox* methods don't need to be modified to use it.

```
private String[][] display = { // a list of lists. It will be modified
      // during a game to show the Fox. Warning: NOT rectangular
      { "      ","1","--", "4", "--", "7"},
      { "    /|\\ | /|\\"},
      { "   / | \\|/ | \\"},
      { "  ", "0", "--", "2", "--", "5", "--", "8", "--", "10" },
      { "   \\ | /|\\ | /" },
      { "    \\|/ | \\|/" },
      { "      ", "3", "--", "6", "--", "9"}
      }; // seven rows and various length columns

private Point[] mapper = {
      new Point(3, 1), // 0
      new Point(0, 1), // 1
      new Point(3, 3), // 2
      new Point(6, 1), // 3
      new Point(0, 3), // 4
      new Point(3, 5), // 5
```

```
        new Point(6, 3), // 6
        new Point(0, 5), // 7
        new Point(3, 7), // 8
        new Point(6, 5), // 9
        new Point(3, 9), // 10
        };
```

2. Find a better name for the first parameter of the *smaller* method of the MemoryManager. Names of variables should be in terms of the problem itself, not the way we choose to solve the method. The name *row* refers to a row in the array, not anything in the problem. Hint. How does the client code use this?

3. We could replace the entire body of the *holding* method of Police with the following. Investigate why this is true and the meaning of each part of it. The single '&' is not an error. It is an operator of Java.

```
int police = computeValue();
int where = (int)pwr(position);
return (police & where) != 0;
```

4. Investigate writing a Tic-Tac-Toe game in exactly the same way. The person can play first and the computer tries to move as well as it can, knowing its own history. The game is also called Noughts and Crosses. The game can result in a *draw*, with no winner.

5. A Scanner object can be created pointed at a String (among other things) rather than a File. This makes it more convenient than a StringTokenizer in many ways. It also lets you combine file-at-a-time input with scanning. Refactor the input of the MemoryManager class to use this idea.

6. Consider sorting the allMoves array when it is created. Look in java.util.Collections for the sort method. You might find it easiest to use an *ArrayList* rather than an array to do this. You can then use the *binarySearch* method as well, which is faster than the sequential search we used in *computeValue*. While you are carrying out your investigations, try to learn why we want to suggest this.

11 Collections

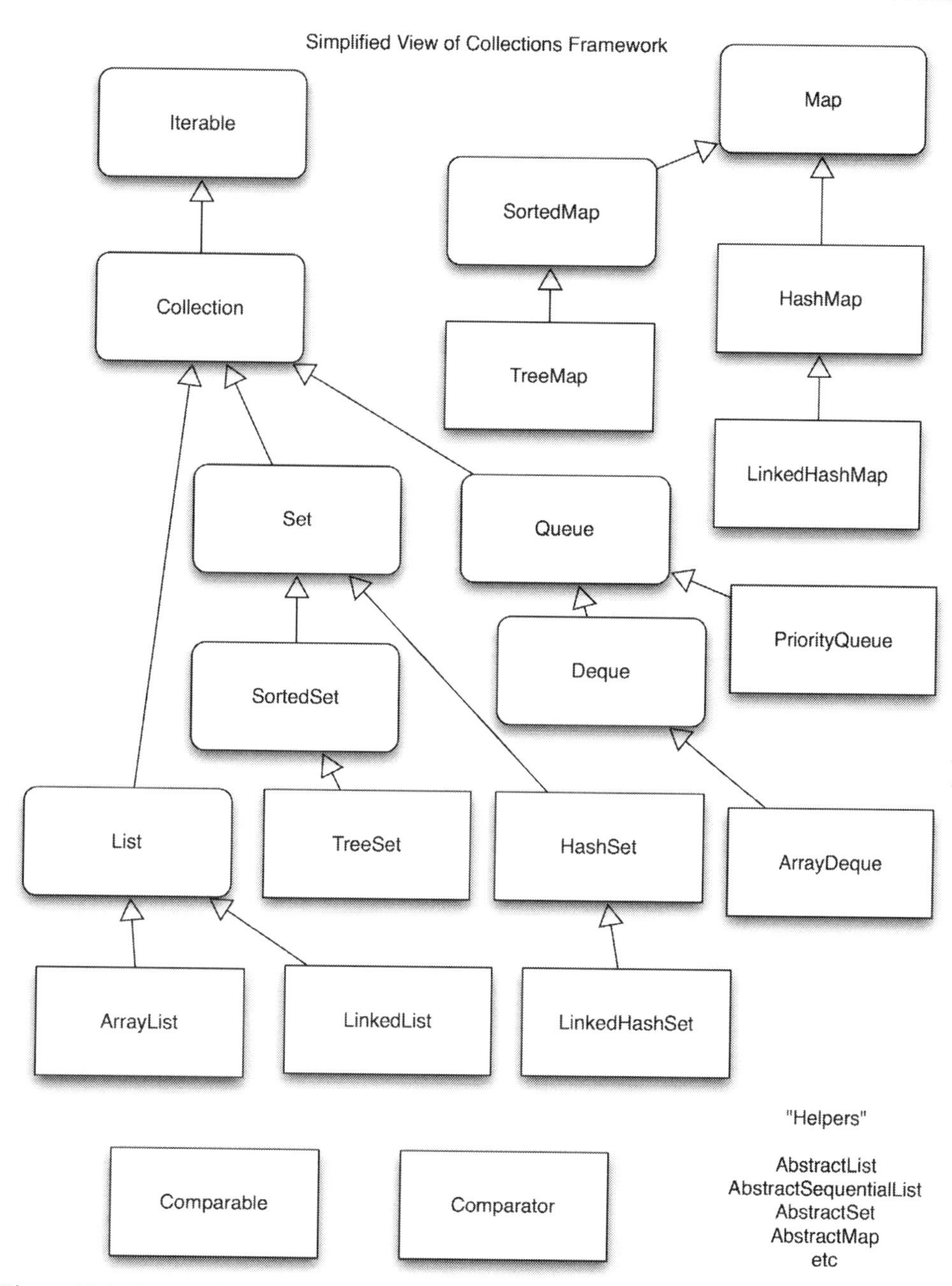

Figure 11.1. Java Collections Framework

11.1 Collections Framework Overview

The Java Development Kit (JDK) comes with nearly 4000 classes. Of these, an important subset is devoted to helping the programmer manage information structured in many ways: the Java Collections Framework. We have seen one and two dimensional arrays so far, which are built into the language itself, not the libraries. There is some support for them in the libraries as well. In this chapter we will look at a very small number of the collection classes and at their characteristics. Figure 11.1 shows some of the most important of the collections classes, though we will study only a few of these and mention a few others. Note that the "rounded rectangles" in the figure are actually interfaces so most of the overall design is just design. The arrows imply extension. Arguably perhaps, the two most important interfaces here are List and Map, since they find the most common usage. The four classes ArrayList, LinkedList, TreeMap, and HashMap are the most important implementations. With those you can do nearly anything.

There are two main groupings here: those that derive from Iterable, and those that come from Map. These represent two quite different ideas. Maps are sets of associations between keys and values, much like our associations between variables and the objects they point to. Associations are like the relationships between people's names (keys) and their selves (values). A map is a way to get access to a value by knowing its key. The bank uses something like a map to relate customer numbers (keys) to the account information for an account (values).

The idea of *iterable*, on the other hand is that of a collection that can be accessed an element at a time using an iterator that knows how to *yield* the items in some order that may be important or not, depending on the collection. You can think of a single dimension array as iterable (though Java does not) with an index that you increment as the iterator. The current value of the index can be used to yield the next value in the array. The reason that Java doesn't consider arrays to be iterable, however, is that arrays don't have a way to control when to stop. That is up to you, perhaps with a for loop that you repeat exactly the right number of times (the length of the array).

Technically Iterable means that a class has a method iterator() that returns an Iterator object. Iterator is itself an interface that defines three methods. It is much like the Enumerations we saw in Chapter 4, but has named its methods differently and has an additional method to remove items. The methods of Iterator are *hasNext*, which return true until the iterator has yielded all the elements, *next*, which returns the next element that has not yet been yielded, and *remove*, which removes the item most recently returned by *next*. Things aren't so simple as that, however, since some iterators will throw an exception (UnsupportedOperationException) if the collection doesn't permit removals.

The order in which *next* returns the values depends on the collection. For a HashSet there is no implied order at all as it is much like a mathematical set. For a List, it will be in the position order within the list, much like an array, with positions 0 through size() –1 as the legal positions. A TreeSet, on the other hand, keeps the values in an order dependent on the values themselves as we shall see and the iterator returns them in this order. If the TreeSet contains Integer objects the order will be the value order with a 5 coming before a 9. Strings in a TreeSet are alphabetized.

While Maps are not Iterable, they do have iterators. For example, a Map will return its keySet() to you and this Set does have an iterator.

Things are still more complex, however. Prior to Java 5 (Java version 1.5) the libraries only had a few collections, like Vector and Hashtable. These were similar to ArrayList and HashMap in more recent versions, but they only held Object values. If you put something in to a Vector and then later retrieved it, the program itself retained no information about what kind of thing it was, so you would have to remind it with a cast. This was irksome to program. Here is an example from Java 1.4. A Vector is a sequential collection.

```
Vector robots = new Vector();
Robot karel = new Robot(1, 1, North, 0)
robots.add(karel); // insert karel into the end of the list
. . . // later in the program
Robot worker = robots.lastElement(); // error here
```

The problem is that the Vector holds Objects, not Robots, so the last line needs to be re-written as:

```
Robot worker = (Robot) robots.lastElement(); // cast
```

All of the new collections support a new feature called genericity (or generics) in which we can indicate when we create a collection what kind of thing we intend to put into it and the program will remember this. The older collections such as Vector now support this also. So here is the above example in Java 1.5.

```
Vector<Robot> robots = new Vector<Robot>();
Robot karel = new Robot(1, 1, North, 0)
robots.add(karel); // insert karel into the end of the list
. . . // later in the program
Robot worker = robots.lastElement(); // OK now
```

We will make use of this shortly.

Another difference between the older and newer collections is that the operations of a Vector are synchronized and so are safe to use in multi-threaded programs whereas the, conceptually similar, ArrayList methods (like most of the methods in the framework) are unsynchronized. This is a trade-off, for not synchronizing the methods makes them run faster and most programs only use a single thread in any case. There is some infrastructure to wrap (Decorator Pattern) a collection in another that provides synchronization when needed (see the Collections class in java.util). Because we seldom need synchronization, we usually prefer to use ArrayList over Vector.

Note that genericity makes collections somewhat like arrays in that we specify what sort of element we will put into an array when we create it. We can now do this with collections as well, though all of the types we use as generic parameters, must be class types. You cannot have ArrayList<int> for example, though you can have ArrayList<Integer>. While that sounds like a flaw, other features make up for it as we shall explore. For the most part you can consider these two the same, though you can only write the latter.

On the other hand, an ArrayList, while similar conceptually to an array has a major benefit in that it is automatically expandable. An array has a fixed length determined when you create it and never changed. An ArrayList, on the other hand will automatically expand and contract depending on how much data you put in to it. It does this by creating new arrays internally as needed to hold the elements but does this in a particularly efficient way. So you need not specify a capacity for an ArrayList, but can keep sending it the *add* message and it will adapt, growing longer and longer.

Finally a last, perhaps major, advantage of collections over arrays is that you manipulate them with the usual message passing syntax, rather than the older subscripting form with square brackets. So, to get the third element from an array named *values*, the expression is `values[2]`, but from an ArrayList with the same name it is `values.at(2)`, similar to what we have been doing since the beginning of the book.

11.2 Collections Exploration – Part 1, Variations

Let's see what we can do with some of the collections and maps in the framework. We shall transform the FMG game of the Intermezzo into a more modern form, replacing many of the arrays we used with objects from the framework. There are many ways to do this, so some of it will be exploratory, looking at tradeoffs: costs and benefits.

First, we shall not touch the MoveRules class as it seems like the best solution we can think of. It is an ideal application of a two dimensional array. It is rectangular; it has fixed values; it is well matched to its problem of determining the legality of a matching (move) between two values. So we leave it be. The Fox and FMG classes will have few changes, none structural. We shall change these only to react to changes elsewhere. We will also be careful not to require gratuitous changes in these. The reason for leaving them is that there are really no collections of data within them and our purpose here is to explore collections.

One class that is simple and admits quite a few reasonable alternatives is the Display class, so we will start with it. In Problem 1 of Chapter 10, we suggested an alternate array for the display itself, and we prefer that one since most of the rows of the two dimensional array have fewer elements. The rows that never change, in fact hold a single cell. However, using a different array for the display requires that we also use a different array for the mapper, since the mapper points into the display array. We repeat the mapper here.

```
private Point[] mapper = {
        new Point(3, 1), // 0
        new Point(0, 1), // 1
        new Point(3, 3), // 2
        new Point(6, 1), // 3
        new Point(0, 3), // 4
        new Point(3, 5), // 5
        new Point(6, 3), // 6
        new Point(0, 5), // 7
        new Point(3, 7), // 8
        new Point(6, 5), // 9
        new Point(3, 9), // 10
        };
```

Recall that we need this mapper so that we can indicate where the fox is in the display when we draw it. If the fox is a logical game cell 7, then we want to place the "F" string at cell `display[0][5]` and the mapper holds these subscripts in a Point object. While there is nothing wrong with using an array for the mapper we can, at least, look at some alternatives in the Java Collections Framework.

First, though, we should note that an array is itself a mapping. It maps a contiguous set of integers starting at 0 to the elements that are contained in the array. The map for an array named *values* is: x -> values[x]. In fact, then an array is a finite mathematical function from a *domain* of integers starting at 0 to a *range* consisting of the values stored. In the above, the mapping is from {0, . . . , 10} to a set of Point objects. Lists do the same thing actually, so we could also represent mapper with a List, either an ArrayList or a LinkedList, as either would work. To use an ArrayList the declaration would be as follows:

private List<Point> mapper = new ArrayList<Point>;

Note that we prefer to use the interface name on the left side, so that mapper is only known to the rest of the program as a List, but need to name a class on the right side since an object is being created. Among other things this makes it easier to replace the ArrayList with a LinkedList later if we choose to do so.

However, this only creates an empty ArrayList, but doesn't put values in to it. There is no nice Java syntax equivalent to the array initializer to do this, so we need to put the creation of the Point objects into the Display class constructor.

```
public Display(int theFox){
    this.theFox  = theFox;
    mapper.add (new Point(3, 1));
    mapper.add (new Point(0, 1));
    mapper.add (new Point(3, 3));
    mapper.add (new Point(6, 1));
    mapper.add (new Point(0, 3));
    mapper.add (new Point(3, 5));
    mapper.add (new Point(6, 3));
    mapper.add (new Point(0, 5));
    mapper.add (new Point(3, 7));
    mapper.add (new Point(6, 5));
    mapper.add (new Point(3, 9));
    Point where = mapper.get(theFox);
    display[where.x][where.y]  = "F";
}
```

This appends each new value to the end of the list. The *get* message near the bottom retrieves the point representing theFox position, usually 5 when we start.

There is another way we could do this with a list, however, which makes the mapping more apparent.

```
public Display(int theFox){
    this.theFox  = theFox;
    mapper.add (0, new Point(3, 1));
    mapper.add (1, new Point(0, 1));
    mapper.add (2, new Point(3, 3));
    mapper.add (3, new Point(6, 1));
    mapper.add (4, new Point(0, 3));
    mapper.add (5, new Point(3, 5));
    mapper.add (6, new Point(6, 3));
    mapper.add (7, new Point(0, 5));
    mapper.add (8, new Point(3, 7));
    mapper.add (9, new Point(6, 5));
    mapper.add (10, new Point(3, 9));
    Point where = mapper.get(theFox);
    display[where.x][where.y]  = "F";
}
```

Here we use an alternative form of add in which we name the cell at which to insert the new item, much as we do with arrays. This explicit version is probably less error prone, so we prefer it. Thus *add* with only one argument adds the item at the end, whereas *add* with two adds the second at the location of the first. And *get* is the basic retrieval operation on lists. In either case, add makes space for the new item, moving existing items if necessary so that there is empty space at the specified index to do the insert.

You need to be careful with this second form of add, however. You can only add between existing items or at the immediate end of the list. If we tried to do the above in the opposite order, adding cell 10 first, we would get errors. The rule is that you can add between the 0 and size positions only. To modify the contents of an existing location use the *set* method, which has the same parameter structure as this second form of add; first the index, then the value.

While we said that we could easily switch to a LinkedList for this with almost no changes (except the original declaration and the imports) we should not do so in this case. This is due to the nature of the ArrayList and the LinkedList and how they match (or not) with our use. The fox starts at cell 5 of the game board. Its first move could take it to any cell except 0 and 10 (depending on what the other player does, of course). This means that we can go directly from the 6th entry in the mapper list to any other but the first and last in the next move of the game. Array like things are well suited to randomly accessing cells, but linked structures are not.

Arrays, and by extension ArrayLists, utilize a densely packed storage mechanism in which it is possible to compute the location of any cell from its index with a simple computation. This is due to the fact that all of the things in the array have the same size, so knowing that you want cell 7 (the eighth cell) says that you can find it at a location 7*sizeOfCell memory locations from the beginning of the structure in the computer's internal memory. This is because 7 cells (0 through 6) precede cell 7 and all have the same size. This is fast for a computer to do since it knows the beginning and the size of the cells.

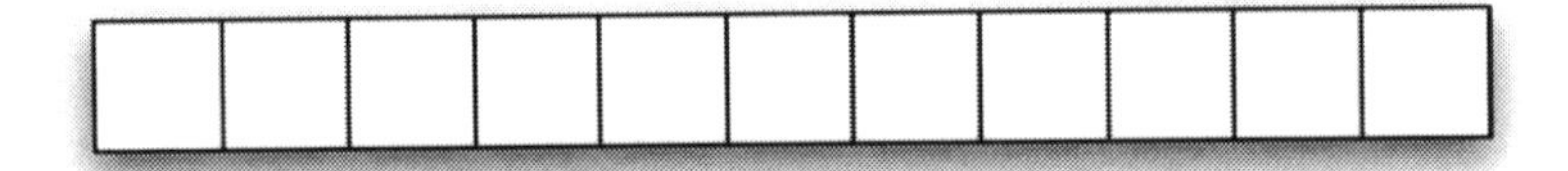

Figure 11.2. Dense Storage

While it is possible to *add* data into a dense structure, between two existing items, it is relatively expensive (time consuming) to do so, as the elements to the right of the new location need to be moved farther right to make room and we need to assure a cell exists at the farthest right. Adding at the end (right) of an ArrayList is normally quite fast, as the structure maintains some extra space to permit this to happen fast, though if you exceed the capacity for that, it will take a while to create new capacity. The time for it will be proportional to the number of cells currently in use since the old data will need to all be copied into a new array. While this sounds very bad, it doesn't happen very often, so on the average it works out. If a cell already exists, we can modify its contents with the *set* method.

Linked structures, on the other hand, are stored completely differently. A linked structure contains a small amount of data (one value) along with a reference to the location of the next such cell. This makes it possible to easily expand such a structure, since we don't need a contiguous block of memory cells to hold it, but can put the next cell anywhere in the memory that is free. But the cost is that to find cell 7 you need to start at cell 0 and follow its link to cell 1 and from there to cell 2, etc, until you count to the 8th such cell. This is slow by comparison. So the tradeoff is memory flexibility against operational speed and if you need to access cells in arbitrary (often called random) order you want something that uses dense, not linked storage. On the other hand, if we were only processing mapper in the order of the cells, then linked might be preferable.

Figure 11.3 shows linked storage with a single link from each cell to the next. The program keeps track of the first cell (at the upper left) separately. The Java LinkedList, however, is doubly linked with a reference in both directions, so that it is possible to move either direction in the list, but only from cell to cell. So, to go from the 6th to the 10th you have to move through all of the intervening cells, one step at a time.

Linked structures are nothing new to you, in fact. Any object that holds a reference to another is linked. That other may be linked to a third, etc. What makes linked lists special, if at all, is that the items in the list have the same type, or more precisely, the same parent type. Back in Chapter 4 we actually built a linked list of decorators of a strategy. The last item in the list was a simple strategy and terminated a chain of decorators that form the bulk of the list. Problem 21 in Chapter 4 is the clearest example of this. A *node* in a list holds some data, perhaps, but also a link to the next node. Many implementations of lists terminate them with the *null* value, which is not an object. Terminating a list with a special object that has no next link is a superior way, however. This is called the Null Object Pattern and in our decorator chain, the innermost Strategy took the role of the Null Object. The problem with the null value is that it can't be polymorphic, so you need to explicitly check for it with an **if** at every step. With a Null Object the innermost (last) item just handles the message in a different way, but, being an object, it CAN handle a message whereas null cannot.

However, if you need to find a given element in a linked structure you need to start at the beginning and search one node at a time. This the time it takes you to find your data requires time proportional to the number of nodes. This *linear* time behavior (since the graph of time vs. number of nodes is a straight line) is much worse than the *constant* time required to access an item in a dense structure such as an array or ArrayList.

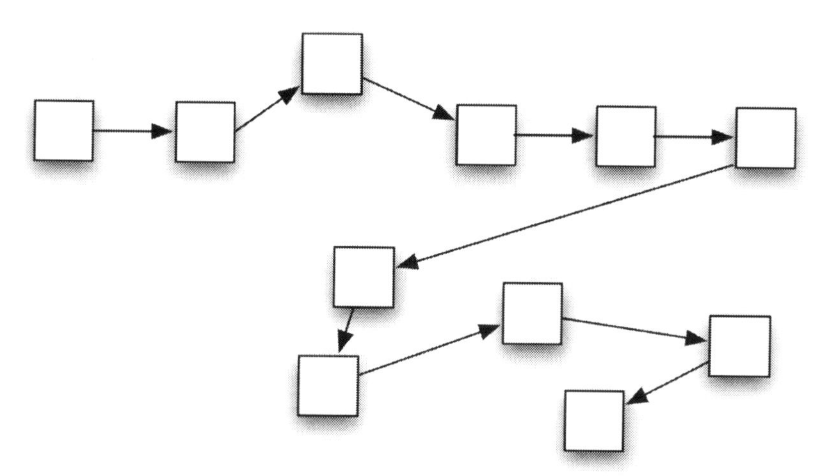

Figure 11.3. Linked Storage

While we have seen options for the Display class mapper structure, none of this has yet had any real benefit for our program, other than in learning about these options. It is hard to justify either of these as better in this situation. The number of cells on the game board is fixed, so the size of the structure we use need not be adaptable. There is a bit more overhead in the list actions than in the array actions. The only real benefit is that we are sending messages when we use objects and so the usual message "dot" syntax that serves for everything else we have done works here also. And, of necessary we open the possibility of using polymorphism too, though it is very unlikely to be of benefit here.

The final variation we will look at for Display is to replace the mapper array with a Map, actually a HashMap. This will have little real benefit either, since the keys will be integers, just as the indexes in arrays are integers. In any case, the declaration would look like this:

```
private Map<Integer, Point> mapper = new HashMap<Integer, Point>();
```

Here there are two parameters in the generic angle brackets. The first gives the key type, Integer, and the second the value type. Note again that it has to be Integer, not int, since we need a class type and Integer is the *wrapper* for int. In fact, in Java 1.5, we can use int values and Integer objects almost interchangeably. It was not so easy in earlier versions of Java in which explicit conversions needed to be done. We shall see this in use in a moment.

Just like with the list solution, the map declaration creates the map, but not the contents, so again we must fill the map in the constructor. It looks very similar to the list version, but for the names of the insert method: *put*, rather than *add*. The retrieval method is *get* in both cases. A map has no *set* method. The *put* method is used both to insert a new key and to change the association of one already stored.

```
public Display(int theFox){
    this.theFox  = theFox;
    mapper.put(0, new Point(3, 1));
    mapper.put(1, new Point(0, 1));
    mapper.put(2, new Point(3, 3));
    mapper.put(3, new Point(6, 1));
    mapper.put(4, new Point(0, 3));
    mapper.put(5, new Point(3, 5));
    mapper.put(6, new Point(6, 3));
    mapper.put(7, new Point(0, 5));
    mapper.put(8, new Point(3, 7));
    mapper.put(9, new Point(6, 5));
    mapper.put(10, new Point(3, 9));
    Point where = mapper.get(theFox);
    display[where.x][where.y] = "F";
}
```

The put method inserts the second argument value (a Point) into the map associated with the first argument (an Integer) as key. The order of insert here is immaterial, unlike the list version, since a map has no sequential structure. The *get* method is passed a key and returns the value, assuming the key is actually stored, or null if the key can't be found. We used a HashMap as the implementation, but we could change it to a TreeMap just by changing the declaration, as everything in both is defined in the Map interface. There is no reason to do so, since a TreeMap is a bit less efficient for this purpose and keeping the elements in key order internally is not needed here, so there is no benefit to the tree.

There is one thing we need to note about the above, however, The Map was declared to have Integer keys and we have used simple int values. We wrote this:

```
mapper.put(3, new Point(6, 1));
```

whereas the following would be more correct:

```
mapper.put(new Integer(3), new Point(6, 1));
```

However, in Java, since version 1.5, this transformation between primitive values and their wrapper object types is automatic. This is called *auto-boxing*. The Integer object is thought of as a box that holds the value. The following are both legal now, but would not have been prior to Java 1.5

```
Integer value = 5; // boxes 5
int other = value; // unboxes the Integer back in to an int value
```

Hash and tree structures are quite different from each other, as well as being different from list structures we saw earlier. A hash structure works by doing a computation on the key to determine where in the structure to store the value. Actually both the key and value are stored together as we shall see. The computation is quite different from the one done in dense structures, however, since the keys don't need to be integers and we don't need to store in key order. Instead, the hashCode method that is possessed by every object is used to start the computation process. Figure 11.4 has a schematic of one kind of hash map, though there are others as well.

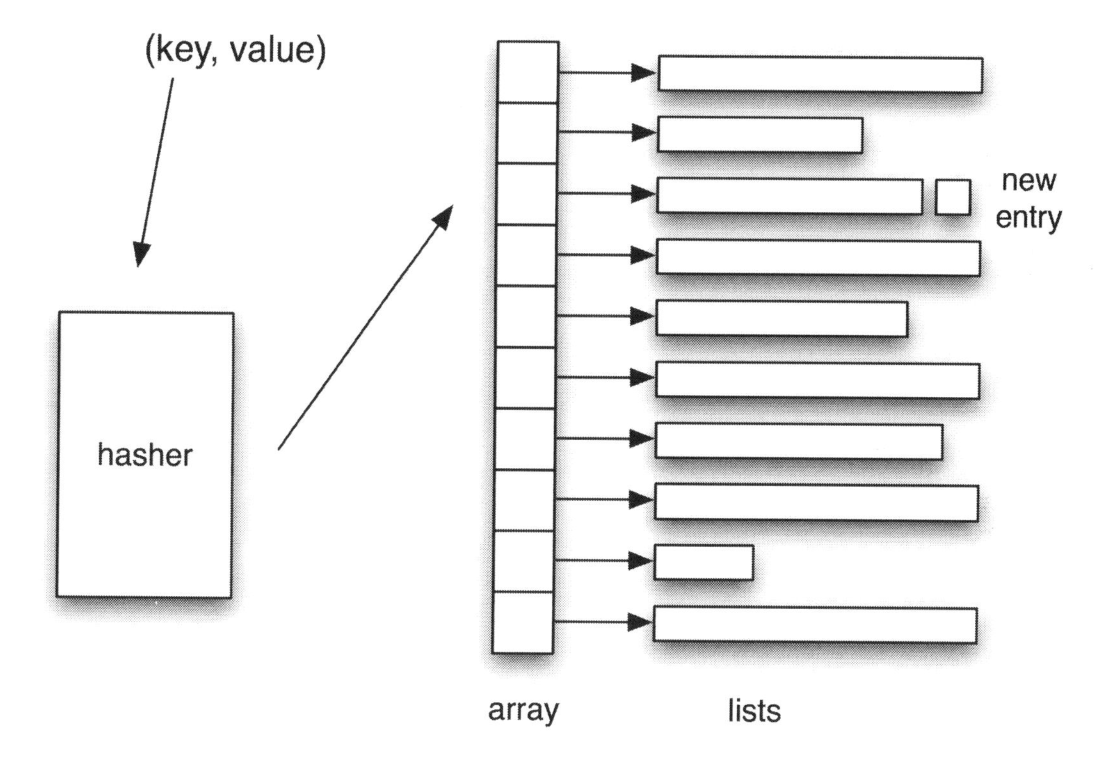

Figure 11.4. HashMap (schematic)

In this structure the key is sent to the hasher, which is just a computation method. It computes an array index by taking the hashCode of the key and then computing a remainder upon division by the length of the so called *bucket* array. The array holds references to lists (either linked or dense). The array is then searched to see if there is already a record in that bucket with the same key. If so, the new key-value pair replaces the original (and the original value is returned from the put method). If it is not stored, then a new entry is created on the list and the key-value pair is inserted there. When two different keys compute the same bucket number it is called a *collision* and we don't like a lot of collisions, since then the lists get long and the searching gets slow. For this reason, the number of buckets is kept to a more or less constant fraction of the number of entries stored (the load factor) by expanding the size of the bucket array periodically. While this reorganization takes time, it guarantees fast look up. And in fact the *reason to be* of a HashMap is to minimize the *get* time. One variation on this, though not the one used in Java at this time, assures that the average length of a bucket list is one, making lookup very fast.

There is one caveat here however. While the search operation is going on within a bucket list, the *equals* method is employed to see if the key being stored is already there. For each stored key we ask is it *equals* to the one being stored. An implication of this is that within the logic of your program, if two distinct objects should compare true for the equals method, then they had better return the same hashCode. If not, then lookup might fail, since the program will be searching the wrong bucket list. The built in objects have this property, of course and since our keys are Integer objects we need not worry. But it is a concern if you use your own class objects (say Robots) as keys in a HashMap.

Another implication of the above, is that if your *equals* method in your own class depends on mutable state within the object, then if you put such an object into a HashMap as a key and then change its state you won't find it again with get. This is because its new value isn't *equals* to its old value even though it is the same object.

Finally, you need to be a bit careful about your hashCode method. It needs to be stable, in the sense that if the mutable state of the object doesn't change, neither should its hashCode. So don't try to use a randomizer to create a hashCode. And you want, as much as reasonable, different objects to return different hashCodes. This is so that the hasher will spread the data more or less evenly among the buckets. If your hashCode always returns 0 for example then all of your data will end up in the first bucket and you can do no better than linear search of this bucket to find it again. This will defeat the entire purpose of a hashMap: fast lookup. So, our HashMap version of the mapper in Display is pretty good, but still, not likely to be as good as an array index lookup.

But a hash map with a decent hasher and an adaptive method for modifying its structure as we add new items will achieve approximately constant time retrieval on the average, though not necessarily for each lookup (get). Inserts are also quite fast on average, though if an insert (put) forces a reorganization, that insert will take longer. An ArrayList, also has such behavior. Lookup (at) is constant time, but insert (add) at the end, while usually fast may force a reorganization/expansion and so take longer.

The TreeMap implementation is built on a completely different concept. Integer data have a size, of course: the value of the integer. Other objects can be given a size as well. A circle has a radius, for example, and a person has a height. In fact, some objects have different "sizes" for different purposes. People also have weight and income, etc. The idea of a TreeMap is to keep key-value pairs in order of the "size" of their keys.

A *binary tree* is, conceptually at least, a linked structure in which each node has two links, called the left and right child nodes. Either or both of the children can be null, or preferably a Null Object. The node typically holds some data as well as the links. In a TreeMap, the node will hold a key-value pair.

A *binary search tree* is a binary tree in which the data have a size and the nodes of the tree have an ordering dependent on the size. In a TreeMap the size of a node is determined by only the key in a way that will be explained below. Once we have the size, the ordering of the nodes is such that for any node, the left child holds data that is smaller than this node and the right child has larger values. When values are the same they are resolved in a uniform way, depending on what is needed. For a tree map the keys can only be present once and so if we try to insert a pair with a key already held, the new data replaces the old with the older value returned from the *put* method. Figure 11.5 shows a simple binary tree showing only keys. If we wanted to insert a pair with key 72 into this tree we would do the following: Starting at the top node (the *root*), we see that 72 is larger, so we go down to the right child and examine that. 72 is smaller so we go left. It is also smaller than 78 and when we go left again we find the Null Object (an empty space in the drawing) and so we create a new node to hold the new data and link it as the left child of the "78" node.

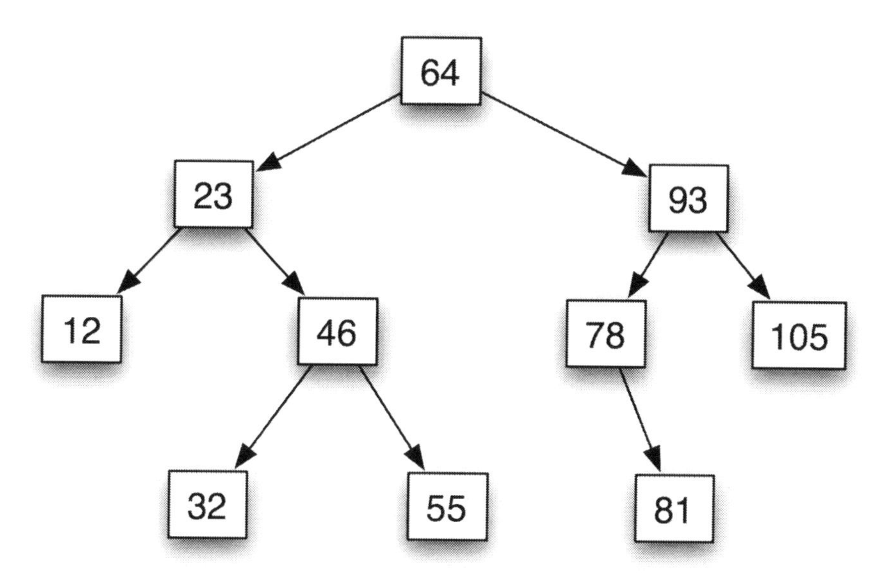

Figure 11.5. A Simple Binary Search Tree

Actually, though, the above simple tree isn't good enough as it can wind up wildly unbalanced. If you start with a small value and repeatedly insert larger and larger values the process described above will always move to the right. The tree will then degenerate to a linked list. On the other hand, if we can keep the tree *balanced*, meaning that each path from the root to a *leaf* (a node with no children) has "about" the same length, then the number of nodes in the tree is exponentially related to the length of such a path. The *height* of a tree is the length of the longest path from root to leaf, counting links, not nodes. Our example tree has height 3. But it is possible to store as many as 15 nodes in this tree without changing the height if we either (a) enter them in correct order (hard) or (b) adjust the shape of the tree so that it stays balanced as we go (also hard). The former method is usually infeasible as we don't often get the data in an appropriate order. The other is possible to do, though the algorithms are complex. In general, it is possible to store as many as $2^{n+1}- 1$ nodes in a tree of height n. Therefore a tree of height 20 can store over a million nodes. Looking at the reverse of this, it is possible to search a tree with a million nodes and take no more than 20 steps to do it. This *logarithmic* behavior is what makes a TreeMap attractive, though it requires the tree be kept balanced as inserts are done. The algorithms to balance on insert need to move the nodes around a bit, but they move only a logarithmic number of nodes, so their performance is also quite good. Not as good as a HashMap, but if you want the data kept in order, very good. The iterator for the keySet of such a tree will yield the keys in order, and given the keys, we can get the associated values *in key order*. The actual implementation of a TreeMap in the Java libraries is currently a Red-Black Tree in case you want to investigate further.

Not everything can be put into a TreeMap as a key since the structure needs to be able to compare the keys for what we have called "size". In fact, there are two ways to make it possible for objects of a class to serve as keys in a TreeMap (or elements in a TreeSet, which we shall see shortly).

The first way is for the potential key type to implement the Comparable<T> interface. The Integer class implements Comparable<Integer> so we have had no difficulties yet. But if you wanted to use Person as a key type you would have work to do. Here is what Comparable looks like:

```
public interface Comparable<T> {
    public int compareTo(T o);
}
```

Therefore we would need to implement this one method. The *contract* for compareTo is this. If the object executing compareTo (i.e. this) should be considered smaller than the argument o, then compareTo should return some negative number. If this should be considered larger, then compareTo should return a positive number, and if this should be considered to have the same size, the method should return 0. This means that two different objects can be compared and the method returns 0. That is to say, compareTo need not be consistent with equals, though it often is. There is another requirement, called *anti-symmetry*. If a.compareTo(b) is negative, then b.compareTo(a) should be positive, and conversely.

In a class that implements comparable, the compareTo method imposes an order on the elements called their *natural order*. TreeMaps use the natural order in the absence of the second solution.

The other way to create a TreeMap for elements that, perhaps, have no natural order or for which we want the ordering to be other than the natural order is to use a special object called a Comparator.

The interface java.util.Comparator looks like this:

```
public interface Comparator<T> {
   int compare(T o1, T o2);
   boolean equals(Object obj);
}
```

A Comparator object can be created for any class T and compares objects of that class to each other. Like the comparable interface, the primary method, *compare*, returns a negative value if o1 is considered less than o2, a positive if the opposite, and zero if they should be considered the same. The difference is in how they are invoked. A comparator is itself an object that compares two other objects of a given class, while *compareTo* is a method of the class itself and compares *this* with another object. A comparator has a similar contract to that of the compareTo method in that it is anti-symmetric and should normally be consistent with equals. The latter is not an absolute requirement, but you are encouraged to document the fact if it the comparator is not consistent with equals.

If you want to use a comparator in a TreeMap you create one before creating the map and then pass the comparator as an argument to the constructor of the TreeMap.

But for all this investigation, we still haven't found a compelling reason to replace the original array with any of these structures. Next, however, let's examine some of the other classes where what we have learned here can make a difference, in one case, a large difference.

11.3 Collections Exploration – Part 2, The MemoryManager

In the MemoryManager class we used two array structures, one to hold *thisGame*, the current game's moves, and *history*, another two dimensional array, to hold the complete history of all moves in all games. Both of these will benefit from transformations, but different transformations. Let's examine thisGame first.

Like all two dimensional arrays, thisGame is a mapping between pairs of integers, the indices, to values of some kind, Here they were also ints, but the in general any element type may be used for such a structure. For every move of the game we compute a value (for the Police position) and the thisGame maps the pair (move, 0) to this value. The computed value of the police position at that time, and maps the pair (move, 1) to the fox's position on the board. The value *move* is the number of the current move, starting at 0. There was nothing absolutely wrong with this, except that by using an array we automatically limited the maximum number of moves that could be recorded. The definition of the game as ending after 20 moves was done partly to accommodate this sort of restriction. However, an ArrayList has no such restriction. So, instead, let's modify the structure to the following simple list of points:

```
private List<Point> thisGame = new ArrayList<Point>();
```

Now, the record method no longer needs to pass the moves value when record is invoked from FMG, as we don't need to specify any row in an array at which to store the data. So it is simpler than before:

```
public void record(Fox fox, Police police){
   thisGame.add(new Point(police.computeValue(), fox.position()));
}
```

Actually, we will later, in *summarize*, only process this list from beginning to end, so a LinkedList would work equally well. But we have two advantages here. We don't need to specify a maximum size, and we don't need to worry about getting the row correct.

We will get an even bigger benefit by changing the history structure to a Map.

```
private Map<Point, Integer> history = new HashMap<Point, Integer>();
```

Recall that in our encoding of the police position values, there were only 165 possible outcomes, but they actually range between 7 and 1792. We didn't want to define an array that large to hold only 165 items so we used the reverse lookup technique to find an number in the range 0 .. 164 that was equivalent. But with a map, we don't need a cell for every possible value, only for the keys we actually want to save. So, the keys will contain (some of) the values between 7 and 1792, along with the fox position, and the values will be a code indicating whether the game was won or lost by the fox. Again, we don't need to tell *summarize* how long the array of moves was in the game, as this is already recorded within the theGame List. Here is the new version of summarize, and it will require a bit of explanation as it uses a new kind of **FOR-LOOP.**

```
public void summarize(int outcome) {
   for(Point where: thisGame){
      Integer value = history.get(where);
      if(value == null){
         history.put(where, outcome);
      }
      else {
         history.put(where, value + outcome);
      }
   }
}
```

In the new Java Collections Framework any Iterable object can yield its contents one element at a time, as discussed above. The new **for** structure takes advantage of this. The form looks like this:

```
for ( <type> <variable> : <iterable object containing type values> ) {
   <list of statements to process the values of variable>
}
```

Here everything matches up: *thisGame* is a List<Point> so it will yield *Point* objects. We use the variable name *where*. Each time around the loop the *where* variable gets a different value from our list that it can then process.

For each such value, we want to increment the corresponding entry in history. However, we may not have stored any such value yet, as this position may not yet have occurred in any game. So when we send history the get message, it might return null. We have to take separate action here.

You need to be careful with maps in this way. If you try to *get* a key that has not been stored you get null instead, so must normally check for it. This will occur elsewhere in this program, so it might be useful to actually write a subclass of HashMap that won't return null in this situation, but rather a value we specify. In the above, it would be most useful if the map returned 0 to us when the key wasn't stored, for then summarize could be simplified to the following:

```
public void summarize(int outcome) {
   for(Point where: thisGame){
      Integer value = history.get(where, 0); // zero if not found
      history.put(where, value + outcome);
   }
}
```

This won't work with a standard HashMap, but we can build the following and use it instead:

```
import java.util.HashMap;
import java.util.Map;

public class DefaultHashMap<K, V> extends HashMap<K, V> {

   public DefaultHashMap(){
      super();
   }

   public DefaultHashMap(int initialCapacity){
      super(initialCapacity);
   }

   . . .

   public V get(K key, V defaultValue){
      V value = get(key);
      if (value == null){
         return defaultValue;
      }
      return value;
   }
}
```

We have supplied various constructors to match those of HashMap, but they don't do much of anything. On the other hand we add a new method, overloading the *get* method to provide a new version to which we pass a value that we want returned if the standard get would otherwise fail. Note that this doesn't lose access to the standard method, since we have a different protocol (signature) for this method, with an additional parameter. We have parameterized this just as HashMap is. The syntax is a bit busy for defining parameterized classes but you get used to it after a while. All parameters and return types of the method are defined in terms of the type parameters of the class. Once this is defined, we can change the declaration of *history* to:

```
   private Map<Point, Integer> history =
               new DefaultHashMap<Point, Integer>();
```

We only use the first constructor of DefaultHashMap, but the other prototypes were just copied from HashMap. All the variations on Java Generics is beyond the scope of our discussions here, however. They can get very complex.

The other main method of the MemoryManager, *smaller*, is used by the fox to evaluate possible moves. With the above changes it becomes especially simple:

```
   public boolean smaller(int police, int current, int trial){
   return history.get(new Point(police, current), 0)
         < history.get(new Point(police, trial), 0);
   }
```

The methods *getMemory*, *saveMemory*, and *readFile* also manipulated the history array in the original, and so require simple updates in this version. We leave them to the reader.

11.4 Collections Exploration – Part 3, The Police class

In the version presented in the Intermezzo, the police class used arrays in two ways. First as a small, one dimension, array to hold the three integers representing police board positions, and second, another one dimension array to do the reverse lookup. This array held the possible values of the police composite position and we searched for a cell holding one so that we could use its index as something like a key for storage in the history array of the memory manager. But this latter use simply disappears in this version since the history structure is now a map, not an array. So the allMoves array simply goes away, and the compute value method will simply return the "raw" value of the sum of powers of the three police positions. We will wait to show this method for a bit, since we also want to change how the three police positions were implemented.

According to the rules of the game, the player representing the police has three pieces on three different squares. Therefore, logically, the player has a mathematical *set* of positions chosen from the set of integers 0 through 10. But a Java Set is like this also, and it is implemented either as a HashSet or as a TreeSet. Since we don't need these to be sorted, we should probably choose a HashSet in this case. The implementations of HashSet and TreeSet are quite interesting. Each uses a map of the corresponding kind internally and only stores the values inserted in the set as keys in the map, using a dummy *value* for every put. This wastes very little space, since the values are all just references to the same object, and is extremely simple to build. This is an example of the Adapter Design Pattern, in fact. The HashSet gives a different interface to a HashMap, adapting it to a new purpose, with more appropriate method names.

```
private Set<Integer> policePosition = new HashSet<Integer>();
```

We need to set this up for the first and every subsequent game, so we do so in the init method as before.

```
public final void init(){ // for a new game
    policePosition.clear();
    policePosition.add(0);
    policePosition.add(1);
    policePosition.add(3);
}
```

The first message makes the set empty in case it was not and the others add elements to the set. It behaves like a set, of course, only permitting one copy of any object to be present. The add method returns true if the object was actually inserted and false if it was already present, leaving the set unchanged in that case. Actually there are some sets in which the add method is unsupported, throwing an exception, since it is possible for a set to be unmodifiable. Sets have a corresponding *remove* method. Since a Set is Iterable, it works with the new FOR-LOOP command we discussed above, so the computeValue method again gets quite simple:

```
public int computeValue() {
    int a = 0;
    for(int value: policePosition){
        a += (int)pwr(value);
    }
    return a;
}
```

We are again depending on auto-boxing here, since technically the contents of the set are Integer objects, not ints. The cast to int is needed for the result of pwr, since pwr returns a long and a long may not fit in an int, so the a *narrowing* conversion must be employed, but it won't be done silently in Java and requires that you *notice* the conversion by supplying the cast. And as we said, there is no reverse lookup required here any more and we can use these values directly.

Finally, here is the legalMove method of the police class, which takes advantage of the new structures:

```
public boolean legalMove(int from, int to, Fox fox) {
    if (! MoveRules.legalPoliceMove(from, to)) {
        return false; // No such move for the police.
    }
    if (fox.position() == to){
        return false; // Already occupied by theFox.
    }
    if(policePosition.contains(to)){
        return false; // Location to is already occupied by Police.
    }
    if(! policePosition.contains(from)){
        return false; // Police not at from location now.
    }
    policePosition.remove(from);
    policePosition.add(to);
    return true;
}
```

As we see, the test for an object being an element of a set is the *contains* method of the set. If we find that the potential move is legal, we remove the *from* value (where the police player currently is) and add the *to* value (where it is moving to).

The other changes to the game are straightforward, though you are invited to complete them and then compare the two versions as a whole.

The Appendix has implementations of some classes that are similar to, but simpler than, some of the important classes of the Java Collections Framework.

11.5 Important Ideas From This Chapter

Adapter Design Pattern
Collection
natural order
Iterable
Null Object Pattern
List
Set
Map
Iterator
Comparator
Comparable

11.4 Problem Set

1. Finish the modification of the FMG class discussed in this chapter

2. Do, or redo, problem 4 of the Primo Intermezzo.

12 Testing and Documentation

It is hard to write programs. It is hard to understand them. It is hard to know when you got it right and when there are unintended consequences of what you have done. It is hard for teams to coordinate efforts. What to do?

12.1 Documentation Overview

Documenting a program or system of programs means providing natural language explanations of what it is, how to use it, and how it works. There are many different kinds of documentation. What is in the documents depends on the audience. If you create a program for end-users, you need to provide explanations of how to use it for common tasks, but you don't need to talk about its internal implementation. On the other hand, if you write a library of classes to be used by other programmers you need more detailed documentation. The explanations we gave in the Intermezzo, however, were neither of these. Rather we tried to provide an explanation of how it is built so that you can learn how to build and structure your own programs.

User level documentation for FMG would talk about how one plays the game, from the initial startup (how to invoke it), through the final end and shutdown. It would explain how to make a move and perhaps some things about strategy. It would explain that the input consists of two numbers in range 0..10 separated by one or more spaces. It would emphasize that the space is critical and that the numbers must be on the same line. Even better, of course, would be to provide more robust input mechanisms, but that is something other than documentation and we shall discuss that later in the chapter.

We are more interested here, however, in how to document a program so that it will be of use to programmers, including yourself. For this, Java provides a tool, JavaDoc, that we will discuss shortly. However, for the most part, we seek to write programs for which very little documentation is needed for other programmers, primarily because we choose both a structure and naming conventions that make it obvious to a skilled reader what is happening. We have tried to emphasize that throughout the book, but it is worth looking back at FMG to see what is working there and what could be improved in terms of having a *self-documenting* program.

The class names are probably fine in the main, Police, Fox, MemoryManager, etc. seem to be accurate names for what objects of the classes do. Most of the methods are fine. The play and oneGame methods are aptly named, etc. On the other hand, we have been suggesting you not abbreviate names, but pwr is clearly an abbreviation. Are there others? How hard is it to fix? Not very, it seems, especially with modern tools in which an editor can easily make global changes. One offender of naming here, is the local variable named just *a* in the Police.computeValue method. Why this name? How is the name related to what it does? If you are trying to learn what the program does, does this name help?

One good reason for encapsulation, by the way, is that it limits the scope of names. We can choose names of things that will be used in smaller scopes and if we do it badly it will have a lesser impact on the overall program. The flip side of this is that names widely seen, such as class and public method names need to be chosen with great care. One convention is to use nouns for the names of methods that return values, with the name descriptive of the value returned. Methods that don't return values should have names that are verbs or verb phrases, describing the action. One reason we don't like methods that do both is that the programs that contain them are harder to reason about, but part of this is the difficulty of finding a good name. The method legalMove of the Police class is such a dual purpose method. It tires to make a legal move and tells us if it did or not. So it is both an action and an accessor of information. You might be misled in your understanding of the program if you think it is just an information getter and later find that the program state was changed when it was invoked. It is difficult to overemphasize the importance of good names. This is especially true when you work in a team. Others need to understand your names, not just yourself.

Some people believe that every line of a program should have a comment on it explaining what it does. In actuality this is a terrible practice, since the program will probably be changed and the comments will probably not be kept in sync. Also, it is difficult to write non-technical comments that capture exactly what the statement does, but nothing more. Better is to have the statement explain itself, through clear naming and straightforward programming. Here is the worst example of per-line commenting:

```
c++;   // increment c
```

Well, of course. If you know the language, you don't need the comment. But what does it *mean*? This one is a bit better:

```
c++; // increment the catheterCount
```

Ah, now we begin to have some understanding. But it should really say this:

```
catheterCount++;
```

in which no comment is needed at all. The variable names a concept in the space of the problem itself. It helps you understand what is going on in this, presumably, medical related program. Strive for this.

12.2 JavaDoc – Automated Documentation

There is a form of programmer documentation, however, that is still needed, even if you write clearly. The purpose of each class and each method needs to be communicated to anyone who needs to work with your program. They need to know how a client needs to interact with your code, because they are likely interested in writing that client code. They therefore need to know what to expect. Java provides a nearly ideal tool for this purpose: *JavaDoc*. JavaDoc actually refers to two things. First it is a kind of comment that you attach to each class and to (at least) each public method. It is also a tool that reads the java files you write with these comments and produces web pages with the extracted information. Therefore a potential user of your code need only consult these web pages to learn a lot about your program code.

JavaDoc comments appear in your code immediately before a class or method and they are just like ordinary multi-line Java comments except that they begin with /** instead of only /*. They end in the usual way with */. Within these comments there are certain key words you can use for special things as we will see shortly, and you can also include html tags to beautify the resulting web pages.

Let's look at an example, by going back and documenting the FMG. The Display class is short so we will use it as an example. First we look at the comment for the class as a whole. It is written immediately before the class header:

```
/** The visual display in ASCII art for the French Military Game.
 * It shows the game board with the fox's current location marked.
 * @author jbergin
*/
class Display{

   private int theFox = 5;

. . .
```

A typical class comment begins with a sentence or two giving the purpose of the class. The special keywords mentioned above include the @author tag, followed by the name of the author of the class.

Constructors and (public) methods should also be documented. Here is the constructor for this class along with its comment:

```
   /**Create a display for the French Military Game with an initial
    * position for the fox
    * @param theFox the initial position of the fox player. Usually 5.
    */
   public Display(int theFox){
      this.theFox  = theFox;
      Point where = mapper[theFox];
      display[where.x][where.y] = "F";
   }
```

Again, it just explains the purpose. @param is followed by the name of a parameter and that followed by some explanation of what the client code is expected to provide as an argument.

Methods that return values can also use the @return tag to explain the nature of the value returned. Of course the type of the parameters and return value is given in the method/constructor protocol. The purpose of the JavaDoc comment, however, is to give logical meaning to those items.

Method comments should also provide some explanation of any special algorithms used so that it will be easier for a reader of the code to get started.

It is possible to document private things as well, but this is of less use to most readers. The most typical usage is by someone who wants to use your code, and for this a discussion of public features is sufficient. In fact, too much documentation can get in the way of seeing the overall picture.

Once you have marked up your code with comments, preferably as you go, you run the JavaDoc tool to produce a set of html pages that can be viewed with any browser. What follows in Figure 12.1 and Figure 12.2 is what was automatically produced from the markup of the Display class.

Package **Class** **Use** **Tree** **Deprecated** **Index** **Help**

PREV CLASS NEXT CLASS FRAMES NO FRAMES All Classes
SUMMARY: NESTED | FIELD | CONSTR | METHOD DETAIL: FIELD | CONSTR | METHOD

fmg

Class Display

```
java.lang.Object
  └ fmg.Display
```

```
 class Display
extends java.lang.Object
```

The visual display in ASCII art for the French Military Game. It shows the game board with the fox's current location marked.

Author:
jbergin

Constructor Summary
`Display(int theFox)` Create a display for the French Military Game with an initial position for the fox

Method Summary	
void	`moveFox(Fox fox)` Move the fox indicator in the display
void	`show()` Print out the current display

Methods inherited from class java.lang.Object
`clone, equals, finalize, getClass, hashCode, notify, notifyAll, toString, wait, wait, wait`

Figure 12.1. JavaDoc for the Display class (part 1)

Note that the extensive Java libraries are all well documented with this technique. You can download these files to your own computer, or browse them online. They are available from http://oracle.com/java, though you may need to search a bit to find them. As this is written the latest online version can be found at: http://docs.oracle.com/javase/7/docs/api/. In addition to what we have shown here, the full web pages come with very useful tables of contents and indexes for everything you might need. Whenever I write programs myself, I always have the JavaDocs available, I keep a desktop icon, in fact, so that they are always easily available.

The command to create the pages for the Display class might be something like the following. We say that we want the author tags included in the output, that the classes can be found relative to the current directory (represented by the period after the –classpath option), that the directory in which to put the html files should be named newdocs. Note that this was run on a UNIX system in which the path separator is the forward slash. On a Windows system it would be the backslash instead.

```
javadoc -author -classpath . -d ./newdocs fmg/Display.java
```

Constructor Detail

Display

```
public Display(int theFox)
```

Create a display for the French Military Game with an initial position for the fox

Parameters:
`theFox` - the initial position of the fox player. Usually 5.

Method Detail

show

```
public void show()
```

Print out the current display

---

moveFox

```
public void moveFox(Fox fox)
```

Move the fox indicator in the display

Parameters:
`fox` - the fox game piece immediately after a move.

Package Class Use Tree Deprecated Index Help
PREV CLASS NEXT CLASS FRAMES NO FRAMES All Classes
SUMMARY: NESTED | FIELD | CONSTR | METHOD DETAIL: FIELD | CONSTR | METHOD

Figure 12.2. JavaDoc for the Display class (part 2)

12.3 Testing Overview

Just as is true of documentation, testing means several different things. Does a program meet the needs of its users and how can we know? Is the program error free? Does it meet the specification that was set for it when it was created? Is it fast enough to handle the required load? Does it make good use of available resources? All of these questions can be answered by testing of various kinds.

Some testing is just letting users use a program, perhaps only partly finished, and getting their feedback on its suitability for their needs and expectations. There is an entire field in the computing industry, Human Computer Interaction (HCI), that looks at programs from the user's standpoint.

Some testing, load testing, tries to break a program by overloading it with data to see how robust it is. Measurements are taken of the amount of work it can (safely) handle. Adjustments to the program may need to be made if we get unhappy results.

Some testing, especially of important programs, is done by specially trained professional testers who work with the finished program and its original specification to see if they match. Your professor does something like this with your programming assignments. He or she may run the program on specially devised data to see if it works in all situations as it should. Some testing, as in load testing, sets out to try and break a program by giving it unexpected inputs.

In fact, one of the major problems in the world of commerce is that too much software is insufficiently tested in this way and hackers gain access to systems by trying improper inputs until something breaks. Once this happens analysis can often show how to exploit the break with carefully crafted inputs. The solution to this problem is not just programmer vigilance, as no one is able to never make a mistake. The solution requires *defense in depth*, with programmer training, good language, good engineering practice, etc. all required to provide layers of safety, each of which is faulty, but in combination provide good security and safety.

However, none of the above testing techniques are very useful in helping a working programmer write good programs. They can tell you later that it is fine or that it is junk, but they don't give you feedback early enough that you can improve your product. So, the kind of testing we want to focus on here, is testing that matters to a working developer. How can you use testing to help you do a better job? One solution that has become popular, because it is both powerful and useful, is *Test Driven Development (TDD)*. TDD usually depends on special testing frameworks that you use as you develop and we will describe one in the next section, but first let's look at the process itself.

What we will describe will sound like more work than developing the application, but in the long run it saves work, as the most frustrating part of programming is finding, analyzing, and removing errors (bugs). TDD can give us the confidence to develop an application to solve a problem one step at a time, knowing that what we add in the next step doesn't break what we added in previous steps. However, like many good things, it takes discipline to become good at it. You don't become a good swimmer, for example, by taking short cuts in training.

Suppose you have a problem to solve and want to use TDD to help. The first step is to find some much smaller problem in the one you are given and think about solving that first. Pick something you know you will need and that you think you have a solution for. In the French Military Game, it would probably not be the memory manager. In fact it probably wouldn't be some particular class, since you are at the beginning and don't yet know what classes you might want or need. For FMG, you might try to first write the user input handler that will handle only one move, for example. You don't worry yet about how the Fox will respond to the move. You don't worry yet about how to represent the three Police pieces, etc. You just handle the input. Once you get that done, you might start to work on a framework for determining if it is a legal move. That doesn't mean getting all the logic right initially, but you will need some methods that will produce some outputs that tell you if a choice was valid or not.

Once you have a small problem within the bigger one that you will work on, the first thing you do is to write a test that, if it passes, will tell you that you got that problem correctly solved. You write the test before you create the solution. The test will initially fail, of course. Once you have a test, however, you then write enough of your application to make that test pass – and nothing more. Then try to think of another test for the same thing. What could go wrong at this point in my application? How will I know if it does? Write a test for that. Run the test. If it passes, good, but if it fails, write a bit more of your solution to make it pass – and nothing more. Once you can't think of how to break this little bit of code any more, and therefore can't think of any more tests, go on to the next little bit of your problem and do the same thing.

But, here is the important point. When you work on the second, third, … parts of the program, run all of the tests for all of the parts at each stage. Then, if you do something today that breaks something you wrote yesterday, you will learn of it immediately. Moreover, since you have just now made only a small change to your program, it should not be too difficult to figure out why it broke. Programmers who write a lot before testing wind up with code that doesn't seem to work, its parts don't fit together, and it is difficult to know why or, more important, what to do. TDD is your friend here.

The real benefit of TDD is not that it helps you a lot in writing a small piece of code correctly the first time. Many programmers are good at that. If that is all it could do, it wouldn't be worth the effort. Where it pays you back, however, is learning immediately when you break something. It gives you the confidence to change a program knowing that it is already correct when you start, and that you will learn immediately if you put a bug into it.

A *suite* of tests that you can run repeatedly is what you want. This is called *regression* testing. It has been used for a long time in program maintenance of valuable programs, but it can also be used in the development of new programs, giving good feedback to the programmers that helps them measure their progress and their success. It is called regression testing, because when a test like this fails, you have *regressed*; gone backwards in your goal of creating a good program. We want to guard against changes making software worse.

Like HCI, there is a complete field of study on Software Testing. It is a viable career path for some people.

In the next section we will look at a tool that enables TDD in Java. Similar things exist for most computing languages. The Robot Programming Language has an extension that fits with this as well.

12.4 JUnit – Automated Testing

One relatively new and very useful tool for TDD is named JUnit (Java Unit). It is available from http://www.junit.org but it is also bundled with many software development packages. There are similar "units" for most programming languages such as Python and C++. JUnit provides a framework for programmer-written tests and was developed precisely to support Test Driven Development.

In TDD with JUnit, the idea is to set up some scenario by creating an object or two and sending the objects a message or two and then making *assertions* about the result. An assertion is just a statement that something is true. The assertions are automated so that you don't need to look to see if they pass (statement true) or fail. If they pass, nothing in particular happens, but if they fail you are made aware of it. You can therefore execute a very large number of assertions about many objects in a few seconds and get confidence that your application passes all of its tests.

There are three things that you need to do to write such an automated test; the setup, the messages in that context, and the assertions about the result. Part of what we need to write for this is determined by JUnit, part from the application we want to test, and part from any extensions to JUnit that we have to simplify our process. An example of the latter is a class provided with Karel J Robot named KJRTest. This class defines assertions about robots that you can use in JUnit. One such assertion is assertFacingEast(UrRobot robot). Here is how it might be used. We will show two forms of it, corresponding to two different versions of JUnit. In the older version, all tests must have names that begin with *test* such as *testRightTurn*.

Let's suppose for an illustration that we are building the StairSweeper class of Chapter 2 of Karel J Robot. Suppose again, that we have decided to write and test a turnRight command first. In JUnit 3, the test class would look like this:

```
import kareltherobot.*;

public class StairClimberTest extends KJRTest implements Directions
{
   private StairClimber karel;

   public void setUp()
   {  World.reset();
      World.readWorld("stairworld.kwld");
      karel = new StairClimber(1, 1, East, 0);
   }

   public void testRightTurn()
   {  assertFacingEast(karel);
      assertRunning(karel);
      karel.turnRight();
      assertFacingSouth(karel);
      assertRunning(karel);
      karel.turnRight();
      assertFacingWest(karel);
      assertRunning(karel);
      karel.turnRight();
      assertFacingNorth(karel);
      assertRunning(karel);
      karel.turnRight();
      assertFacingEast(karel);
      assertRunning(karel);
   }
. . .
}
```

JUnit tests class names usually end in the word Test as above: StairClimberTest. The above is just part of the class, however, and we will add to it as we add more to the application. The class is a subclass of KJRTest, which is supplied with Karel. The object under test is declared as a field of the class but it is normally created in a *setUp* method that is part of the JUnit infrastructure. The code you put in setUp will be executed immediately before any test is run and all of this and the running of the tests themselves will be done automatically.

The test method itself begins with the word test… as is necessary for JUnit 3. This method does two things. First it exercises a method that we are about to create (turnRight) but have not yet written, and second it makes assertions about the results. In this case we want to show that a robot will correctly turn right no matter what position it is initially facing, so we make karel turn around the compass from East back to East.

We emphasize that this test is written before the turnRight method is begun, and when it passes (no assertions fail) we have confidence that we have done our job correctly.

We haven't yet shown the main function that runs this, but it looks like the following in JUnit 3.8.

```
public static void main(String[] args)
{  junit.swingui.TestRunner.run(StairClimberTest.class);
}
```

Running this will produce a graphical application that runs all of our tests (just one here) and displays the results in green, for success and in red for failure. Within any method a test runs until the first assertion fails, but all of the tests are automatically run by JUnit, even if some are failing. But note that since setUp is executed anew before running each test method, we start with fresh new objects for each test, since we did the delivery specification in setUp. Figure 12.3 shows the result of a run. But this occurs only after we write the turnRight instruction and test it. Prior to that, the bar was red.

The run command must assure that everything needed can be found. You need the KarelJRobot.jar file as well as the junit.jar file in addition to the test class itself. A command might look like the following (all one command line):

```
java -cp ".:KarelJRobot.jar:/Applications/testing/junit.jar"
karel.StairClimberTest
```

Alternatively, JUnit is integrated with many software development environments, such as Eclipse and BlueJ. In fact, the graphical version has been dropped from JUnit 4, unless you use one of the integrated environments. If you use one of these, you can usually run your tests from a menu selection or a button. The graphics may be different in such a case, but it will typically show a red or green bar for tests and will also provide a way to point from the output screen back to your failing tests when there is a problem. If you get a red bar then the failure will show up with some explanation in the bottom text area below and double clicking an error line will take you back to the code.

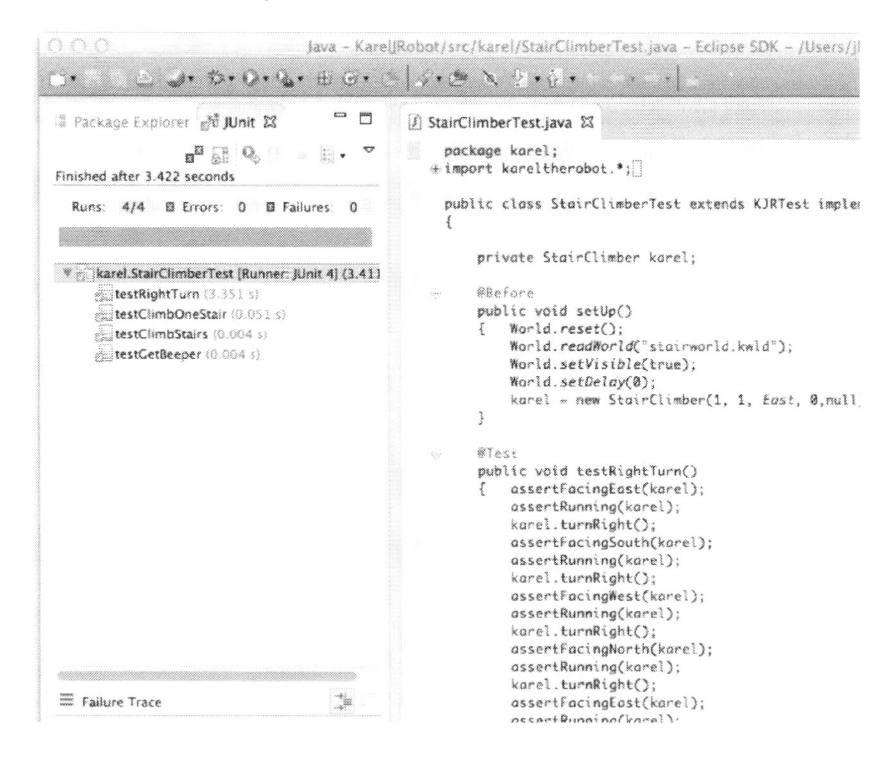

Figure 12.3 The JUnit 4 Eclipae Interface

Of course this tool is available for general programming as well as robot programming. The normal assertions you can make are that a Boolean expression is true, that two values are equal to one another, that a statement throws an exception, etc.

However, there are two restrictions. First is that you can only test public things. For the most part this means you can test public methods that return something and look at the results. The exception to this is when the infrastructure builds in some helps, such as the special robot assertions in Karel. The second is that it is very difficult, though not impossible to test graphical programs and even the output to a console. The application should be developed apart from its presentation layer in any case, separating the *model* (or the logic underlying it) from the *view* (how it looks to the user). So JUnit is most suitable for testing the model. In FMG, for example, the view is the FMG class, along with the Display. The model is everything else: The Fox, the Police, the MemoryManager, and the MoveRules. This is where the logic of the game is. The rest was just presentation. In fact, if we want a really clean separation between model and view, we could remove all of the methods of FMG model classes that write to System.out and replace them with accessors of information that can be used by a view class such as FMG itself. The Fox.showPosition method would be replaced by, perhaps, Fox.getPosition, that returns a String, or even the cell number on which the fox resides. This provides cleaner separation of model and view, and also makes it easier to test, since we can invoke this method and make assertions about the result.

An interesting fact about testing, though, is that when well done, you will have about as much test code as application code; perhaps more. This is due to the fact that a lot of things can go wrong with software and you want to guard against all of them, especially when you are writing your programs a bit at a time, which is, really, the only sensible way to do it.

While this seems like a lot of extra work, it actually isn't, for the following reason. While you may have only a small part of your program to write at this moment, you still need to understand it and plan its solution. If it is at all difficult to understand you will need to ponder what to do. If you do this thinking while you have a test framework open in front of you, then you write tests as you think. You make the test framework part of your design process, capturing design decisions in tests as you go. Since you are writing tests that will exercise the code you are about to write, you get to see how the code looks in use before you actually write it.

For example, to write the turnRight command we need to think about the effect of it first, Then we can capture this in tests, designing its name and any needed parameters. Of course this case seems to simple to bother, but most are not, and the test will still be there to tell us later if we break something in adding a new feature later.

In JUnit version 4, things are a bit different, though the concepts are the same. This version uses new features of Java called *annotations*, and the names of things don't matter so much any more. The setUp method can be called whatever you like, though it is often still called setUp, but it must be preceded by a *Before* annotation.

```
@Before public void setUp()
{  World.reset();
   World.readWorld("stairworld.kwld");
   karel = new StairClimber(1, 1, East, 0);
}
```

Likewise, tests can have whatever name you like, but are preceded by a Test annotation.

```
@Test public void testRightTurn()
{  assertFacingEast(karel);
   assertRunning(karel);
   karel.turnRight();
   . . .
```

Otherwise testing is about the same in these two versions.

12.4.1 Testing Example – The Calculator Again

The CalculatorModel we examined in Chapter 9 was developed using TDD with JUnit 3. Here we will show part of the process of development.

Imagine that we have not yet begun on the project, so have no code at all. We have a list of features that the calculator must have. We presented these as part of the discussion in Chapter 9. The first such *development story* was: A new calculator should have a display of 0. (See Section 9.6.1). Such stories are small and individually simple, but collectively they cover the necessary features of the application. We want to build the application one story at a time, though this sometimes makes it necessary for us to modify things we have done before. We pay that price to gain the benefit of being able to think in smaller parts, rather than try to juggle all of the requirements at once.

We start by creating a JUnit test for an application that doesn't exist. It doesn't yet even have a name. Since we will be using JUnit 3, we create a new file named CalculatorTest.java and put the necessary imports in at the top. The name of the class is also determined by our file name as usual:

```
package com.jbergin.calculator;

import junit.framework.TestCase;

public class CalculatorTest extends TestCase{

   public static void main(String[] args)
   {  junit.swingui.TestRunner.run(CalculatorTest.class);
   }

}
```

The next thing to do is to create an object to test, but we don't have the class name yet, so we think, think, think, and come up with CalculatorModel, for the reasons given back in Chapter 9. We then declare a new field of the test class of this new, as yet undefined, type. We also create the object in the setUp method:

```
public class CalculatorTest extends TestCase{

   CalculatorModel calculator;

   public void setUp() throws Exception{
      calculator = new CalculatorModel();
   }
. . .
}
```

This doesn't compile, of course, since CalculatorModel isn't defined, but it is useful to note that JUnit can still process this file without error, though it will tell us that the file can't be compiled.

We are now ready to write a test, though we could also build just enough of the calculator model to make this work. If you decide to do that, then create another file named CalculatorModel.java with just this:

```
package com.jbergin.calculator;

public class CalculatorModel{
}
```

Everything will now compile and if you run JUnit at this point, it will tell you that there are no tests. Now we can attack the first story. The calculator needs to have a display of zero. Since we are building a model, this means that it should have a method (think of a name.... ah, *getDisplay*) that return zero immediately after a calculator is created. Well, we have just created the calculator in setUp, so we can write a test assertion that this, as yet undefined method, will return zero. So, we add the following to the CalculatorTest class:

```
   public void testDisplay(){
      assertEquals(0, calculator.getDisplay());
   }
```

This can't execute yet, since there is no such method in the Calculator class so we can add that next. We want to write just enough code to make this test pass. There are a variety of ways to do this, some simpler than others, but we shall pick a middle ground here.

```
public class CalculatorModel{
   private int display = 0;

   public int display(){
      return display;
   }
}
```

If we run JUnit now, we will get a green bar. We have an absolutely minimal application, that implements one simple story, for which we have a test, and the test passes. We haven't even needed to look at the other stories, or think about how to build them. We just work in small increments and let the application grow, driven by the stories and the tests.

Now we can proceed to the next story: Give the calculator keys like 5 and 3. When you hit a single key the value of the key should "show" in the display.

Initially, we can give the calculator only those two keys and make them work for only single key presses. The other keys can be added later if we can add those successfully. Other stories will address multiple key presses. So, again, we have narrowed the scope of our development to the smallest possible step. So, we go back to the test class and write another test, or two.

```
   public void testPress5(){
      calculator.pressFive();
      assertEquals(5, calculator.getDisplay());
   }
```

```
   public void testPress3(){
      calculator pressThree();
      assertEquals(3, calculator.getDisplay());
   }
```

Again, we have made a design decision here. The calculator will have a separate method for each key to press. In each test we started with a fresh calculator, since setUp is run between tests, We exercised the new functionality and then we made assertions about changes to the model.

Once we have the test, we can go back to adding methods to the application itself. So add the following to CalculatorModel.

```
public void pressFive(){
   display = 5;
}

public void pressThree(){
   display = 3;
}
```

Our tests will again pass (green bar), since each of these sets the getDisplay field and the display method returns the current value of this field. We haven't considered other keys, nor multiple presses. Of course, this isn't the code we saw in Chapter 9, but this is just the first pass. This code will change as we go. We are willing to modify existing code as we learn that new things are required, but for now, we are meeting all requirements with a simple solution.

The third story talks about multiple key presses: If you press a sequence of number keys, the results should accumulate in the display. A 5 followed by a 3 should display 53. A test for this might look like the following. It is in the test class, of course.

```
   public void testAccumulate(){
      calculator. pressFive ();
      calculator. pressFive ();
      calculator. pressThree ();
      assertEquals("multiple press error", 553, calculator.getDisplay());
   }
```

Here we have shown a slightly different form of the assertEquals method, in that it has a message as the first argument. This message will be printed whenever the assertion fails. Also note that the expected value in an assertion comes before the tested value. The JUnit output messages will make more sense if you do it this way. The above test runs ok, since we have already built all of the methods it uses, but it will fail, since they don't yet do the right thing. So, we need to modify the pressFive and pressThree methods so that they do a better job. We examined the logic of the accumulation process in Chapter 9, so won't repeat it here, but as we start modifying the two methods we see that they both have to accumulate a value. It is therefore wise to factor this out (Say it Once) into a separate accumulate method of CalculatorModel.

```
private void accumulate(value){
   display = 10 * display + value;
}
```

```
public void pressFive(){
   accumulate(5);
}

public void pressThree(){
   accumulate(3);
}
```

We still haven't gotten to the point at which we use objects to represent the keys, or to use strategies, but nothing in our stories yet requires anything like that. We also don't have a way to clear the display, but we have no requirement for that either. If we don't count lines of code consisting of a single close brace, we now have eleven lines of code and fourteen lines of test. But all the tests pass at this point, not just the newest one. JUnit will run them all so a green bar gives us confidence in out development process.

Note that each story is small. It leads to a small test or two, and that leads to a small change or addition to our code base. This is the essence of TDD. And notice how much of our design work is done while we are writing tests.

The fourth story is a bit more extensive: Give the calculator a + key that adds the results of two operands. Other operator keys will be added later (-, *, /). Sum isn't done till you hit equals, though.

At this point in thinking about how to proceed we discover that the numeric keys have to do two different things, depending on whether an operator key has just been pressed. We captured that in the first version of the state transition diagram (Figure 9.1). If we want to develop a polymorphic solution, we realize that we will need more than just the one class, CalculatorModel. So our next step is to *refactor* our code to enable us to move forward more easily. Refactoring is changing the structure of the code without changing its behavior, and we have tests in place to help us make sure we don't change the behavior. At this point we can introduce the interface CalculatorKey and the class NumberKey. Suppose we decide to make them inner classes of the CalculatorModel itself (as we did in Chapter 9).

```
public interface OperatorKey extends CalculatorKey
{
   public void operate();
}

public class NumberKey implements CalculatorKey{

   public NumberKey(int value){
      this.value = value;
   }

   public void press(){
      accumulate(value);
   }

   private final int value;
}
```

We will then also need to create a Number key for the five key and another for the three key and connect them to the corresponding press methods of the CalculatorModel.

```
   private final CalculatorKey five = new NumberKey(5);
   private final CalculatorKey three = new NumberKey(3);

   public void pressFive()
    {
        five.press();
    }

    public void pressThree()
    {
        three.press();
    }
```

We now have a larger collection of objects interacting to solve the current simple problem, but some of the objects (three and five) are hidden. The CalculatorModel can now be called a *façade* for the objects and we have an application of the Façade Design Pattern, the intent of which is to provide a unified face to a bunch of interacting objects. We haven't changed the behavior of the application in this change in its structure. How do we know that? The tests still pass. Now you can go on to implement the new story on this code base by adding strategies and it will be much easier than to do so on the earlier one. But it was the tests that gave us the confidence to make the changes to the new structure knowing that we couldn't break something unnoticed. This too is swell.

12.5 Important Ideas From This Chapter

model
view
JUnit
JavaDoc
Test Driven Development (TDD)
Façade Design Pattern

12.6 Problem Set

1. Find one of your old Karel J Robot programs and document it using JavaDoc. Provide documentation for each class, each public method and for each parameter and return value of your methods.

2. Finish the development of tests for the CalculatorModel that was begun in Section 12.4.1

3. Write user level documentation for FMG explaining to a user exactly how to run the program and interact with it.

Secondo Intermezzo – A Toy Computer

1 Introduction to Machine Language

In this second interlude we will discuss some very low level computer ideas by examining a simulation of simple hardware machine language. To give you an idea of how low level this is, we start by presenting a program that consists of a simple loop that will add some data and print it.

```
00:    zer
01:    push  104
02:    push  105
03:    subtr
04:    jnn   6
05:    jmp   16
06:    push  106
07:    ldd
08:    add
09:    push  104
10:    inc
11:    pop   104
12:    push  106
13:    inc
14:    pop   106
15:    jmp   1
16:    outp
17:    halt
```

Not easy to understand, of course. In fact, it isn't easy even if you understand the language. This language has absolutely no abstraction facility. You can't name a variable, or a method, or anything. You can make only the tiniest of steps at a time, and so the amount of detail required to do anything meaningful becomes overwhelming. Some of the words probably make sense; add and halt, for example, others are gibberish. Let's get started in trying to understand a system in which this can make sense. All of your computer programs are translated into something not too different from this, Each line is an instruction, and even a simple Java program might contain thousands of such instructions. This particular language, by the way, has no special merit. I just created it for purposes of this discussion. But it is similar to real *machine languages*.

First, the leftmost column is not part of the language. I've just labeled the lines, but the labels are significant. The 6 on the right of line 04 refers to line 06, in fact. The names in the middle column are called *opcodes* and a machine language comes with a fixed, not extendable, list of these. Each does some simple thing. The right column numbers are called *operands*, though not every opcode needs an operand. In this language an instruction consists of a single opcode and zero or one operands.

In reality it is even a bit harder than we have shown. The machine codes are really just numbers, though we have shown names above to make it a bit easier to follow below. We shall return to this idea, however.

2 The Memory and Its Contents

This computer has only a few parts. One is its memory, which is really just an array of cells. Each cell can hold either an *instruction* or a piece of *data*. The instructions are like those above. All of the operands in the right column of our program are actually indexes into this memory array. We normally call them addresses. The numbers in the left column, which label the instructions, are also addresses, and the implication is that at address 08 you will find the "push 104" instruction. Figure 1 shows the parts of this computer. The heavy line between the Stack and the Memory is a *data bus* that transfers data between the two. The PC (program counter) was discussed earlier, in Section 9.2. The meaning is the same here.

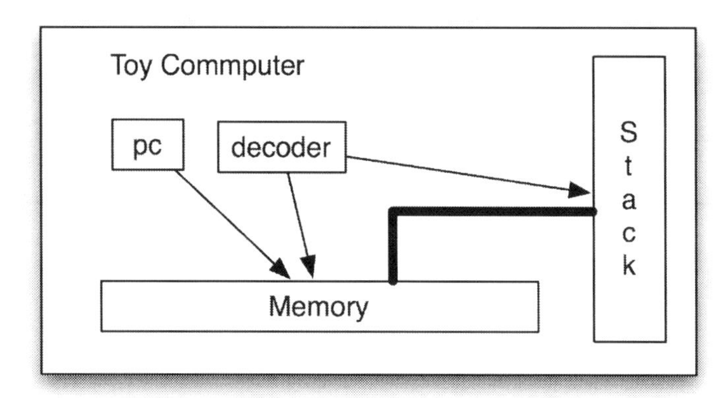

Figure 1. Schematic of the Toy Computer

The data used in this computer is of the type *double*.

In Java, a double is a 64 bit number that represents an approximation to a real number with a decimal part. Some examples of doubles are 65.3 and 3.1416. The type float is similar, though it is stored in 32 bits and so has both less range and less precision. The most important thing to know about doubles is that they really are approximations. It is not possible to represent all of the real numbers, even just those between 0 and 1, in a computer, since in any range of real numbers there are infinitely many values. But computers are finite.

An implication of this is that if you add up .01 a thousand times, you won't get 10 like you expect. Though you will get a number close to 10. Doubles are good for measurements, such as temperature, which are seldom perfectly precise, but they are not good for things like money, which does require precision.

We will actually build a computer simulator that executes programs like those above. We will need some data structures to hold some of its elements, such as its memory. Rather than use an array for the memory or a Java ArrayList, both of which would be good choices, we will use instead the classes given in the Appendix. These classes were built for no reason but to give you something to read that is fairly sophisticated, but a bit less so than those in the Java libraries. They are very similar to the corresponding Java collections classes and are in fact interchangeable with them for our purposes here. We will represent the memory of the computer with a DenseList, which is like an ArrayList. We shall, however encapsulate it a bit more, wrapping it in a façade to present a more "memory like" face to the computer simulator itself.

We will, in fact encapsulate both the data stored in the array and the instructions in Java classes. They are quite simple. Since we want either of them to be storable in a memory cell, we want a common superclass or interface to represent them. We call this empty interface *Code*. We have also provided JavaDoc comments for the important parts.

```
package computer;

/** A super type for things inserted into the memory
 * of the toy computer.
 * @author jbergin
 *
 */
public interface Code{

}
```

```
package computer;

/** Represents data cells in the memory of the toy computer.
 * Holds a single double value. We depend on auto-boxing of
 * Java 5 here as the typical use is double, not Double.
 * @author jbergin
 *
 */
public class Data implements Code{
   private Double data;

   /** Create a data cell holding a double that may be
    * inserted into the memory
    * @param d
    */
   public Data(Double d){
      this.data = d;
   }

   /** Retrieve the double value of this cell
    * @return the double value
    */
   public Double value(){
      return data;
   }

}
```

```
package computer;

/** Represents an instruction cell in the memory of the toy
 * computer. An instruction has an opcode and an operand.
 * The operand might not be used by every instruction
 * @author jbergin
 *
 */
public class Instruction implements Code{
   private int opcode;
   private int operand;

   /** Create an instruction cell that may be placed in
    * the memory of a toy computer
    * @param operation the opcode
    * @param onWhat the operand
    */
   public Instruction(int operation, int onWhat){
      opcode = operation;
      operand = onWhat;
   }

   /** Retrieve the opcode of this instruction
    * @return the instruction code itself in integer form
    */
   public int opcode(){
      return opcode;
   }

   /** Retrieve the operand of this instruction. It will
    * likely be 0 if the opcode
    * doesn't use any operand
    * @return the operand, which is always an address in the
    * memory of the toy computer.
    */
   public int operand(){
      return operand;
   }

}
```

So, Data has just a value, but an Instruction has both an opcode and an operand

The memory of the computer can now be defined as a DenseList of $1024 = 2^{10}$ cells, each of which can hold an item of type Code.

```
package computer;

import com.jbergin.generic.DenseList;

/** A dense array-like structure representing the memory of a toy
 * computer. The memory may hold cells of type Code, either
 * Data cells or Instruction cells.
 * @author jbergin
 *
 */
public class Memory{
   private DenseList<Code> storage = new DenseList<Code>(1024);

   /** Create a memory of size 1K or 1024 cells.
    */
   public Memory(){
      for(int i = 0; i < 1024; ++i){
         storage.add(null);
      }
   }

   /** Insert a cell into the memory at a fixed address
    * @param code the cell to be inserted. It may be Data or
    * Instruction
    * @param cell the address at which to put the item in
    * range: 0..1023
    */
   public void put(Code code, int cell){
      storage.set(cell, code);
   }

   /** Retrieve a data cell from the memory. An error will occur
    * if it isn't a data cell
    * @param cell the address of the desired cell
    * @return the cell at the required address
    * @throws ClassCastException if the cell has the wrong type
    */
   public Data getValue(int cell){
         return (Data)storage.get(cell);
   }

   /** Retrieve an instruction cell from the memory. An error will
    * occur if it isn't an instruction cell
    * @param cell the address of the desired cell
    * @return the cell at the required address
    * @throws ClassCastException if the cell has the wrong type
    */
   public Instruction getInstruction(int cell){
      return (Instruction)storage.get(cell);
   }
}
```

We can put something into memory by setting the DenseList cell with the new value. We don't record which kind of thing we put there, however, so if we want to retrieve it with one of our get methods, we need to know what we put in that cell. Nothing will help us keep track of this. This is one of the difficult features of low level programming; there is no nice language like Java to help keep you from misusing data.

3 The Execution Stack

The next major feature of our computer is its *stack*. A Stack is a data structure, that can be either densely stored or linked, but it has a special data protocol called Last-in, First-out, or LIFO. You insert data into a stack with a *push* operation, and it is then saved. For us the data will be doubles. You retrieve data with a *pop* operation. And pop returns the item most recently pushed, as well as removing it from the storage. The name Stack is supposed to remind you of a stack of plates. You can put a plate on the top (push) but if you want a plate you normally retrieve (pop) the one most recently placed on the top. Java has a Stack class, which extends java.util.Vector, but we shall build our own, also based on the DenseList, just to see how it is done. Since our DenseList is automatically expandable, so will the stack be. Note, however, that it is an error to try to pop from a stack that is empty. A push adds the new element at the end, and a pop retrieves it from the end, but also removes it. The version we present here is generic, though our use will be Stack<Double>.

```
package computer;

import com.jbergin.generic.DenseList;

/** A LIFO storage structure. Useful in such things as
 * language translation and in execution of
 * arithmetic expressions. Insertions are only at the "top".
 * Removals are only at the "top".
 * @author jbergin
 *
 * @param <T> the type of element stored
 */
public class Stack<T>{
   private DenseList<T> storage = new DenseList<T>();

   /** Enter an item into the storage at the top.
    * @param element the item to be inserted
    */
   public void push(T element){
      storage.add(element);
   }

   /** Remove and return the item most recently pushed that
    * has not yet been popped
    * @return the top of the stack
    * @throws IllegalStateException if the stack is empty
    */
   public T pop(){
      if(storage.isEmpty()){
         throw new IllegalStateException("Pop of empty stack");
      }
      int last = storage.size() - 1;
```

```
        T result = storage.get(last);
        storage.remove(last);
        return result;
    }

    /** Get a reference to the top of the stack without removing it.
     * @return the item at the top of the stack
     * @throws IllegalStateException if the stack is empty
     */
    public T top(){
        if(storage.size() == 0){
            throw new IllegalStateException("Pop of empty stack");
        }
        return storage.get(storage.size() - 1);
    }

    /** Tells if the structure is empty.
     * @return whether or not the stack is empty (has no elements)
     */
    public boolean isEmpty(){
        return storage.isEmpty();
    }

    /** Empty the stack
     */
    public void clear(){
        storage.clear();
    }
}
```

The computer will have both a Memory and a Stack and the reason we want the latter is that is where all computation is done in this computer. To add two numbers you push both of them on to the stack and then issue an *add* instruction. The add instruction itself pops two items from the stack, adds them and pushes the result back onto the stack. The size of the stack shrinks by one in this operation, of course. This also explains why the add instruction at location 07 of our little program didn't need any operands. They are implicit, being the two top stack cells. A computer like this is called *stack-based*. The high level language Forth is based on similar principles, in fact.

4 The Toy Computer

The only other important piece of our computer is an int called the *pc* (program counter), previously discussed in Section 9.2. Normally we spell out the names of things in programming, but the name pc has become so entrenched among people who do this kind of programming that we will keep it. The idea is that the pc always maintains the address of the next instruction to be executed. When our computer starts, the pc is always 0, meaning that the instruction in memory cell 0 will always be the first one executed. The pc then steps through the program to execute the instructions one after the other. Some instructions can change this order of execution, as we shall see.

With this background we can explain some of the instructions in our program. Instruction *zer* pushes 0.0 onto the stack. Instruction *inc* adds 1.0 to whatever is on top. Recall that the stack contains double data. Instruction *push* has an operand and the meaning is that the operand represents the address of a data cell in memory and the contents of that cell, a double, are to be pushed. The contents of the original cell are not modified, however. Only the stack changes.

Notice that in our definition of Instructions, the opcodes are represented as ints. here is a complete listing represented as Java constants.

```
private static final int push = 0;
private static final int pop = 1;
private static final int toss = 2;
private static final int outp = 3;
private static final int dupl = 4;
private static final int add = 5;
private static final int subtr = 6;
private static final int halt = 7;
private static final int inp = 8;
private static final int jmp = 9;
private static final int jnn = 10;
private static final int ldd = 11;
private static final int zer = 12;
private static final int inc = 13;
private static final int lda = 14;
```

However, in order to simulate the execution of a program like the one we began with, we need methods in the computer simulator to carry them out. These are part of the class ToyComputer, as are the constants above. The comments explain each operation.

```
/** Copies a memory cell and pushes it onto the stack
 * @param mem the address of the memory cell desired
 */
public void push(int mem){
   stack.push(memory.getValue(mem).value());
}

/** Pop the stack and put the result into memory
 * @param mem the memory cell address into which to put the
 * stack top
 */
public void pop(int mem){
   memory.put(new Data(stack.pop()), mem);
}

/** Discard the top of the stack. Pop, but throws away the result
 */
public void toss(){
   stack.pop();
}
```

```
/** Pop the stack and print the result on standard output
 */
public void outp(){
   System.out.println(stack.pop());
}

/** Duplicate the top of the stack. i.e. push a copy of the top
 * onto the top
 */
public void dupl(){
   stack.push(stack.top());
}

/** Pop the two top elements from the stack, add them and push
 * the result
 */
public void add(){
   stack.push(stack.pop() + stack.pop());
}

/** Pop the two top elements from the stack and subtract them.
 * The original top is the left operand and the one below is
 * the right operand. Push the result
 */
public void subtr(){
   stack.push(stack.pop() - stack.pop());
}

/** Unconditionally jump to an instruction at the specified address
 * @param where the address of the next instruction to be executed
 */
public void jmp(int where){
   pc = where;
}

/** Push a zero onto the top of the stack.
 */
public void zer(){
   stack.push(0.0);
}

/** Add 1.0 to the top of the stack. Increment.
 */
public void inc(){
   stack.push(stack.pop() + 1.0);
}
```

```
/** The top of the stack is an address. Pop it, extract the
 * data item at that address and push the result. Replace
 * an address with the item it points to
 */
public void ldd(){
   int where = stack.pop().intValue();
   push(where);
}

/** Pop the stack. If the result is non-negative then jump
 * to the specified address
 * @param where the address of the next instruction of the
 * stack top was non-negative
 */
public void jnn(int where){
   if(stack.pop().intValue() >= 0){
      pc = where;
   }
}

/** Terminate execution of the running program
 */
public void halt(){
   running = false;
}

/** Retrieve a double from standard input and push the result
 * @throws NumberFormatException if the input can't be
 * interpreted as a double
 */
public void inp(){
   Scanner in = new Scanner(System.in);
   stack.push(in.nextDouble());
}

/** Load the address of an operand. Primarily used to get the address
 * of a label onto the stack
 * @param where the address to be loaded
 */
public void lda(int where){
   stack.push((double)where);
}
```

Next, we need a way to actually load the memory preparatory to running a program. Both the program and the data it will manipulate need to be loaded in to the memory. Since this simple device isn't connected to a disk drive we need some way to put instructions and data into individual memory cells. In the early days of computing, this was done using strictly numeric codes, 1 instead of pop, for example. They were entered physically using a set of switches on the front of the computer. Here we have four methods for handling this. They depend on a field called the loadAddress that represents the next cell into which to put an instruction. It is automatically incremented each time you put in an instruction, and it always starts from zero. Data cells are put into cells specified in the method itself, however.

```
/** Load an instruction into the next available memory
 * location starting from zero
 * @param opcode the opcode of the instruction
 * @param operand the operand (memory address) that
 * the opcode will operate on
 */
public void loadInstruction(int opcode, int operand){
   memory.put(new Instruction(opcode, operand), loadAddress++);
}

/** Load an instruction into the next available memory
 * location starting from zero. The
 * operand will be set to zero in this instruction
 * @param opcode the opcode of the instruction
 */
public void loadInstruction(int opcode){
   loadInstruction(opcode, 0);
}

/** Load a data cell at an arbitrary memory address
 * @param data the double value to be stored (a Data cell
 * will be created)
 * @param location the memory address into which to put the new cell
 */
public void loadData(double data, int location){
   memory.put(new Data(data), location);
}

/** Reset the load address so that a new program may be loaded
 * over the current one
 */
public void reset(){
   loadAddress = 0;
}
```

Using this, our original machine language program would be loaded like this. I chose to load the data first, but it doesn't matter.

```
ToyComputer computer = new ToyComputer();

computer.loadData(1.0, 100); // data to be added
computer.loadData(2.0, 101);
computer.loadData(3.0, 102);
computer.loadData(4.0, 103);
computer.loadData(0.0, 104); // control counter
computer.loadData(3.0, 105); //const number of items - 1
computer.loadData(100.0, 106); // data loc of beginning of data

computer.loadInstruction(zer);
computer.loadInstruction(push, 104);
computer.loadInstruction(push, 105);
```

```
computer.loadInstruction(subtr);
computer.loadInstruction(jnn, 6);
computer.loadInstruction(jmp, 16);
computer.loadInstruction(push, 106);
computer.loadInstruction(ldd);
computer.loadInstruction(add);
computer.loadInstruction(push, 104);
computer.loadInstruction(inc);
computer.loadInstruction(pop, 104);
computer.loadInstruction(push, 106);
computer.loadInstruction(inc);
computer.loadInstruction(pop, 106);
computer.loadInstruction(jmp, 1);
computer.loadInstruction(outp);
computer.loadInstruction(halt);
```

See if you can now trace out this program using the definitions of the opcodes given in the JavaDoc comments. Its purpose is to add the data in cells 100 through 103 of the memory, printing 10.0 at the end.

5 Running the Program

Now that we have the program in the memory, let's look at how a computer actually executes a machine language program. Our simulation will be quite close to this. A computer is driven by a clock and we can think of the clock making four ticks per cycle. The computer also has a program counter (pc) that is always used to point to the next instruction to be executed as well as an instruction decoder that can hold one instruction: the one currently in execution.

On the first tick of the clock, the instruction in memory pointed to by the pc is loaded into the decoder. In our program an error will occur if that location doesn't hold an instruction, but in a real computer, it just loads whatever is there and will interpret it as an instruction even if it isn't. This tick is called *load*. The next, or *increment*, tick causes the pc to be incremented so that it now points to the next instruction in sequence. If we just loaded from cell 22, then the increment tick will put 23 into the pc. The third tick, *decode*, gives the computer a chance to extract the parts of the instruction and, in a real computer, start the electrical signals flowing through the machine. The last tick, *do*, is where the instruction is actually performed. The clock then goes around again, with a new *fetch* tick.

On the do tick, an add instruction causes two values to be popped from the stack and the result pushed back on. The only thing that is very different here, is what happens on jump instructions. Recall that the increment made the pc point to the next instruction after the current one. If a jump is executed, however, the pc itself may be modified. On an unconditional jump, *jmp*, the operand is written into the pc. Since this happens just before fetch, the next instruction executed will be the one whose address was in the *jmp*. Conditional jumps like *jnn* only write into the pc when their condition is met.

Here is the code that implements run. Note that we have broken the cycle down. The loop in *run* is potentially infinite, broken only by an error or by the execution of a *halt* instruction.

```
/** Execute the program currently stored in the memory.
 * Starts at address 0 in  all cases. It uses a typical
 * fetch-increment-decode-do cycle
 */
public void run(){
   pc = 0;
   running = true;
   stack.clear();
   while (running){
      fetch();
      increment();
      decodeDo();
   }
}

/** Fetch an instruction using the program counter (pc).
 * Put it into the decoder in the CPU (Central Processing Unit)
 */
private void fetch(){
   decoder = memory.getInstruction(pc);
}

/** Increment the pc
 */
private void increment(){
   pc++;
}

/** Decode the instruction in the decoder (break it into parts)
 * and execute it
 */
private void decodeDo(){
   perform(decoder.opcode(), decoder.operand());
}
```

There is one last piece. We need to connect the numerical operation codes, like 5 for add, to the actual methods that carry out the instruction. Think of the method itself as the wiring that knows how to execute a particular instruction, but we still need to get the decoder connected to this infrastructure. The final piece is then this:

```
/** The internal map between opcode numbers and the
 * operational methods. Think of this as the internal
 * wiring of the computer that connects the decoder
 * to the various operational units such as an adder,
 * the stack, etc. The polymorphic replacement of this
 * is beyond the scope of the book.
 * @param op an opcode
 * @param opnd the (optional) operand for this opcode
 */
private void perform(int op, int opnd){
   switch(op){
   case push: push(opnd);
      break;
   case pop: pop(opnd);
      break;
   case toss: toss();
      break;
   case outp: outp();
      break;
   case dupl: dupl();
      break;
   case add: add();
      break;
   case subtr: subtr();
      break;
   case halt: halt();
      break;
   case inp: inp();
      break;
   case jmp: jmp(opnd);
      break;
   case jnn: jnn(opnd);
      break;
   case ldd: ldd();
      break;
   case zer: zer();
      break;
   case inc: inc();
      break;
   case lda: lda(opnd);
      break;
   default:
      throw new UnsupportedOperationException("Unknown instruction");
   }
```

This is the first switch statement we have seen in this book. It is a low level device that is, actually, much like machine language itself. The numeric expression in parentheses after the keyword switch (here *op*) is evaluated to an integer, the control, and the various cases are just integers (or the names of integer constants, as here). The case whose value matches the computed control value is the place where execution begins. It continues from that place until you either reach the end of the structure or a *break* statement, at which point it is finished. Switch statements are rather error prone. The default clause, if present, is executed if none of the case values match the control. The *default* clause is optional and if missing nothing is done if the control matches none of the case tags. The *decodeDo* method uses this to translate a numeric opcode in an instruction to a Java method used to execute that instruction. There is a polymorphic solution that would replace this switch, but it is quite advanced.

6 More Convenient Programming – Assembly Language

Machine language has no programmer abstraction facility. The only abstraction we have shown is names for opcodes. Real machine code doesn't have even this. If we extracted our program from the computer it wouldn't have the names of the operations, but their numeric opcodes:

```
12 0
0  104
0  105
6  0
10 6
9  16
0  106
11 0
5  0
0  104
13 0
1  104
0  106
13 0
1  106
9  1
3  0
7  0
```

Well, the original was bad enough. But we can do a bit better. Assembly language is an attempt to add a couple of simple abstraction facilities to machine code to make it a bit easier to understand. In addition to the names of opcodes, that we have already shown, but which are built in to the language, it is possible for a programmer in assembly code to give names to machine addresses also. This means that the 104 and 106 in the above program can be made a bit more decipherable. Here is an assembly program that has the same effect as our original, though slightly different structure, since it takes advantage of the new facility. It also shows a zero operand for those instructions that don't require an operand, but that is to make this easier to read by a program: the Assembler.

```
   zer 0
   lda data
   pop point
label loop
   push calc
   push stop
   subtr 0
   jnn more
   jmp done
label more
   push point
   ldd 0
   add 0
   push calc
   inc 0
   pop calc
   push point
   inc 0
   pop point
   jmp loop
label done
   outp 0
   halt 0
label data
   double 1.0
   double 2.0
   double 3.0
   double 4.0
label calc
   double 0.0
label stop
   double 3.0
label point
   double 0.0
```

As an historical note, Assembly language got its name from the way programs were submitted to computers in the early days of computing. Decks of punch cards were "assembled" with user code as well as system code and data and then read through card readers into the computer. The name has persisted.

This example shows not only the program, but also the data that it will manipulate. There are two new features here that are not part of machine code. A *label* is just a symbolic address. The first label, loop, will be associated with the address 3, since it immediately precedes the instruction that will be loaded into cell 3.

This sort of thing is much easier to understand, though still far from easy. The names let us decipher it a bit. The *data* consists of four values. The *calc* is where we shall save a counter that tells us when we have added enough values. *Stop* is the value of *calc* that will cause us to leave a counting loop, and *point* is going to be a pointer to the next data value to be added. The earlier labels are also supposed to be instructive. The label *loop* indicates that we return to it to complete a loop structure, The label *done* indicates that we have left the loop and want to output our result and exit. The *more* label is needed since the jnn instruction is a bit awkward for us in this program and we need to skip over the jmp instruction. This is a canonical two way branch in this language, similar to an IF-THEN instruction in Java.

The second feature is the *double directive* that gives instructions to the assembler about what to do with the number that follows. It is not a machine instruction, nor does it correspond to one. Instead, it says that a double value is to be loaded into the computer memory at the current loadAddress. The first such, will be at the address specified by the *data* label, the next immediately after, etc. Label *data* will be 20, so the 1.0 will be at address 20, etc. The labels themselves are not instructions, so don't contribute to the instruction count.

We want to examine a program, the Assembler, that will translate this into machine code. The input will look like the above. But note that an assembler is very unforgiving. Errors will result in gibberish. We could provide output in many different forms. We could produce something like our first example in the intermezzo, or something like the first example in this section (real machine code), but we will actually do something much more useful. Our output will actually be a Java fragment that can be pasted into a main program and then run. Here is the output for the program above.

```
computer.loadInstruction(zer, 0);
computer.loadInstruction(lda, 20);
computer.loadInstruction(pop, 26);
computer.loadInstruction(push, 24);
computer.loadInstruction(push, 25);
computer.loadInstruction(subtr, 0);
computer.loadInstruction(jnn, 8);
computer.loadInstruction(jmp, 18);
computer.loadInstruction(push, 26);
computer.loadInstruction(ldd, 0);
computer.loadInstruction(add, 0);
computer.loadInstruction(push, 24);
computer.loadInstruction(inc, 0);
computer.loadInstruction(pop, 24);
computer.loadInstruction(push, 26);
computer.loadInstruction(inc, 0);
computer.loadInstruction(pop, 26);
computer.loadInstruction(jmp, 3);
computer.loadInstruction(outp, 0);
computer.loadInstruction(halt, 0);
computer.loadData(1.0, 20);
computer.loadData(2.0, 21);
computer.loadData(3.0, 22);
computer.loadData(4.0, 23);
computer.loadData(0.0, 24);
computer.loadData(3.0, 25);
computer.loadData(0.0, 26);
```

The version we will show here could use some fixing. While we will read an input file and write an output, we won't make this process very general or robust. Otherwise, this matches what happens in principle in a real assembler program.

Such a program is driven by a table, a map, actually, of symbols. The symbols are strings and the data are the numeric equivalents. When the assembler starts, the table is initialized with the opcode names and their values. We will use the classes from the Appendix for much of this, but we didn't build a HashMap and we need one for the table, so we will use the one from the Java Libraries.

```
public class Assembler {

   private Map<String, Integer> table = new HashMap<String, Integer>();
   private DenseList<String> program = new DenseList<String>();
   private boolean translateOK = true;
   private DenseList<String> translated = new DenseList<String>();

   public Assembler(){
      table.put("push", 0);
      table.put("pop", 1);
      table.put("toss", 2);
      table.put("outp", 3);
      table.put("dupl", 4);
      table.put("add", 5);
      table.put("subtr", 6);
      table.put("halt", 7);
      table.put("inp", 8);
      table.put("jmp", 9);
      table.put("jnn", 10);
      table.put("ldd", 11);
      table.put("zer", 12);
      table.put("inc", 13);
      table.put("lda", 14);
   }
```

We will read the assembly language program into the *program* list, one token per entry. The *translated* list will hold our output prior to writing it.

A typical assembler works in two steps, called *passes*. Each pass processes the input, which is why we capture it in a list. On the first pass, the program looks for symbols used in the program other than the opcodes and tries to give them numeric values. These values are always derived from the instructionCounter we discussed earlier, and which is used to assign instructions to addresses when loading. Something identical is used in the assembler to compute, on each pass, where each instruction will be put.

The assembler examines each instruction, one after the other. With the instruction counter initialized to zero it counts each instruction as it processes. Our sample program begins like this:

```
   zer 0
   lda data
   pop point
label loop
   push calc
   push stop
```

The instruction counter is 1 after processing the zer instruction, 2 after the lda, and 3 after the pop. So, when it encounters the label, it assigns 3 to the label named loop. The instruction counter is not incremented except for machine language instructions (which a label is not), so the label loop is actually the address of the push instruction. There is not much more to an assembler than this.

At the end of the first pass the program checks that all symbols used were actually put into the table. If a symbol appears in an operand position before it appears in a label, we need to assure that the label eventually shows up.

At the beginning of the second pass, the table should hold all symbols used in the program and the pass just uses this information to translate each label into numeric form. So all occurrences of *loop* in our program above will translate to 3 in the output.

Using traditional names for the passes, the main driver of the process, then is just this:

```
public void assemble() throws IOException{
    readProgram();
    pass1();
    pass2();
    writeResult();
}
```

The structure of such an application is often called a *pipeline*. Each of the four invocations advances the computation and hands off the results to the next piece. As was mentioned above, the read and write methods could use improvement, but here is what I used as this was developed:

```
private void readProgram() throws FileNotFoundException {
    Scanner scan = new Scanner(new File("prog.txt"));
    while(scan.hasNext()){
        String next = scan.next();
        program.add(next.trim());
    }
}
```

This puts each token into a single string, not each line. This means that we have two tokens for each line of the input. This is why we put the extra 0 arguments with instructions such as add. It isn't pretty, but it makes the following easier. The alternative is to give the assembler knowledge about how many operands each opcode has.

```
private void writeResult() throws IOException {
    if (! translateOK){
        return;
    }
    BufferedWriter writer = new BufferedWriter(
            new FileWriter("translated.txt"));
    for(String instruction: translated){
        writer.write(instruction);
        writer.newLine();
    }
    writer.close();
}
```

Given this, pass1 just fills the table, being careful to count instructions as it goes. It is looking for labels, so it ignores the numeric values, but everything in the input file is a string, so it needs to try to extract integers from the operands to see if they really are integers encoded in the strings. Our for loop counts by two to account for the fact that we have exactly two strings in the program list per line of the input. This pass also ignores the *double* directives. If we find a symbolic operand we will wind up in the catch block, since trying to extract an integer from it fails. We put the string into some kind of list We used a stack for this, but don't really need it to be a stack. any Iterable will do. These saved operands are then checked at the end, when the first loop completes, to make sure they have been put into the table. The instruction counter is used to assign a value to each label that it finds as we discussed above.

```
private void pass1() {
   Stack<String> toBeDefined = new Stack<String>();
   int instructionCounter = 0;
   for(int count = 0; count < program.size()-1; count+=2){
      String opcode = program.get(count);
      String operand = program.get(count + 1);
      if(opcode.equalsIgnoreCase("label")){
         table.put(operand, instructionCounter);
      }
      else {
         instructionCounter++;
         if(opcode.equalsIgnoreCase("double")){
            continue;
         }
         try{
            int value = Integer.parseInt(operand);
            // don't process numeric operands yet
         }
         catch(Exception e){
            toBeDefined.push(operand);
         }
      }
   }
   while(!toBeDefined.isEmpty()){
      String value = toBeDefined.pop();
      if(table.get(value) == null){
         System.out.println("Label: " + value + " not defined.");
         translateOK = false;
      }
   }
}
```

Now, if there have been no errors, we can do the actual translation on pass 2. It is possible to produce many different output formats, as mentioned above. You can modify pass2 in a variety of ways to do this. In pass2, we again need to keep track of the instruction counter, for now it also determines where things are actually loaded. We have to process opcode lines and double directive lines differently, of course.

This is a process that has quite a lot of structure. At the limits of understandability. It would benefit by extracting helper methods, perhaps.

```
private void pass2() {
      if (! translateOK){
         return;
      }
      int instructionCounter = 0;
      for(int count = 0; count < program.size(); count+=2){
         String opcode = program.get(count);
         String operand = program.get(count + 1);
         if(opcode.equalsIgnoreCase("label")){
            continue;
         }
         else{
            if(opcode.equalsIgnoreCase("double")){
               translated.add("     computer.loadData(" +
                     operand + ", " +
                     instructionCounter + ");");
            }
            else{
               int value = 0;
               try{
                  value = Integer.parseInt(operand);
                  // don't process numeric operands yet
               }
               catch(Exception e){
                  value = table.get(operand);
               }

               translated.add("     computer.loadInstruction(" +
                     opcode + ", " + value + ");");
            }
            instructionCounter ++;
         }
      } // end for
   }
```

To use this, you just create the Assembler object and send it an assemble message, though it reads from a file with a fixed name and, likewise, writes to a fixed file. But you can then copy the output into a program that will drive the operation of the Toy Computer.

7 Important Ideas From This Intermezzo

Stack
Machine Language
Assembly Language
double

8 Problem Set

1. Make the Stack class here Iterable<T>, and give it an Iterator<T> returned from the iterator() method. A stack iterator should probably work from the top of the stack toward the bottom.

2. Give the machine language a new instruction *jez* that will jump if the stack top is zero, while also popping the stack.

3. Give the machine multiply and divide instructions: *mul* and *div*.

4. Modify the output of the Assembler so that it puts a comment to the right of each output line showing at what address that instruction or data cell will be loaded.

5. Modify the output of the Assembler program so that it writes a complete and correct Java class with a main function that can be directly executed. The current output is the only variable part of this output.

6. Write a program in our little assembly language to do the following. A section of memory has a sequence of values, starting at a known location. The last number in the sequence is 0.0, but there are no other zero values. Start at the beginning of this sequence and sum all of the values. Stop when you get to the zero and print the result. You might also print out the count of values. You then could modify the program to print the average. Assemble the program and run it on the simulator. Are there additional, simple, instructions that would help you do this exercise?

13 Queues, Priority Queues, and Huffman Coding

In this chapter we will examine two additional storage structures as well as get additional practice working with Strings and doubles. We shall see another application as well, one that tries to make data transmission as efficient as possible by carefully coding the information sent.

13.1 Queues and Priority Queues

In spite of the similarity of names, these are two quite different things. Normally the term Queue refers to a First-in, First-out (FIFO) data structure in which the next item to remove is the one that has been stored the longest, but not yet removed. It is like a waiting line that one enters at the back (tail) and exits at the front (head). Queues are used in event simulation, such as a program that simulates the effect of customers arriving at a bank and waiting in line for service. The usual purpose of such a simulation is to determine average waiting times, for example. In the Java libraries, Queue is an interface, extended by Deque, short for Double Ended Queue. In a Deque (pronounced deck, as in deck of cards) an element can enter at either the front or rear and exit at either end as well. A deque that utilizes only one "end" behaves like a stack, in fact. And a deque is also like a deck of cards in that a card can easily be inserted at either the top or bottom and likewise removed from either end.

None of our sample implementations in the Appendix is suitable for the implementation of a Deque, but a LinkedList from java.util is a good example, that has efficient operations in all cases. Generally speaking a doubly linked list is a good candidate for implementing either a queue or a deque. It is possible to use array-like structures for these, especially when they only require a bounded number of elements, though the implementations are a bit tricky.

The key operations on a queue are *add* (adds an element at the tail), *remove* (removes and returns an item from the head) and *peek* (retrieves, but does not remove the item at the head). It is an error to try to remove from an empty queue (NoSuchElementException), but peek will just return null. Another important operation is *poll*, which is like remove, except that it just returns null for an empty queue. A deque has additional operations for inserting at the head, removing from the tail and peeking at the tail, along with a few others. Since a java.util.LinkedList implements both these interfaces, it has all of these operations.

A *priority queue* on the other hand, is not FIFO. The typical use of a priority queue is a situation in which a process has work to do but additional work comes in while the process works on the current item. When the process is ready for more work it goes to he queue to get the next item. However, in this case, it is better if the process work on high priority items, not just old items. It *polls* the queue to get the desired, highest priority, item.

You can think of the insert point in a priority queue as the tail. However when you *poll* a priority queue the item you get is the one with smallest *priority*. This item is thought of as the head, but it need not have been in the queue the longest amount of time. The priorities are associated with the elements themselves and don't change while the item is in the queue. In the Java implementation, the priorities are in fact determined by either the natural ordering of the elements (using *compareTo*), which requires that the elements be Comparable, or by using a supplied Comparator object. The PriorityQueue class in Java implements the

Queue interface, though it doesn't imply FIFO. In fact, you need to be a bit careful with the word *queue*, as it is used in a variety of ways.

When implemented as a doubly linked list all of the major operations on a queue or deque take constant time. You simply need to add or remove a node. Priority queues, on the other hand are quite different and their operations are normally logarithmic in terms of the number of items stored. This is due to the fact that a priority queue is stored as a height balanced binary tree (which may well be stored in an array in a certain way). The highest priority item (the smallest value) is always at the root of the tree, and when you insert or delete an element the tree is re-balanced and the new high priority item is brought to the root.

The usual implementation is called a Priority Heap which is a binary tree stored in an array. If you store root of a binary tree in cell 1 (not 0) of an array or dense list and store the children of the node stored in cell k in cells 2*k and 2*k +1, then it is easy to find both children and the parent from any given array cell, just knowing the index. It is also possible to do this with no empty cells in the array. We leave it to you to investigate this.

13.2 Huffman Coding – The Problem

Suppose you want to send textual information across a communication *channel*, such as downloading a message to a cell phone. Your channel may have lots of *bandwidth* (capacity), but never enough. So you would like to encode the information efficiently. The time it takes to transfer a message depends on the number of bits it contains, with each character of information normally requiring 8 or 16 bits, if normal encoding is used. In Java, the encoding of a character uses UNICODE, requiring 16 bits, though many systems still use something like ASCII, requiring only 8 bits, but less suitable for use in international commerce with many languages and therefore many alphabets. An 8 bit code only has room for $2^8 = 256$ different encodings. This is enough for English, but not for English and Swedish, Norwegian, Japanese, Urdu, etc. Therefore UNICODE is becoming more popular, though it has to make some compromises in the case of Chinese.

The problem we want to address, however, is that these codes all use a fixed number of bits for each character, but the relative frequencies of the various characters is not uniform. There are a lot more 'a' characters sent across the net than '%' characters. A key insight is that a code that uses fewer bits for frequently used symbols and longer codes for uncommon ones should be a win overall. The problem is knowing where such a character begins and ends within a stream of bits. The key trick for that is devising a code in which the coding of no character is the prefix of the coding of any other character. Thus, once you have discovered a valid code by reading a few bits, you can assume that you have what you want and go on from there for the next code.

To make it a bit more concrete, let's take an example. Here is the first paragraph of *The Adventures of Huckleberry Finn* by Mark Twain. Aside from being an interesting story, the book is noteworthy for its treatment of a variety of American English dialects of the early 19th century.

> YOU don't know about me without you have read a book by the name of The Adventures of Tom Sawyer; but that ain't no matter. That book was made by Mr. Mark Twain, and he told the truth, mainly. There was things which he stretched, but mainly he told the truth. That is nothing. I never seen anybody but lied one time or another, without it was Aunt Polly, or the widow, or maybe Mary. Aunt Polly--Tom's Aunt Polly, she is--and Mary, and the Widow Douglas is all told about in that book, which is mostly a true book, with some stretchers, as I said before.

This short paragraph contains 559 characters. but they are not evenly distributed. Here is what we mean

char	freq
;	1
D	1
O	1
S	1
U	1
W	1
Y	1
I	2
'	3
f	3
g	3
P	3
v	3
-	4
A	4
c	4
M	4
k	6
.	7
T	7
,	11
m	12
b	14
w	14
y	15
d	16
l	16
u	16
s	20
r	21
i	22
n	24
h	30
a	34
e	38
o	39
t	47
space	110

So the space character alone accounts for nearly 20% of the text. A code that used a few bits for space, t, o, etc but more for semicolon, D, O, and the like might be advantageous. The method we will show can encode the 559 characters in 2451 bits, or about 4.4 bits per character, rather than the 8 of ASCII.

Here is the beginning of that 2451 bits of encoding:

```
1111110100111111001011111100000011111101
```

And it goes on for quite a while. It looks like gibberish, but the code itself, looks like this:

```
char code
space : 00
' : 11011101
, : 110110
- : 1001100
. : 011010
; : 1111110111
A : 0110111
D : 1111110101
I : 10011100
M : 1001101
O : 1111110010
P : 10011111
S : 1111110011
T : 1111111
U : 111111000
W : 1111110110
Y : 1111110100
a : 1000
b : 01001
c : 0110110
d : 01111
e : 1010
f : 10011101
g : 11011100
h : 0101
i : 11010
k : 1101111
l : 10010
m : 111110
n : 11110
o : 1011
```

```
r : 11001        v : 10011110
s : 11000        w : 01000
t : 1110         y : 01100
u : 01110
```

And the encoding begins with: 1111110100 1111110010 111111000, which is YOU, using letters that were very infrequent and so with codes 10 bits long. The next two "bits" are 00, a space. And notice that 00 does not begin any other code. This is why it works. No character code is the prefix of any other.

We want to be able to create such a code and use it to encode and later decode texts. The process is named Huffman coding, named for its inventor. One interesting feature of a Huffman code is that it is created tailored precisely to the text that will be sent. That is interesting, and achieves very good compression of the encoding, but leaves you with the problem that the receiver of the encoded text has to also have the key that encoded it in order to decode it and in the example we are using of encoding for data transmission it means that the code has to be sent along as well, lowering the benefit.

Edgar Allen Poe wrote a story, *The Gold-Bug*, in which he discusses some similar things in a different context. Poe was interested in what was then known as Secret Writing, now known as encryption. Poe's discussion in The Gold-Bug is also based on relative frequencies of letters in text. If we devise a Huffman code for typical English (German, French, ...) text, rather than for a particular example of text, then the same encoder can be shared once and several different texts can be exchanged and decoded with some benefit. By the way, Poe's story is fun and interesting, but he got the relative frequencies for English wrong.

13.3 Huffman Coding – The Data Structures

We will require quite a few different ways of storing data for the creation of a Huffman coder. The main coding mechanism itself is a binary tree. The leaves of this tree are also referenced from a Map. The tree has, in each node, a reference pointer to each child, but also a reference to the parent node (except at the root, of course). The way that a character is encoded is to work up the tree from leaf to root. The "turnings" at the nodes give us the bits of an encoding. For example, the t is encoded in a leaf that requires three right turns and one left turn to reach the root. A right turn moving upward means that the path is upward from the right child. The hash map referencing the leaves lets us easily find the beginning of a path for an encoding.

This tree will be purpose built. There is no way to use a general purpose data structure for something like this. The operations are too specialized. It also will not be well encapsulated. Just the fact that we have references from outside the tree to the leaves makes this fairly obvious. The implication of this is that the programming we will do will be more error prone because we can't depend on abstraction and encapsulation to guide us. We have to "get it right" all the time. The tree has two interesting aspects. One is that we can both encode and decode using the same tree. Encoding works up the tree from the leaves and decoding down from the root. The other interesting aspect is that this tree will have "no missing nodes". A node is either a leaf or it has exactly two child nodes. The process we use to create it should make that obvious. A property of such trees is that they always have exactly one more leaf nodes than they do internal nodes. You can easily prove this by mathematical induction on the number of nodes in such a tree. Figure 13.1 shows a part of this resulting tree.

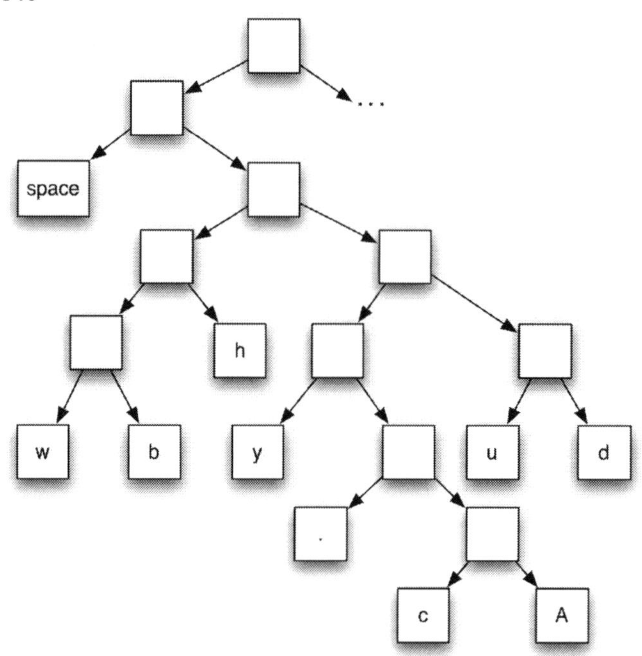

Figure 13.1. Part of the Huffman Tree

In order to create this tree, we need two additional structures. One will be a PriorityQueue and the other will be an ordinary Queue. There are various replacements we could use for the PriorityQueue, but this one works for the purpose and you might enjoy thinking about what we could do to replace it. Recall that a queue has constant time operations. It is implemented as a LinkedList, of course. The priority queue on the other hand has logarithmic time insertions and removals. This is not bad, but slower than constant time, generally.

The queue and the priority queue will hold nodes from our tree structure, and since the tree itself isn't encapsulated, having a reference to any node means you have a reference to the "tree" that is rooted at that node. So, conceptually, the queue and priority queue contain trees. We also want to sort these trees (actually we sort the leaves) using the probability that the character represented by the node will occur in the text. Since our nodes don't have a natural ordering, we will us a Comparator when we create the priority queue so that it knows which node is "smaller."

We will also do a fair amount of processing of Strings, but only one character at a time. Our inputs and outputs will all be represented as strings, though it would make more sense for the output (the encoded bit pattern of 0's and 1's) to be stored in a BitSet. For illustrative purposes, a String will serve. Strings are immutable, and there is one place in which we need to make modifications to a string passed as an argument, so we will use the mutable equivalent *StringBuffer* instead.

Finally, node probabilities are numbers between 0 and 1 so we will represent them using double values. The probability is just the frequency of a letter in the text divided by the length of the text. These probabilities will be the basis for choosing the length of the coding of each character. A character with a high likelihood of appearing will get a short code, Infrequent characters get long codes.

The coding tree will be built from the bottom up. We will start with the leaves. We will start processing the characters of lowest frequency and these will get more processing, meaning that the paths to them from the eventually created root node will be longer. This is how we achieve short codings for frequent items.

Suppose we put some things into a priority queue in arbitrary order, but all at once, and then retrieve them all. The results will be in sorted order from smallest to largest. If we enqueue n items and the time to enqueue or dequeue an item is proportional to lg(n) (the base two logarithm of n), then over all, the time is proportional to n*lg(n). This is about as good as you can do with a sorting algorithm. In fact we could have put the nodes in an ordinary list and sorted them to achieve the same effect as our use of the priority queue.

It would be good to consider something important here. The Huffman coding process, if considered all at once, is quite difficult. but almost all of the difficulty is in managing the data. By using data abstractions, such as queue and priority queue we isolate our problem solving from the low level details of precisely where in the structure the next insertion should be placed so that we may think at a higher level. The priority queue object will get it right and we can think about what to do with the values we extract rather than the details of the storage. This is a very big idea.

The data declarations of our coder class are these:

```
private DefaultHashMap<Character, Integer> characterFrequencies =
      new DefaultHashMap<Character, Integer>();
private Queue<Node> rightQueue = new LinkedList<Node>();
private Map<Character, Node> encodings =
      new TreeMap<Character, Node>();
private NodeComparator compare = new NodeComparator();
private PriorityQueue<Node> leftQueue =
      new PriorityQueue<Node>(30, compare);
private Node codeTree = null;
```

The two queues will be called the leftQueue and the rightQueue, imagining that you are sitting at a desk with physical data structures in front of you. The hash map will be used as we compute frequencies, and the TreeMap to keep the character codings in order. The NodeComparator tells us about larger and smaller probabilities of the characters, and the codeTree is the goal of this processing. We want to create this tree, represented simply by its root node, without encapsulation.

We have seen the DefaultHashMap previously (Chapter 11). We will see the other class definitions below.

13.4 Huffman Coding – The Process

The program we will build for this will also use a pipeline architecture. We will have a number of phases, run one after another to finally get the coding tree and associated structures. Then we will be able to encode the string whose frequencies defined that particular tree. We can encode other strings with the same tree as well, provided that they don't use additional characters than the original, but the savings in total bits won't be as large.

The class we will build will be called HuffmanCoder. The pipeline method, which is what you usually call, looks like this:

```
public String codeIt(String text){
   getFrequencies(text);
   makeLeaves(text.length());
   buildTrees();
   return mapIt(text);
}
```

The parameter is the string to be encoded and the return result is the encoding. First we read the original text and compute simple frequencies of the characters in it. A Map is good for this. Next we will make all of the leaf nodes in the tree we are about to create. There will be one leaf for each distinct character in the text. The one "space" node will represent all of the space characters in the text, etc. Our text has 38 different characters, but the process will discover that. Then we build the trees using the two queues and finally we use the tree in the *mapIt* process to do the actual translation.

Getting frequencies is quite easy. We hold them in a DefaultHashMap with the characters as keys and the current count of occurrence as the value.

```
public void getFrequencies(String text){
   for(int i = 0; i < text.length(); ++i){
      char character = text.charAt(i);
      int current = characterFrequencies.get(character, 0);
      characterFrequencies.put(character, current+1);
   }
}
```

We use a default hash map to make it easy to handle a character the first time we see it. It won't bě in the map yet, so a standard map would return null from the get method. Here we get back 0 instead. In any case we just increase the count and put it back with the same key. this process replaces the current entry in the map. When this completes, the map holds our frequencies. Next we want to create the leaves, one for each entry in the map.

The Nodes of the binary tree will hold a variety of things, but the leaf nodes represent individual (distinct) characters from the text and their probability of occurrence. The probability is just the frequency divided by the length of the text, but we need to be careful. We can't use an integer for this (or it would always be zero) so we need to force the division to be done with *floating point* data. Here we will use doubles, The node will hold the probability value and the character the node represents.

To create the leaves we can iterate over the keys of the map, extract the frequency, compute the probability, create the node, and put it into the left queue, which is a priority queue.

```
public void makeLeaves(int textLength){
   for(char character:characterFrequencies.keySet()){
      int frequency = characterFrequencies.get(character);
      Node node = new Node(frequency*1.0/textLength, character);
      leftQueue.add(node);
      encodings.put(character, node);
   }
}
```

Note that in the above we compute: `frequency*1.0/textLength`. The reason we multiply by 1.0 is to force the computer to use floating point arithmetic. If we just compute `frequency/textLength`, where both operands are integer types, the arithmetic will be integer and the fractional part will be lost. But in this case the result will always be zero, since the textLength is larger than the frequency. Multiplying the numerator by 1.0 (before the division is done) yields a floating equivalent of the frequency and the division will then be done retaining the fractional part. This is a common trick when you need both integer and floating point data in the same program.

We also have an additional map called *encodings* that we will later use to encode the characters. As was mentioned earlier, we encode a character of the text by moving upward from the leaf. This encodings map makes it easy for us to get the leaf knowing the character. Once we have the leaf we can move upward in the tree (Node) structure by following *parent* references.

The fact that the leaves are also in a priority queue using a comparator that gives the smallest probability the highest priority is also important. We want to process the leaves from least to most likely, which will have the effect of giving the unlikely characters longer codings. Alternatively we could sort the leaves, but the priority queue works just as well for this, with about the same amount of time required. You can experiment with this of course. An ArrayList in Java can be easily sorted, using methods you write yourself, or using methods of the Collections class in java.util.

The NodeComparator class itself is quite easy, as Comparators only need one method: compare.

```
private class NodeComparator implements Comparator<Node>{

   public int compare(Node o1, Node o2) {
      return Double.compare(o1.value(), o2.value());
   }

}
```

Even easier, as the Double class has a compare method we can use to build this. Recall that this will return a negative value if the first operand is considered smaller and a positive value if larger, with zero being returned if the values have the same "size". For Doubles, same size means same value, of course, but it need not.

Finally we reach the real deal: creating the tree itself.

We start with all the leaves in the left queue, effectively sorted using this comparator. High priority for a priority queue means small value, which exactly matches our problem. The right queue is empty, but we will put things in to it. In fact, we will put things in to it in order of increasing size. In fact, we want the contents of both queues sorted, but for the one on the right it will be automatic. So, as we go along, there will be entries on both queues and if we *peek* at either queue we will see the smallest value in that queue. The right queue, unlike the left, will have nodes in it but they won't be leaf nodes.

The process itself is quite simple. Of all the nodes we have created (leaves or not) we select the two with the smallest probability value. From these we create a new node (non-leaf) with these two as children, but with a value equal to the sum of the probabilities of the two children. We put the result into the right queue. If you think about this for a moment it should be clear that larger values are going in to this queue than what it holds already, since we work from smallest value up. The process ends when there is only one node left. It will be in the right queue, of course, and we set this to be the value of the codeTree field.

```
public void buildTrees(){
   while (leftQueue.size() + rightQueue.size() > 1){
      Node small = getNode();
      Node next = getNode(); // two smallest values
      Node newNode = new Node(small.value() + next.value(),
            small, next);
      rightQueue.add(newNode);
   }
   codeTree = rightQueue.poll();
}
```

We used a different node constructor here, of course, since we are creating a non-leaf, but we also depend on a private method getNode that retrieves the smallest value from either of the queues:

```
private Node getNode(){ // pre at least two elements
   if(leftQueue.isEmpty()){
      return rightQueue.poll();
   }
   else if(rightQueue.isEmpty()){
      return leftQueue.poll();
   }
   else if (compare.compare(leftQueue.peek(),rightQueue.peek()) < 0){
      return leftQueue.poll();
   }
   else {
      return rightQueue.poll();
   }
}
```

Strange, perhaps, that this is the longest method we have seen so far. While we are doing something quite profound, the methods that achieve it are extremely simple. But this one has several cases to consider, hence its structure. Note that we use the comparator explicitly here. It is also used within the leftQueue object to keep the priorities straight. Recall that *peek* retrieves a value, but doesn't remove it, whereas *poll* both retrieves and removes the head of a queue (including a priority queue).

The tree has a leaf for each character, so 38 leaves and 37 internal nodes. The codes we saw in Section 13.2 actually tell us where these leaves appear in the tree. The space node, with code 00 appears down two nodes to the left from the root: the leftmost grandchild of the root. To find the "Y" node, different from the 'y' node, with code 1111110100, you need to descent 6 levels moving to the right, then one to the left, right again for one and finally two more to the left. This is what makes the code work: purely the structure of the tree and nothing else.

But moving down the tree is useful for finding a character knowing it's code, We first want to go in the other direction to discover the code for a character. So here is the final step in our pipe line. It uses a helper that does all the work. We left the helper public in this case, since it is useful for finding codes of individual characters.

```
   public String mapIt(String text){
      String result = "";
      for(int i = 0; i < text.length(); ++i){
         result += codeFor(text.charAt(i));
      }
      return result;
   }

   public String codeFor(char ch){
      String result = "";
      Node node = encodings.get(ch);
      if(node != null){
         result = node.code();
         while(node.parent() != null){
            node = node.parent();
            result = node.code() + result;
         }
      }
      return result;
   }
```

Because of the way we created the tree and filled the encodings map, we should never see null for the node. That would imply we see a character in the text that doesn't have a node. This might occur only if you try to use a Huffman tree to encode a text other than the one it was created from and it has additional characters not in the original.

So codeFor just walks up the tree, from leaf to root, extracting one bit for each step. The code extracted from each node will be just a zero or a one and we just catenate them together. Since we work up the tree, we attach the new code "bit" to the left, rather than the right of the result. The code stored in the root is the empty string, by the way.

But wait, there is magic here. What is this *code* method? We haven't seen anything like that yet! And the *parent*. We talked about that, but haven't seen it yet.

Ok, all of that his handled internally by the tree nodes themselves. Each node in the tree (except the root) knows whether it is the left or right child of its parent. Left children have a 0 for the code and right children have a 1. Note that in general, nothing in Java does this automatically and you have to set up structures so that a Node can know is location.

The complete Node class is below. We won't discuss much of it, as it is mostly just accessors for fields, but note that we have as few mutators as we can and still carry out the process in buildTrees.

The first constructor creates only leaves. The other only non-leaves. Note that we didn't use a polymorphic solution here, instead using data to distinguish the kinds of nodes. A polymorphic solution would have Node as an interface with leaf and non-leaf classes as implementations.

When a non-leaf node is created, two child nodes are attached to it. If they aren't null, then their codes are set depending on whether they are put to the left or right. It happens that it isn't important to the algorithm which of the two nodes goes to the left and which to the right, as long as we can remember which is which. Each such node is also given a parent when it is attached.

```
class Node{

   private double value = 0.0;
   private char symbol = '\0';
   private Node left = null;
   private Node right = null;
   private Node parent = null;
   private String code = "";
   private boolean isLeaf = true;

   public Node(double value, char symbol){ // leaf nodes
      this.value = value;
      this.symbol = symbol;
   }

   public Node(double value, Node left, Node right){
      this.value = value;
      this.left = left;
      if(left != null){
         left.code = "0";
         left.parent = this;
      }
      this.right = right;
      if(right != null){
         right.code = "1";
         right.parent = this;
      }
      this.isLeaf = false;
   }

   public String code(){
      return code;
   }

   public void setLeft(Node node){
      left = node;
      node.parent = this;
      node.code = "0";
   }

   public void setRight(Node node){
      right = node;
      node.parent = this;
      node.code = "1";
   }

   public boolean isLeaf(){
      return isLeaf;
   }
```

```
public Node parent(){
        return parent;
    }

    public void setParent(Node parent){
        this.parent = parent;
    }

    public double value(){
        return value;
    }

    public char symbol(){
        return symbol;
    }

    public Node left(){
        return left;
    }

    public Node right(){
        return right;
    }
}
```

Note that the character '\0' is called the null character, not to be confused with the null value. It is the UNICODE symbol whose bit pattern is all zeroes. We use it as a filler here until a real value is supplied, but note that only leaf nodes have a symbol. The internal nodes are aggregate nodes over the probabilities of the children, rather than themselves representing any character.

It is important to be aware of what private means in Java. In the constructor for a node, we are modifying private fields of other Node objects. There are no setters (mutators) for the nodes. We just assign to the field of the other object. The privacy boundary, hence the encapsulation boundary, in Java is the class, not the object. Visibility markers like private are there to permit a programmer to enforce invariants on a class. The invariants are maintained by making it more difficult for programmers (including the one who writes this) to break them. The one that writes the Node class, however, is expected to *do the right thing*. So the system doesn't protect you from yourself in all cases.

13.5 Decoding the Result

All we have seen so far is the means of creating a coding from an original text. Presumably this code can be sent or stored somewhere, but eventually someone will want to see the original. So we need to decode the encoding to get back the original exactly. Our encoding, by the way, is called *lossless*. It loses no information at all in encoding in fewer bits. This is unlike something like mp3 music files or jpeg photo encodings, both of which are *lossy* compressions. You can't extract the original exactly from either of these formats. But a Huffman encoding loses none of the information in the original text.

We decode a Huffman encoding using the same tree that encoded it, just walking the tree from top down, rather than bottom up. The input is the 0-1 encoded version and the output should be the original. We look at each bit in the input, a 0 or a 1. Starting at the root of the tree a 0 tells us to move down to the left child, and 1 to the right. We keep this up until we reach a leaf and then we output that (attach it to the result) and start over at the root of the tree, looking at the next bit of input. Note that the input *bit stream* isn't divided up in to characters, It is just a continuous stream of 0's and 1's. It is the prefix property of the encoding that keeps us out of trouble in this. When we reach a leaf we have a character and it is the only one possible for that pattern of bits. No other character has a coding that begins with the 0-1 pattern we just followed to get to that leaf.

```
public String decodeIt(String coded){
    String result = "";
    Node node = codeTree;
    int i = 0;
    while( i < coded.length()){
        while(! node.isLeaf()){
            if(coded.charAt(i) == '0'){
                node = node.left();
            }
            else{ // must be 1
                node = node.right();
            }
            i++;
        }
        result += node.symbol();
        node = codeTree;
    }

    return result;
}
```

We must note here for completeness, that we have encoded our 0-1 "bit stream," not as actual bits, but as characters. As such we haven't really saved anything since, in Java, a 0 takes 16 bits to store. However, Instead of using String as our output type, we could, with minor modifications (and some change in the methods we have needed to employ from the libraries) used BitSet instead and then we would see the savings.

13.6 Encoding the Translation Tree – More Recursion

There is a bit of a flaw in our scenario above. We talk about sending the encoded bit-stream across the net for to save time of transmission by sending fewer bits. But we also made clear that you need the same tree to decode the text that you used to encode it. So somehow, the tree needs to get to the receiver as well. There are a variety of ways to handle this, and we will see an additional application of recursion here. Indeed recursion is often used to process linked structures such as linked lists and trees. In processing of binary (especially) trees, there are four orderings that we can think of for the nodes. They are called pre-order, post-order, in-order, and level-order. The first three are similar to each other and often useful in following a tree. The last, level-order is important in priority queues as it is the means of taking a binary linked tree and mapping it to an array in an especially efficient way.

In each of the first three orderings of a tree, we will walk through the structure following the parent and child relationships (which may be represented by links). We shall pass by each node more than once, perhaps, but one of these is distinguished, and called the *visit*. Any action we perform at the node occurs during the visit.

With that concept is mind, we *traverse* a binary tree in pre-order, by visiting a node and then traversing the tree rooted at its left child (also in pre-order) and then traversing the tree rooted at the right child.

To make it more explicit, consider the following tree.

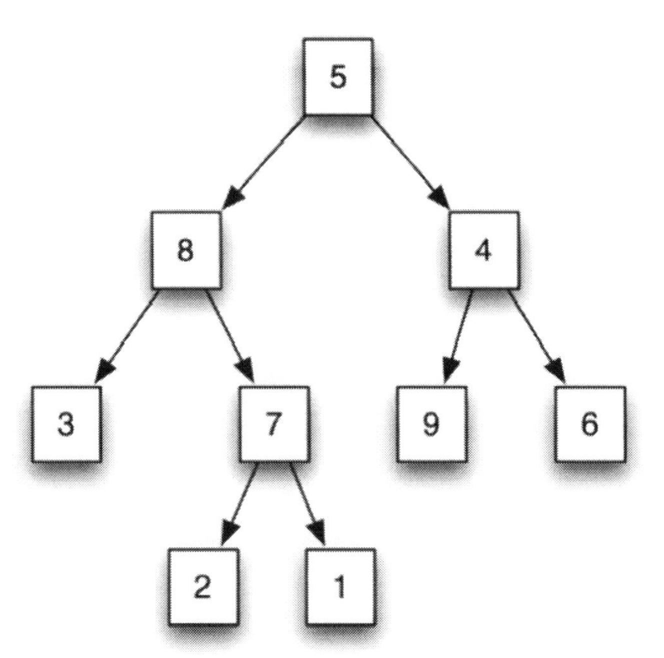

Figure 13.2. A Simple Binary Tree

To walk this in pre-order we start at the root and visit it. Here that means we just report the node. So 5 is our first node. Then we traverse the left tree rooted at 5 so we next visit 8. But then, since we are doing this recursively, after we visit the root of that tree we traverse its left tree, so visit 3. We are now done with the left child of 8 so we visit 7 and then 2 and, after the 2, the 1 node since it is the right child of the 7. But now we have completed the right child of the 8 node as well and thus the left child of the 5 so we can begin on the right child. We next visit 4 then 9 and finally 6: So, in all: 5, 8, 3, 7, 2, 1, 4, 9, 6. Make sure you can follow this.

Post-order, on the other hand, visits a node after traversing both the left and right trees. So in post order, we start with the left tree and get to the 8, but don't visit it yet, since we haven't yet traversed the sub-trees. We then get to 3, which has no children so we visit it. We now begin on the right child of 8 and visit these nodes in order 2 then 1 and finally 7. Now, having traversed both sub-trees of the 8 we can finally visit the 8 and then start on the right sub tree of the 5 without yet visiting it. We let you fill in the rest, but the result is 3, 2, 1, 7, 8, 9, 6, 4, 5. Is it clear why pre-order is sometimes called top-down, and post-order called bottom-up? Think about it and become familiar with the terminology.

In-order traversals visit a node between traversing its left and right child trees. So in particular the 8 will be visited between (though not immediately between) the 3 and 7 nodes. The order here is 3, 8, 2, 7, 1, 5, 9, 4, 6.

All of these are important for various reasons. In a binary search tree, such as a Java TreeSet, inorder gives the nodes in order of value. It sorts the values.

Finally level order reports the nodes by height, and moving left to right within a level. It doesn't follow the links at all. Here the root is reported, then its children (left to right) then their children, etc. 5, 8, 4, 3, 7, 9, 6, 2, 1.

What we want to do here with our code tree is create a version of it that can be sent across a transmission line and then re-constituted at the other end. The tree will be encoded as a character stream (a String) that "knows" the structure of the tree. What we will do is a recursive pre-order traversal of the code tree, outputting information about each node we visit and the path we take. It is actually a common processing method. In fact, compilers that translate languages like Java into a lower level form use something like this.

Not to lose focus, here, now we are going to encode the tree itself that was used to encode the text. It uses a completely different process.

Here *visiting* a node will simply be represented by a recursive invocation in which the node is an input parameter. As part of this, and the basis of the recursion, the same method will be invoked on both the left and right children. We show two versions of this. The first, though longer may be easier to decipher. The method is called encodeTree and it invokes itself twice. This is a method of the HuffmanCoder class.

```
public String encodeTree(Node node, String soFar){
    String tempLeft = "";
    String tempRight = "";
    if(node.isLeaf()){
        soFar += "L"+node.symbol();
    }
    else {
        if(node.left() != null){
            tempLeft = "0" + encodeTree(node.left(), soFar);
        }
        else{
            tempLeft = "x"; // should never appear
        }
        if(node.right() != null){
            tempRight = "1" + encodeTree(node.right(), soFar);
        }
        else{
            tempRight = "x"; // should never appear
        }     }
    return soFar + tempLeft + tempRight;
}
```

The original invocation of this, assuming our HuffmanCoder object is *this*, is

```
this.encodeTree(codeTree, "");
```

So, the first node we visit is the root of the codeTree, and the soFar parameter is the empty string. It is intended to be the tree encoding we have created "so far." Perhaps it is easiest to understand this if we look at the last line first. What we will do in between is create an encoding of the left child of the current node and save it in tempLeft and an encoding of the right child and then just paste them to the end of what we have done so far. For a leaf node, the encoding is just the letter "L" followed by the character in the Node itself. Recall that these were the characters from the original text that form the leaf nodes of our code tree. For a non-leaf node we recursively process the left and right sub trees, with, for example `encodeTree(node.left(), soFar)`, but we also mark the left tree with a "0" and the right tree with a "1", just as we marked the nodes themselves this way to enable decoding of our coded text. The output of this for our example tree is this:

```
00L 1000Lw1Lb1Lh100Ly10L.10Lc1LA10Lu1Ld1000La10Ll100L-
1LM100LI1Lf10Lv1LP10Le1Lo1000Ls1Lr10Li10L,100Lg1L'1Lk
10Lt10Ln10Lm1000LU10LO1LS100LY1LD10LW1L;1LT
```

It isn't so easy to understand, but it really is an encoding of the tree. Notice for example, the 00 before the "space" leaf.

Because the encoding tree actually has no missing nodes, we should never wind up in either of the else clauses in the above, and never see an "x" in the encoding. It indicates an error somewhere. Because of that, the following is equivalent to the above. It is more compact, but probably less understandable.

```
public String encodeTree (Node node, String soFar){
   if(node.isLeaf()){
      return soFar + "L"+node.symbol();
   }

   return soFar + "0" + encodeTree(node.left(), soFar)
                + "1" + encodeTree(node.right(), soFar);
}
```

Here is a third, non-equivalent version, that will let you see where the sub trees begin and end in the encoding. This latter form could also be decoded, but we shall use the above.

```
public String encodeTree (Node node, String soFar){
   if(node.isLeaf()){
      return soFar + "L"+node.symbol();
   }

   return soFar + "0(" + encodeTree (node.left(), soFar)
                + ")1(" + encodeTree (node.right(), soFar) + ")";
}
```

Here we just wrap parentheses around the result of each recursive call. The output then shows more clearly where the sub-trees begin and end. Each is within parentheses. The presentation here shows the break of the root node. The first two lines, beginning with 0 holds the entire left sub-tree. the first parenthesis matches the last on the second line. There is a space following the first L character, of course. The third line begins the right sub-tree (hence the 1), but it is much larger. The first parenthesis on that line matches the last in the entire string. While this may be slightly easier for you, the computer can process the shorter version above, and it is the one we will use.

```
0(0(L
)1(0(0(0(Lw)1(Lb))1(Lh))1(0(0(Ly)1(0(L.)1(0(Lc)1(LA))))1(0(Lu)1(Ld)))))
1(0(0(0(La)1(0(Ll)1(0(0(L-
)1(LM))1(0(0(LI)1(Lf))1(0(Lv)1(LP))))))1(0(Le)1(Lo)))1(0(0(0(Ls)1(Lr))1(0
(Li)1(0(L,)1(0(0(Lg)1(L'))1(Lk)))))1(0(Lt)1(0(Ln)1(0(Lm)1(0(0(0(LU)1(0(LO
)1(LS)))1(0(0(LY)1(LD))1(0(LW)1(L;)))))1(LT)))))))
```

Now, suppose that we have created the code tree and used it to encode the text and then used the above process to encode the tree itself. Then we send both across our transmission line and, at the other end, we want to be able to reconstruct the tree and then recover the original text.

This will also use a recursive process, but it will be recursive on the coded tree string. We want to start with the entire string and *consume* it, a character at a time (or two characters in case of a leaf node), re-creating left and right sub trees as we see 0's and 1's respectively. This will also be a top down tree traversal, except that we will be creating the tree as we go, not just walking an existing tree.

We have considered the possibility of error in the following, so it is a bit longer than it should be, but the errors indicate bugs in the program, though they could also indicate that the tree coding wasn't received accurately.

The code will use a new data structure: a *StringBuffer*. Unlike a String, a StringBuffer is mutable. You can modify it. In general this isn't as good an idea as it might sound like because it is fundamentally error prone. For almost all processing, working with immutable objects is a big win. Here, however we want to start with the entire string and gobble up characters of it from the beginning, creating nodes as we go, but passing the remainder to recursive calls, rather than the whole. We could, of course, create new strings for each recursive call, but that creates a lot of objects that will be almost immediately discarded. The delete(0, 1) invocation removes the first element of a StringBuffer. In general delete(k, m) starts removing at k, but ends just before m. And m-k is the number of elements removed. This inclusion of the first index, but not the last is a fairly common practice, so watch out for it.

Previously we created the HuffmanCoder class. Here we see the companion HuffmanDecoder. It contains the decoder method we saw previously, to re-create the text, but two methods to re-create the tree.

The first method is just an organizer for the main work. It begins by creating a new non-leaf node, that has null child nodes to be filled in as we go, and passes this and the encoded tree to the recodeTree method which does the work recursively.

```
public class HuffmanDecoder {

private Node codeTree;

public void createCodeTree(String codedTree){
   this.codeTree = recodeTree(
         new Node(0.0, null, null),
         new StringBuffer(codedTree));
}

private Node recodeTree(Node node, StringBuffer codedTree){
   if(! codedTree.equals("")){
      char ch = codedTree.charAt(0);
      if(ch == 'L'){
         char symbol = codedTree.charAt(1);

         codedTree.delete(0, 2);
         return new Node(0.0, symbol);
      }
      if(ch == '0'){
```

```
            codedTree.delete(0, 1);
            Node another = new Node(0.0, null, null);
            node.setLeft(recodeTree(another, codedTree));
         }
         else{ // x)
            System.out.println("error l");
         }
         ch = codedTree.charAt(0);
         if(ch == 'L'){
            char symbol = codedTree.charAt(1);

            codedTree.delete(0, 2);
            return new Node(0.0, symbol);
         }
         if (ch == '1'){
            codedTree.delete(0, 1);
            Node another = new Node(0.0, null, null);
            node.setRight(recodeTree(another, codedTree));
         }
         else{ // x
            System.out.println("error r");
         }
      }
      return node;
   }

   public String decodeIt(String coded){ // as before
      String result = "";
      Node node = codeTree;
      int i = 0;
      while( i < coded.length()){
         while(! node.isLeaf()){
            if(coded.charAt(i) == '0'){
               node = node.left();
            }
            else{
               node = node.right();
            }
            i++;
         }
         result += node.symbol();

         System.out.print(node.symbol());
         node = codeTree;
      }

      return result;
   }
}
```

When *recodeTree* is invoked sending a node, it will either send back the original node with child nodes attached to it, or it will return a leaf node instead, Don't forget this important fact. When it is invoked the original tree encoding may have been partially consumed already, of course, in previous invocations. If in the current state we see an "L" character at the beginning of what remains of the encoding we get the next character and create a leaf node with it as symbol, and return it. But we also must consume the two characters that we processed. This is key to understanding how it proceeds. We advance the computation by consuming the input. If we forget to do this, our program will fail. We give 0.0 as the probability here, since we no longer need it. That was only used to create the tree from the original frequencies of the text, but we are beyond that now.

If we don't see an "L" at the beginning then it is either a 0 or a 1. In fact a 0 will be followed by a tree encoding followed by a 1 followed by another. At any point, that "tree" could be a leaf or not, and if not, another 0, etc.

So, if we see a "0" then we create another empty, but non-leaf, node and recurse, getting back either a completed tree (completed by further recursions) or a leaf. Since we saw a 0, we attach the result as the left child of the current node. This recursion, of course, consumes more of the StringBuffer, so it is no longer the same as what we sent. Well, actually, it IS the same object, but we have changed its state. It has fewer characters in it now. It is this that we pass on. In fact, it should have consumed one sub-tree worth of characters. If we were using the parenthesized version of the coding, it would process everything up to the matching parenthesis.

After processing the left child (starting with the 0) we expect a right child as well, since the tree has no missing nodes. But this child might itself be a leaf, so we have to repeat that logic.

When the process completes we have in the decoder program a codeTree that is identical in structure to the one that was used in the coder program. Therefore we can now take the coded text and re-create the original. Whew.

13.7 Important Ideas From This Chapter

queue
priority queue
Huffman tree
coding
decoding
recursive tree processing
in-order
pre-order
post-order
level-order

13.8 Problem Set

1. We built the Huffman tree using frequencies derived from a specific text. Modify the program by making it possible to use a set of predetermined frequencies instead.

2. Instead of walking the tree for each occurrence of a character while encoding a text, do this instead. Provide a hash map of with character keys and the encodings as values. Then just look up the code while

encoding. Given what you know about trees and maps, which of these would be faster. Suppose you take into account the fact that you also need to create the map.

3. Provide a polymorphic solution for Nodes, distinguishing Leaf and NonLeaf Nodes. Why are the Leaf Nodes not an instance of the Null Object Pattern?

4-7 Completely distinct from providing a means of encoding, the Huffman tree provides a bit of raw material on which to practice recursive programming. The next few exercises explore this.

4. Write a recursive pre-order tree walk that will count the number of nodes in the Huffman tree (or any binary) tree. The prototype for this method follows. It is invoked by sending the root node and zero for the count so far.

```
public int nodeCount(Node root, int count);
```

Try it again for a post-order walk. Do you need the count paramenter? Note that post-order tree walks are good for passing information up the tree from below.

5. Verify that the number of leaf nodes in the Huffman tree we created is one more than the number of internal nodes. Do this by actually counting them with recursive tree walks.

6. Verify, using mathematical induction, that the number of leaf nodes is one more than the number of internal nodes in any binary tree with the property that all nodes have either exactly two children or none.

7. Write a recursive tree walk that will print out the leaf nodes values of the Huffman tree. Note that this walk can use any of the tree walking protocols: pre-order, in-order, or post-order. You might try them all for practice.

8. Suppose that we want to encode a character using the Huffman tree, but, for some reason, have lost the encodings map. Start from the root of the tree, use a tree walk to search for your character, and return the encoding if you find it.

Chapter 14 Project and Case Study – MiniKarel

This chapter presents a course-long project that can be carried out as you study the various chapters here. We will describe a robot world, similar to the Karel World. It won't be exactly the same, however. Some things will closely track the simulator you have been using and other things will differ greatly.

The project will start with a skeleton application that has some features already implemented. Your work will be to read and understand what is here, and then to extend it. Unlike the earlier chapters in which the exercises appear at the end, here they will appear in-line as it becomes feasible to do them. We will also arrange this according to the dependencies on earlier chapters. We will also ask you to do some investigations outside this book, using the Sun-supplied JavaDocs for the Java system. Some of the exercises here will depend on your having done earlier ones, as well.

This is how much real-world programming goes, by the way. You don't start with nothing, but with an application that may have been in use for a while and needs updating and extension. You might someday find yourself on a project that is new to you, but which has been in development for weeks or months.

14.1 Overview

In this section we will see the basic skeleton of the robots and the world. Everything will be put into a package: com.jbergin.robot. All of your code should be in a package. This makes it possible to import from one project to another.

We need a way to represent robot directions. We will use an enum, which was introduced in Java 1.5.

```
package com.jbergin.robot;

/** Robot Directions. Enums are like public static final fields. It is
 * a shorthand for a simple class structure. To make use of these in
 * another class they should be imported static as in
 * import static com.jbergin.robot.Direction.*
 * @author jbergin
 *
 */
public enum Direction {
   North, West, South, East;
}
```

Java enums are really a shorthand for a class with predefined constants. The above is approximately equivalent to the following, though enums have additional options, such as methods and constructors. Either of these will work in the same way here. Numbering them (either automatically in the above or explicitly as below) in the order of left turn enables some processing.

```
public class Direction {
   public static final int North = 0;
   public static final int West = 1;
   public static final int South = 2;
   public static final int East = 3;
}
```

For example, as a robot turns left, its next direction is `(direction + 1) % 4`, where *direction* is the current direction the robot is facing.

In fact, in an enum, the values are objects, not ints, but they have an *ordinal* method that will return the values above. In addiiton, there is a *name* method, so direction.name() might return the String "North" and direction.ordinal() would then return 0;

Next we want a way to specify what are the capabilities of the simplest kind of robots. We will do this with an interface defining the basic five actions, plus a display method. We call it the UrSpecification and the simplest kind of robot will implement this. Note that we have provided comments to explain each method. These comments are in the special JavaDoc format discussed in Chapter 12. Except for *report*, this is just like the specification of UrRobot in Karel J Robot.

```
package com.jbergin.robot;

/** Defines the basic capabilities of a simple robot
 * @author jbergin
 *
 */
public interface UrSpecification {
   /** Robot moves forward one block or halts and turns off
    *  if its front is blocked, , signaling an error
    */
   public void move();

   /** Robot turns 90 degrees to its left
    */
   public void turnLeft();

   /** Robot turns off. If later sent any message except another
    * turnOff message, it will throw a RobotException
    */
   public void turnOff();

   /** Robot picks one beeper from the current corner if any
    * are available. If not, it turns off, signaling an error.
    */
   public void pickBeeper();

   /** Robot puts one beeper on the current corner if it has any
    * in its beeper-bag. If not, it turns off, signaling an error.
    */
   public void putBeeper();
```

```
   /** Robot prints its current state to System.out
    */
   public void report();
}
```

Since errors can occur in robot programs we want an exception class so that we can throw robot specific exceptions. This is a minimal subclass extension of RuntimeException, doing nothing but initializing constructors.

```
package com.jbergin.robot;

/** Exception thrown by robots when they encounter errors
 * @author jbergin
 *
 */
public class RobotException extends RuntimeException {

   public RobotException(String message) {
      super(message);
   }

   public RobotException(Throwable cause) {
      super(cause);
   }

   public RobotException(String message, Throwable cause) {
      super(message, cause);
   }

}
```

If a robot tries to move through a wall, for example, we will throw a RobotException. Only the first form of the constructor will be used here, giving a message to be printed when the exception is seen.

To avoid confusing things too much, the simplest kind of robot here is called MiniKarel. Here is the complete class in this skeleton form. Notice that some methods have TODO comments in them. This will be work for you to do. We also give a String name to each robot as we create it. This will be useful in reporting the state of a robot, especially if your robot program has more than one robot.

```
package com.jbergin.robot;

import static com.jbergin.robot.Direction.*;

/** The simplest kind of robot. A minimal implementation
 * of UrSpecification
 * @author jbergin
 *
 */
public class MiniKarel implements UrSpecification {
```

```
   private String name = null;
   private World myWorld = null;
   private int currentStreet = 1;
   private int currentAvenue = 1;
   private Direction direction = North;
   private boolean onState = true;
   private int beepers = 0;

   /** Create a robot at the origin, facing North
    * @param name A name for the robot to be used in reports
    * @param beepers the number of beepers in the beeper bag initially
    * @param world the world that this robot will be delivered to
    */
   public MiniKarel(String name, int beepers, World world){
      this(name, 1, 1, North, beepers, world);
   }
   /* Note: Use World.INFINITE to represent an infinity of beepers
    */

   /** Create a robot is an arbitrary situation
    * @param name A name for the robot to be used in reports
    * @param street the initial street
    * @param avenue the initial avenue
    * @param direction the initial Direction North, South, East, or West
    * @param beepers the number of beepers in the beeper bag initially
    * @param world the world that this robot will be delivered to
    */
   public MiniKarel(String name, int street, int avenue,
            Direction direction, int beepers, World world){
      this.name  = name;
      this.currentStreet = street;
      this.currentAvenue = avenue;
      this.direction = direction;
      this.beepers = beepers;
      this.myWorld = world;
      report();
   }

   public void move() {
      if(!onState){
         throw new RobotException(name +
               " tried to move when not running.");
      }
      if(! frontIsClear()){
         onState = false;
         report();
         throw new RobotException(name +
               " tried to walk through a wall.");
      }
      System.out.println(name + " moved.");
      if(direction == North){
         currentStreet++;
```

```
    }
    else if (direction == West){
       currentAvenue--;
    }
    else if(direction == East){
       currentAvenue--;
    }
    else{ // South
       currentStreet--;
    }
 }

 public void turnLeft() {
    if(!onState){
       throw new RobotException(name +
             " tried to turn left when not running.");
    }
    System.out.println(name + " turned left.");
    if(direction == North){
       direction = West;
    }
    else if (direction == West){
       direction = South;
    }
    else if(direction == East){
       direction = North;
    }
    else{ // South
       direction = East;
    }
 }

 public void turnOff() {
    System.out.println(name + " turned off.");
    onState = false;
 }

 public void pickBeeper() {
    if(!onState){
       throw new RobotException(name +
             " tried to pickBeeper when not running.");
    }
    if(myWorld.hasBeeper(currentStreet, currentAvenue)){
       // TODO finish this
    }
    else{
       // TODO finish this
    }
 }
```

```
   public void putBeeper() {
      if(!onState){
         throw new RobotException(name +
               " tried to putBeeper when not running.");
      }
      // TODO finish this
   }

   public void report() {
      String beepersCount = beepers<0?"infinite":
            new Integer(beepers).toString();
      String clearState = frontIsClear()?"clear.":"blocked.";
      String runningState = onState?"running.":"halted.";
      System.out.println(name + " is facing " + direction +
            " at row " + currentStreet +
            " column " + currentAvenue + " with " +
            beepersCount + " beepers. " +
            " Front is " + clearState + " Run state is " + runningState);
   }

   /** Package visible method to determine if the robot's front is clear
    * @return true if the front is clear
    */
   boolean frontIsClear() {
      return direction == North &&
         ! myWorld.wallOnAvenueNorthOf(currentStreet, currentAvenue)
      || direction == South &&
         ! myWorld.wallOnAvenueSouthOf(currentAvenue, currentStreet)
      || direction == East &&
         ! myWorld.wallOnStreetEastOf(currentStreet, currentAvenue)
      || direction == West &&
         ! myWorld.wallOnStreetWestOf(currentStreet, currentAvenue);
   }

   /** Package visible snapshot of the robot's state then this
    * object was created
    * @author jbergin
    *
    */
   class RobotState{
      // TODO finish this
   }

   /** Obtain a snapshot of the robot's state when this is invoked
    * @return the robot's instantaneous state - a snapshot
    */
   RobotState getCurrentState(){
      // TODO finish this
      return null;
   }

}
```

Note that the methods like *move* throw RobotExceptions when they can't be properly executed. Some of them need to interact with World objects as well. Each robot created is also told what world it will be delivered to. This is different from what we have seen before. A robot also prints out its progress each time it executes one of the methods.

Robots need to exist in a World, of course. The world maintains information about beepers and walls. It can also keep information about what streets and avenues are legal, and a variety of other information. Maps and Sets are discussed in Chapter 11. As you begin simply note that a *Set* is much like a mathematical set. It holds elements that you can insert and remove. A map is a set of associations between *keys* and *data*. Knowing a key gives you access to the data using the *get* method.

```
package com.jbergin.robot;

import java.awt.Point;
import java.util.HashMap;
import java.util.HashSet;
import java.util.Map;
import java.util.Set;

/** The robot world. Knows where the beepers are as well as the walls.
 * TODO make it learn the locations of all robots
 *
 */
public class World {

   public static final int INFINITE = -1;

   private Map<Point, Integer> beepers = new HashMap<Point, Integer>();
   private Set<Point> eastWestWalls = new HashSet<Point>();
   private Set<Point> northSouthWalls = new HashSet<Point>();

   /** Place a single beeper at a specific corner
    * @param street the street on which to place the beeper
    * @param avenue the avenue on which to place the beeper
    */
   public void placeBeeper(int street, int avenue){
      Point where = new Point(street, avenue);
      Integer howMany = beepers.get(where);
      if(howMany == null){
         beepers.put(where, 1);
      } else {
         beepers.put(where, howMany+1);
      }
   }

   /** Remove a single beeper from a corner. Throws and exception if
    * there is no beeper
    * there
    * @param street the street from which to remove the beeper
    * @param avenue the avenue from which to remove the beeper
    */
```

```
public void removeBeeper(int street, int avenue) {
   Point where = new Point(street, avenue);
   Integer howMany = beepers.get(where);
   if(howMany != null){
      if(howMany == 1){
         beepers.remove(where);
      } else{
         beepers.put(where, howMany = 1);
      }
   } else {
      throw new RuntimeException(
      "Tried to remove beepers from world where there were none.");
      // should not be thrown. Robots should catch this.
   }
}

/** Place a single wall segment north of a given corner
 * @param northOfStreet the street just below the new wall
 * @param blockingAvenue the avenue that will be blocked
 */
public void placeWallEastWest(int northOfStreet, int blockingAvenue){
   eastWestWalls.add(new Point(northOfStreet, blockingAvenue));

}

/** Place a single wall segment east of a given corner
 * @param blockingStreet the street that will be blocked
 * @param eastOfAvenue the avenue just west of the new wall
 */
public void placeWallNorthSouth(int blockingStreet, int eastOfAvenue){
   northSouthWalls.add(new Point(blockingStreet, eastOfAvenue));
}

/** Determine if there is a wall just East of a given corner
 * @param street the street of the corner
 * @param avenue the avenue of the corner
 * @return true if there is a wall just East of this corner
 */
public boolean wallOnStreetEastOf(int street, int avenue){
   return northSouthWalls.contains(new Point(street, avenue));
}

/** Determine if there is a wall just West of this corner
 * @param street the street of the corner
 * @param avenue the avenue of the corner
 * @return true if there is a wall just West of this corner
 */
public boolean wallOnStreetWestOf(int street, int avenue){
   return wallOnStreetEastOf(street, avenue - 1);
}
```

```
   /** Determine if there is a wall North of a given corner
    * @param street the street of the corner
    * @param avenue the avenue of the corner
    * @return true if there is a wall just North of this corner
    */
   public boolean wallOnAvenueNorthOf(int street, int avenue){
      return eastWestWalls.contains(new Point(street, avenue));
   }

   /** Determine if there is a wall just South of a given corner
    * @param street the street of the corner
    * @param avenue the avenue of the corner
    * @return true if there is a wall just South of this corner
    */
   public boolean wallOnAvenueSouthOf(int street, int avenue){
      return eastWestWalls.contains(new Point(street - 1, avenue));
   }

   /** Determine if there is one or more beepers on a given corner
    * @param street the street of the corner
    * @param avenue the avenue of the corner
    * @return true if the corner has any beepers
    */
   public boolean hasBeeper(int street, int avenue){
      return beepers.containsKey(new Point(street, avenue));
   }
}
```

These skeletons form the basis of a simulator that you can extend by doing the exercises in the next sections.

14.2 State, Building MiniRobot

The exercises here are all accessible after you have worked through Chapter 9.

Exercise 14.1 Finish the inner class RobotState within MiniKarel. It's fields should form a snapshot of the state of the containing robot when the RobotState object is created. Its constructor should initialize all fields. There should be an accessor for each field, but no setters at all.

Exercise 14.2 Finish the *currentState* method of MiniKarel by creating and returning a RobotState object.

Exercise 14.3 Complete the MiniRobot class, building all methods. Each uses currentState to get a snapshot of its own state as the basis for making its decision. Here is skeleton code for this class:

```
package com.jbergin.robot;

import static com.jbergin.robot.Direction.*;

/** A robot that has sensing capabilities in addition to the Ur spec.
 * @author jbergin
 *
 */
public class MiniRobot extends MiniKarel implements RobotSpecification {

   public MiniRobot(String name, int street, int avenue,
         Direction direction, int beepers, World world) {
      super(name, street, avenue, direction, beepers, world);
   }

   public MiniRobot(String name, int beepers, World world){
      super(name, beepers, world);
   }

   public boolean anyBeepersInBeeperBag() {
      RobotState state = getCurrentState();
      // TODO finish this
      return false;
   }

   public boolean nextToABeeper() {
      RobotState state = getCurrentState();
      // TODO finish this
      return false;
   }

   public boolean facingEast() {
      RobotState state = getCurrentState();
      // TODO finish this
      return false;
   }

   public boolean facingNorth() {
      RobotState state = getCurrentState();
      // TODO finish this
      return false;
   }

   public boolean facingSouth() {
      RobotState state = getCurrentState();
      // TODO finish this
      return false;
   }
```

```
   public boolean facingWest() {
      RobotState state = getCurrentState();
      // TODO finish this
      return false;
   }

   public boolean frontIsClear() {
      return super.frontIsClear();
   }

}
```

Exercise 14.4 Take advantage of the "direction arithmetic" discussed in the first section to remove the if statement in the turnLeft method of MiniKarel.

14.3 Arrays and I/O, Extending the World

The exercises here apply to the material in Chapter 10 especially, as well as the Primo Intermezzo.

Exercise 14.5 The constructors of MiniKarel robots weren't careful enough. It is possible to pass null as the world, for example, or to initialize a robot on an illegal corner. In reality the constructor should throw an exception when this sort of thing happens. Make these changes, and search the code for other opportunities to improve its safety of use. Which class should be responsible for knowing what is a legal corner?

The Assertion interface defines a set of assertions that can be implemented by the MiniKarel class to make it easy to make assertions about the state of robot programs as they run:

```
package com.jbergin.robot;

/** Allows an implementing robot class to make assertions about the
 * state of "this" robot. Used primarily in JUnit testing, but applicable
 * elsewhere
 * @author jbergin
 *
 */
public interface Assertion {
   /** Assert that the robot is on a given street
    * @param street the street in question
    * @throws RobotException if the robot is not on that street
    */
   public void assertOnStreet(int street) throws RobotException;

   /** Assert that a robot is on a given avenue
    * @param avenue the avenue in question
    * @throws RobotException if the robot is not on that avenue
    */
   public void assertOnAvenue(int avenue) throws RobotException;
```

```
    /** Assert that a robot has no beepers in its beeper bag
     • @throws RobotException if the robot has any beepers in
     * its beeper bag
     */
    public void assertHasNoBeepers() throws RobotException;

    /** Assert that a robot has some beepers in its beeper bag
     * @throws RobotException if there are no beepers in its beeper bag
     */
    public void assertHasBeepers() throws RobotException;

    /** Assert that the robot's front is clear
     * @throws RobotException if the front is blocked
     */
    public void assertFrontIsClear() throws RobotException;

    /** Assert that the robot is facing North
     * @throws RobotException if the robot is facing any other direction
     */
    public void assertFacingNorth() throws RobotException;

    /** Assert that the robot is facing West
     * @throws RobotException if the robot is facing any other direction
     */
    public void assertFacingWest() throws RobotException;

    /** Assert that the robot is facing South
     * @throws RobotException if the robot is facing any other direction
     */
    public void assertFacingSouth() throws RobotException;

    /** Assert that the robot is facing East
     * @throws RobotException if the robot is facing any other direction
     */
    public void assertFacingEast() throws RobotException;

    // more might be helpful
}
```

Exercise 14.6 Modify MiniKarel so that it also implements the Assertion interface. Build all of the required methods. They throw RobotExceptions if their assertion fails, but do nothing otherwise.

Exercise 14.7 Give the World class a method

```
    public void readWorld(String filename) throws IOException
```

that will read Karel J Robot world files and insert the walls and beepers specified there into the world. A sample such file appears in Section 10.3.

Here is a sample world file:

```
KarelWorld
Streets 6
Avenues 5
northsouthwalls 4 2 3
beepers 3 4 3
eastwestwalls 3 2 4
```

Except for the first line, the order of the others is irrevelant. The beepers specification first gives the corner (street, avenue) and then the number of beepers. The eastwestwalls specification gives the corner just below the first segment, here (3, 2) and, using the same street, the corner just below the last (3, 4). The northsouthwalls specification first names an avenue (careful here) and the two streets. The wall then extends just east of (2, 4) to just east of (3, 4). The result can be seen in Figure 14.1.

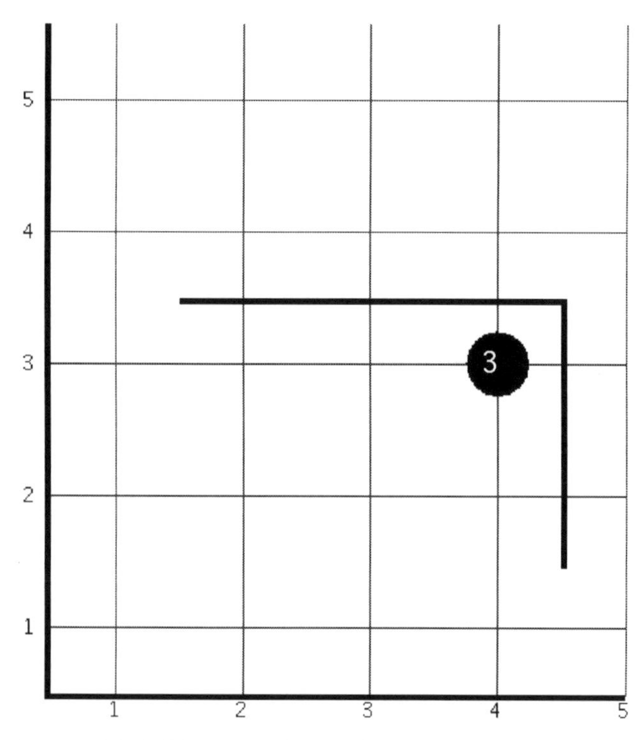

Figure 14.1. A Simple World Read From a File

Exercise 14.8 Finish the pickBeeper and putBeeper instructions. Be sure to throw RobotExceptions when the message is received in an illegal state. Don't forget to update the world in each of your methods also.

Exercise 14.9 Build the StairSweeper program of Chapter 3 and test it with this new environment.

Exercise 14.10 Give the World a method

```
public void writeWorld(String filename) throws IOException
```

that will write files compatible with the Karel J Robot World files using the current state of the world (walls and beepers). Robot are not written to such files.

Exercise 14.11 (After studying the Primo Intermezzo) Give the world a method

```
public void display(
      int startStreet,
      int startAvenue,
      int numberOfStreets,
      int numberOfAvenues)
```

that will print out an ASCII art representation of the world. Show corners as periods, walls as sequences of dashes (horizontal) or vertical bars (vertical), the beepers as *'s, and the robots using one of ^, >, V, <, according as the direction is North, East, South, or West, respectively. Here is a world with a beeper at 3, 3, a horizontal wall above 2, 1, a vertical wall East of 2, 2, and a North facing robot at the origin.

```
| .     .     .     .     .     .     .
|
| .     .     .     .     .     .     .
|
| .     .     .     .     .     .     .
|
| .     .     *     .     .     .     .
|___
| .     .  |  .     .     .     .     .
|          |
| ^     .     .     .     .     .     .
|_______________________________________

Lower-left corner is Street: 1 Avenue: 1.
```

One good way to do this is to use a two dimensional array of chars with extra spaces between streets and avenues. Note that this exercise is quite challenging.

Exercise 14.12 Give the world a way to tell the robots whether they should be printing out their progress on every move, turnLeft, etc. Currently they always do so. The robots should actually consult the world to see if they should *trace*. If not, the System.out.println commands in these methods should not be executed.

14.4 Collections, Neighbors

These exercises expand on your knowledge from Chapter 12.

The next few exercises detail changes that can form the basis of a graphic version of this, though we won't follow up on that. However, whenever a robot moves, for example, the world needs to know about it, and then inform a graphic layer to make the corresponding visual changes. This is actually how the Karel J Robot simulator is built.

Exercise 14.13 Modify MiniKarel so that it extends java.util.Observable. The notify method will have a RobotState object as the data parameter.

Exercise 14.14 Modify the methods of MiniKarel so that each method that causes a change in the state of the robot (such as move), sends itself the setChanged message and notifies all observers passing a new RobotState object.

Exercise 14.15 Modify World so that it serves as an observer of all robots. The world can itself either implement java.util.Observer or can create an object that does and to which it delegates observation.

Exercise 14.16 Give the world a Map<Robot, Point> that keeps track of where each robot is. The notify method of Observer can help you here. This map should be updated whenever any robot moves.

Exercise 14.17 Give the RobotSpecification interface a nextToARobot method to determine if the receiver is next to another robot. Implement it in MiniRobot.

Exercise 14.18 Provide for a method like *neighbors* as in Karel J Robot. Create a collection "on the fly" to hold the current neighbors of the robot executing the method. Don't forget not to include the robot itself. Think about what sort of collection you should use. It needs to be Iterable. The collection is not a permanent field but is created and returned within the method itself.

Exercise 14.19 Analyze the collections used in the World class for their appropriateness.

14.5 Documentation and Testing

These exercises apply to the material of Chapter 13.

The skeleton code was documented with JavaDoc comments. You may not have kept these comments up to date as you worked. Now is the time to do that.

Exercise 14.20 Update documentation as needed for all of the methods you have created and/or modified.

We now have enough infrastructure, especially in the Assertion interface to do a good job of testing all of the code here. A simple JUnit file has been provided that tests turnOff. We want to extend that test class to provide good tests for all of the code, especially the MiniKarel code. Here is a start on your test class (using JUnit 4).

```
package com.jbergin.robot;

import org.junit.*;
import org.junit.runner.*;
import static org.junit.Assert.*;
import static com.jbergin.robot.World.*;

public class RobotTest {
   private World world = null;
   private MiniKarel chuck = null;
   private UrSpecification sue = null;
```

```
   @Before
   public void setUp() throws Exception {
      world = new World();
      chuck = new MiniKarel("Charles", INFINITE, world);
      sue = new MiniKarel("Susan", 0, world);
   }

   public void populateWorld(){
   }

   @Test
   public void testTurnOff(){
      sue.turnOff();
      try {
         sue.move();
         fail("Should have thrown an exception");
      } catch (RuntimeException e) {
         System.out.println(e);
      }
      try {
         sue.turnLeft();
         fail("Should have thrown an exception");
      } catch (RuntimeException e) {
         System.out.println(e);
      }
      try {
         world.placeBeeper(0, 0);
         sue.pickBeeper();
         fail("Should have thrown an exception");
      } catch (RuntimeException e) {
         System.out.println(e);
      }
   }

   @Test
   public void testMoves() throws Exception{
      chuck.move();
//    chuck.assertOnStreet(1);
   }

   public static void main(String [] args){

      JUnitCore runner = new JUnitCore();
      runner.run(RobotTest.class);
   }
}
```

Exercise 14.21 Provide tests in the RobotTest JUnit test class for the move method of MiniKarel. Test the method in all possible configurations, including when the robot is not blocked and when it is, both by a boundary wall and by a wall within the world.

Exercise 14.22 Provide good tests for *turnLeft*. Check all possible turns.

Exercise 14.23 Provide tests for *pickBeeper*.

Exercise 14.24 Provide tests for *putBeeper*.

Exercise 14.25 In the same JUnit test file or in another, if you prefer, test all of the methods of MiniRobot.

14.6 Dialogs, Refactoring, and Polymorphism

This section collects exercises of a somewhat more advanced nature.

Usually the main task block creates robots with *new* invocations. It is also possible, instead, to call for a dialog when you need a robot and have the user fill in the dialog with the delivery specification parameters. This might be useful in testing a robot in a number of initial configurations.

Exercise 14.26 Create a dialog for the initialization of a MiniRobot. The dialog will have input fields for street, avenue and number of beepers. You can explore various options for inputting the direction. One that will require some research is to use a javax.swing.JList, which is like a pop-up menu. The listener for such a thing is a ListSelectionListener, which you will also need to investigate. The client of such a dialog will take the values entered to create a new MiniRobot.

Exercise 14.27 In MiniKarel a turnLeft was implemented using a sequential IF structure. Here is another way. You can provide a hash map (for example) that maps each direction to the next direction. North maps to West, etc. Then turnLeft can consult this map rather than execute an if statement. Implement this idea. Note that this map can be static, since robots can share it. It is the same for all robots and never changes.

Exercise 14.28 Note that both moving and turning depend on which direction a robot is facing in this implementation. We can delegate a lot of work to some strategy-like objects called DirectionManagers that implement this interface:

```
private interface DirectionManager{
   public void manageMove(); // precondition: It is legal to move
   public void manageTurnLeft();
   public boolean manageFrontIsClear();
   public boolean manageFacing(Direction direction);
   public void manageAssertFacing(Direction direction);
   public String directionName();
}
```

A robot will have four objects that implement this: northManager, etc. The manageTurnLeft in the northManager will set the currentManager to westManager (among other things, perhaps). The northManager will implement manageMove by increasing the street number by one, etc. The MiniKarel then delegates things like move and turnLeft to its current DirectionManager object. You might also want a map to associate managers with the corresponding directions. Note that now the "direction" implementation is really just the current direction manager. Externally the client code still uses North, etc, but internally it is the direction managers that handle everything. They have behavior, rather than just being tags. You may want to build the manager infrastructure entirely within the MiniKarel class (inner classes).

Exercise 14.29 Create a class diagram of all of the classes in your simple robot project.

Appendix

Here we will show some simplified implementations of a few of the important classes in the Java Libraries. Each of them here is rich enough to implement the Collection interface. We have left out quite a lot of things here, but the reader should get an idea about how to build such things from reading this code. Some of it is a bit complex, but most is easy.

Note as you read these that some of the methods are identical in quite different classes. That is because some of these are implemented in terms of others. In fact, the Java libraries contain partial implementations of many of these that can be extended and in which you only need to build a few of the key methods that differ according to the concept of the class, with the others being inherited from the abstract super class. We have built them anew each time, though it goes against the "say it once" principle, simply so that the reader can find everything in one place.

While we use these in sample code in the latter part of this book, the author recommends that you use these only for study, but build your own code using the official Java libraries.

1 A Dense List Implementation

Here we present a class that is a bit like the ArrayList class of the Java Libraries. It is, however, much less sophisticated. It has many of the frequently used methods. It expands as needed as you add items. An ArrayList will also shrink as you remove them, but we don't do that here. The specification of these methods is close to that of the ArrayList.

```
import java.util.Collection;
import java.util.Iterator;

public class DenseList<T> implements Iterable<T>, Collection<T>{

   private int size = 0;
   private int capacity;
   private T[] store = null;

   public DenseList(int initialCapacity){
      capacity = initialCapacity;
      store = (T[])new Object[capacity];
   }

   public DenseList(){
      this(1);
   }
```

```
public void add(int index, T value){
   if(index < 0 || index > size){
      throw new IndexOutOfBoundsException();
   }
   if(size == capacity){
      expand();
   }
   for(int i = size - 1; i>= index; --i){
      store[i + 1] = store[i];
   }
   size++;
   store[index] = value;
}

private void expand(){
   T[] newStore = (T[])new Object[2*capacity];
   for(int i = 0; i < size; ++i){
      newStore[i] = store[i];
   }
   store = newStore;
   capacity = 2 * capacity;
}

public void clear(){
   size = 0;
   store = (T[])new Object[1];
}

public boolean add(T value){
   if(size == capacity){
      expand();
   }
   size++;
   store[size-1] = value;
   return true;
}

private void indexCheck(int index){
   if(index < 0 || index >= size || size == 0){
      System.out.println("index " + index + " size " +size);
      throw new IndexOutOfBoundsException();
   }
}

public T get(int index){
   indexCheck(index);
   return store[index];
}
```

```
public Iterator<T> iterator(){
   return new Iterator<T>(){
      int nextToYield = 0;

      public boolean hasNext() {
         return nextToYield < size;
      }

      public T next() {
         T result = store[nextToYield];
         nextToYield++;
         return result;
      }

      public void remove() {
         throw new UnsupportedOperationException();
      }

   };
}

public T remove(int index){
   indexCheck(index);
   T result = store[index];
   for(int i = index; i < size-1; ++i){
      store[i] = store[i+1];
   }
   size--;
   return result;
}

public boolean remove(Object value){
   for(int i = 0; i < size; ++i)
      if(store[i].equals(value)){
         remove(i);
         return true;
      }
   return false;
}

public T set(int index, T value){
   indexCheck(index);
   T result = store[index];
   store[index] = value;
   return result;
}

public int size(){
   return size;
}
```

```
public boolean addAll(Collection<? extends T> c) {
   boolean changed = false;
   for(T value:c){
      boolean temp = add(value);
      if(temp){
         changed = true;
      }
   }
   return changed;
}

public boolean contains(Object o) {
   for(T value:this){
      if(value.equals(o)){
         return true;
      }
   }
   return false;
}

public boolean containsAll(Collection<?> c) {
   for(Object value:c){
      if(!contains(value)){
         return false;
      }
   }
   return true;
}

public boolean isEmpty() {
   return size == 0;
}

public boolean removeAll(Collection<?> c) {
   boolean changed = false;
   for(Object value: c){
      boolean temp = remove(value);
      if(temp){
         changed = true;
      }
   }
   return changed;
}
```

```
    public boolean retainAll(Collection<?> c) {
        boolean changed = false;
        DenseList<T> toRemove = new DenseList<T>();
        for(T value: this){
            if(!c.contains(value)){
                toRemove.add(value);
                changed = true;
            }
        }
        removeAll(toRemove);
        return changed;
    }

    public Object[] toArray() {
        Object[] result = new Object[size];
        int count = 0;
        for(Object value: this){
            result[count] = value;
            count++;
        }
        return result;
    }

    public <T> T[] toArray(T[] a) {
        throw new UnsupportedOperationException
              ("toArray is beyond the scope of this discussion.");
    }

}
```

Anonymous Inner Classes: To create the Iterator returned by the iterator method, we have used another feature of Java not yet seen in the book. It is possible to create an object of a subclass of an existing class or implement an existing interface without naming the new class or even giving it any purpose other than to create the one object.

In spite of its length, the body of the iterator method above has only one statement in it. this is its structure:

```
return new Iterator<T>(){
    . . .
};
```

Between the braces we see the definition of three methods of an Iterator. This creates and returns a new object, not of Iterator type (an interface in any case), but an anonymous implementing class. The braces after the parentheses are all that signifies this. The semicolon at the end is required, since this is just an object creation statement. Here Iterator is an interface, but the same trick can be used to create an object of an anonymous subclass of an existing class as well. It is even possible to pass parameters if that is needed. The syntax is, perhaps, too dense, but it is used, so you should watch for it.

2 A Linked List Implementation

Here are two classes that implement a linked list similar to the Java LinkedList. This is less sophisticated but has many of the most commonly used methods. Like the library version it is generic. A linked list is built of nodes. First the Node class.

```
public class ListNode<T>{
   private T value;
   private ListNode<T> next;

   public ListNode(T initialValue, ListNode<T> initialNext){
      value = initialValue;
      next = initialNext;
   }

   public T getValue(){
      return value;
   }

   public void setValue(T newValue){
      value = newValue;
   }

   public ListNode<T> getNext(){
      return next;
   }

   public void setNext(ListNode<T> newNextNode){
      next = newNextNode;
   }
}
```

Since this class has getters and setters for each field, it is not well encapsulated in spite of the private fields. It is really just raw stuff from which to build a list. It could be an inner class within the list itself. In a public form it is impossible to maintain invariants on it or on the class that depends on it.

Next is the list class. It has just the same interface as the DenseList class above. Compare the corresponding methods after you get a sense about each one.

This list is only singly linked, where the LinkedList class of the libraries is doubly linked. Each node has a reference to both the next and previous nodes there. With single linking some operations are necessarily more complex and inefficient. The *add* method here puts the new cell on the farthest end of the list so that it is easier to index from the "near" end. In fact, the Java definition of lists is not as well suited to a linked list of any kind as it is to a dense list. It was decided to do it this way so that they could be unified with a single API (Application Programmer Interface).

Not only is the Java LinkedList class doubly linked, but it has more sophisticated iterators than what we show here. A *ListIterator* permits movement in both directions (*previous* as well as *next*) and permits insertions, deletions and modifications to the list itself at the current location of the list iterator. A location of a list iterator should best be considered to be between elements, rather than at elements. But the simple code here only uses regular iterators, but we do show a remove method in this iterator. The iterator we will use is a small extension of Iterator that is appropriate for a singly linked list. It permits the most recently yielded item to be replaced (set) and a new node to be inserted immediately before the next item that would otherwise be yielded by next (add). This permits additions at the beginning.

```
import java.util.Iterator;

public interface ModifyingIterator<T> extends Iterator<T> {

   public void set(T element);
   public void add(T element);
}

import java.util.Collection;
import java.util.Iterator;

public class LinkList<T> implements Iterable<T>, Collection<T>{
   private ListNode<T> head = null;
   private int size = 0;

   public void clear(){
      head = null;
      size = 0;
   }

   public int size(){
      return size;
   }

   public boolean add(T value){
      ListNode<T> node = head;
      if (node == null){
         head = new ListNode<T>(value, head);
         size++;
         return true;
      }
      ListNode<T> listNode = node;
      while (listNode.getNext() != null){
         listNode = listNode.getNext();
      }
      listNode.setNext(new ListNode<T>(value, null));
      size++;
      return true;
   }

   private void indexCheck(int index){
      if(index < 0 || index >= size || size == 0){
         throw new IndexOutOfBoundsException();
      }
   }
```

```
public T get(int index){
   indexCheck(index);
   T result = null;
   ListNode<T> listNode = head;
   for(int i = 0; i < index; ++i){
      listNode = listNode.getNext();
   }
   result = listNode.getValue();
   return result;
}

public void add(int index, T value){
   indexCheck(index);
   if(index == 0){
      head = new ListNode<T>(value, head);
      size++;
      return;
   }
   ListNode<T> listNode = head;
   for(int i = 0; i < index-1; ++i){
      listNode = listNode.getNext();
   }
   listNode.setNext(new ListNode<T>(value, listNode.getNext()));
   size++;
}

public T set(int index, T value){
   indexCheck(index);
   T result = null;
   ListNode<T> listNode = head;
   for(int i = 0; i < index; ++i){
      listNode = listNode.getNext();
   }
   result = listNode.getValue();
   listNode.setValue(value);
   return result;
}

public boolean remove(Object value){
   ListNode<T> aNode = head;
   if(aNode == null){
      return false;
   }
   ListNode<T> listNode = aNode;
   if(listNode.getValue().equals(value)){
      head = listNode.getNext();
      size--;
      return true;
   }
```

```
      while(listNode.getNext() != null){
         ListNode<T> nextNode = listNode.getNext();
         if(nextNode.getValue().equals(value)){
            listNode.setNext(nextNode.getNext());
            size--;
            return true;
         }
         if(nextNode.getNext() == null){
            return false;
         }
         listNode = nextNode;
      }
      return false;
   }

   public T remove(int index){
      T result = null;
      if(index < 0 || index >= size){
         throw new IndexOutOfBoundsException();
      }
      if(size == 0){
         return null;
      }
      ListNode<T> listNode = head;
      if(index == 0){
         size--;
         head = listNode.getNext();
         return listNode.getValue();
      }
      for(int i = 0; i < index - 1; ++i){
         listNode = listNode.getNext();
      }
      ListNode<T> nextNode = listNode.getNext();
      result = nextNode.getValue();
      listNode.setNext(nextNode.getNext());
      size--;
      return result;
   }

   public ModifyingIterator<T> iterator(){
      return new Iterator<T>(){
         ListNode<T> nextToYield = head;

         public boolean hasNext() {
            return nextToYield != null;
         }

         public T next() {
            T result = nextToYield.getValue();
            nextToYield = nextToYield.getNext();
            return result;
         }
```

```
        public void remove() {
            if(!okToRemove){
                throw new IllegalStateException(
                    "Iterator illegal state to remove.");
            }
            okToRemove = false;
            if(previous == null){
                return;
            }
            if(previous == head && nextToYield == previous.getNext()){
                previous = head = nextToYield;
                size--;
                return;
            }
            ListNode<T> node = nextToYield;
            previous.setNext(node);
            size--;
        }

        public void set(T element) {
            if(previous.getNext() == nextToYield){
                previous.setValue(element);
            }
            else{
                previous.getNext().setValue(element);
            }
        }

        public void add(T element){
            if(previous == nextToYield){
                head = previous = nextToYield =
                         new ListNode<T>(element, head);
            }
            else if(previous.getNext() == nextToYield){
                previous.setNext(new ListNode<T>(element, nextToYield));
            }
            else{
                previous = previous.getNext();
                previous.setNext(new ListNode<T>(element, nextToYield));
            }
            size++;
        }

    };
}
```

```
public boolean addAll(Collection<? extends T> c) {
   boolean changed = false;
   for(T value:c){
      boolean temp = add(value);
      if(temp){
         changed = true;
      }
   }
   return changed;
}

public boolean contains(Object o) {
   for(T value:this){
      if(value.equals(o)){
         return true;
      }
   }
   return false;
}

public boolean containsAll(Collection<?> c) {
   for(Object value:c){
      if(!contains(value)){
         return false;
      }
   }
   return true;
}

public boolean isEmpty() {
   return size == 0;
}

public boolean removeAll(Collection<?> c) {
   boolean changed = false;
   for(Object value: c){
      boolean temp = remove(value);
      if(temp){
         changed = true;
      }
   }
   return changed;
}

public boolean retainAll(Collection<?> c) {
   boolean changed = false;
   DenseList<T> toRemove = new DenseList<T>();
   for(T value: this){
      if(!c.contains(value)){
         toRemove.add(value);
         changed = true;
      }
```

```
      } // end for
      removeAll(toRemove);
      return changed;
   }

   public Object[] toArray() {
      Object[] result = new Object[size];
      int count = 0;
      for(Object value: this){
         result[count] = value;
         count++;
      }
      return result;
   }

   public <T> T[] toArray(T[] a) {
      throw new UnsupportedOperationException
            ("toArray is beyond the scope of this discussion.");
   }

}
```

3 A Tree Set Implementation

Here we present a very simple binary search tree. It makes no attempt to balance the tree, so can behave poorly if you add things in an order that puts it out of balance. The tree appears after the necessary node class. These nodes, like the list nodes are not well encapsulated. Note that the only real difference between list and tree nodes is the number of "next" references, here called children. The overall effect of this class is to create a sorted set-like class.

```
public class TreeNode<T> {

   private T value;
   private TreeNode<T> leftChild;
   private TreeNode<T> rightChild;


   public TreeNode(T value, TreeNode<T> left, TreeNode<T> right){
      this.value = value;
      this.leftChild = left;
      this.rightChild = right;
   }

   public T getValue() {
      return value;
   }

   public void setValue(T value) {
      this.value = value;
   }
```

```
   public TreeNode<T> getLeftChild() {
      return leftChild;
   }

   public void setLeftChild(TreeNode<T> leftChild) {
      this.leftChild = leftChild;
   }

   public TreeNode<T> getRightChild() {
      return rightChild;
   }

   public void setRightChild(TreeNode<T> rightChild) {
      this.rightChild = rightChild;
   }

}
```

Since this class has getters and setters for each field, it is not well encapsulated in spite of the private fields. It is really just raw stuff from which to build a tree. It could be an inner class within the tree itself.

Note that while this implements the idea of a set, we only implement the Collection interface.

```
import java.util.Collection;
import java.util.Comparator;
import java.util.Iterator;

/** A class similar to, but simpler than a java TreeSet.
 * It is not balanced, however.
 * @author jbergin
 *
 * @param <T> the element type of the data
 */
public class BinaryTreeSet<T> implements Iterable<T>, Collection<T>{

   private Comparator<T> comparator;
   private int size = 0;
   private TreeNode<T> root = null;


   public BinaryTreeSet(){ // requires T implement Comparable<T>
      this.comparator = new Comparator<T>(){

         public int compare(T o1, T o2) {

            return ((Comparable<T>)o1).compareTo(o2);
         }

      };
   }
```

```
public BinaryTreeSet(Comparator<T> comparator){
   this.comparator = comparator;
}

private void fill(TreeNode<T> node, DenseList<T> list){
   if(node.getLeftChild() != null){
      fill(node.getLeftChild(), list);
   }
   list.add(node.getValue());
   if(node.getRightChild() != null){
      fill(node.getRightChild(), list);
   }
}

public Iterator<T> iterator() {
   DenseList<T> copies = new DenseList<T>(size);
   fill(root, copies);
   return copies.iterator();
}

public boolean add(T o) {
   if(root == null){
      root = new TreeNode<T>(o, null, null);
      size++;
      return true;
   }
   TreeNode<T> node = root;
   TreeNode<T> parent = node;
   while (node != null && ! o.equals(node.getValue())){
      parent = node;
      if(comparator.compare(o, node.getValue()) < 0){
         node = node.getLeftChild();
      }
      else{
         node = node.getRightChild();
      }
   }
   if(node != null){
      return false;
   }
   node = new TreeNode<T>(o, null, null);
   if(comparator.compare(o, parent.getValue()) < 0){
      parent.setLeftChild(node);
   }
   else{
      parent.setRightChild(node);
   }
   size++;
   return true;
}
```

```
   public boolean addAll(Collection<? extends T> c) {
      boolean changed = false;
      for(T value:c){
         boolean temp = add(value);
         if(temp){
            changed = true;
         }
      }
      return changed;
   }

   public void clear() {
      root = null;
      size = 0;
   }

   public boolean contains(Object o) {
      if (root == null){
         return false;
      }
      try{
         TreeNode<T> node = root;
         while(node != null){
            T value = node.getValue();
            if(value.equals(o)){
               return true;
            }
            if(comparator.compare((T)o, value) < 0){
               node = node.getLeftChild();
            }
            else{
               node = node.getRightChild();
            }
         }
      }
      catch(Exception e){
         return false;
      }
      return false;
   }

   public boolean isEmpty() {
      return size == 0;
   }

   private TreeNode<T> promote(TreeNode<T> node){
      if(node.getLeftChild() != null){
         node.setValue(node.getLeftChild().getValue());
         node.setLeftChild(promote(node.getLeftChild()));
         return node;
      }
```

```
      else if(node.getRightChild() != null){
         node.setValue(node.getRightChild().getValue());
         node.setRightChild(promote(node.getRightChild()));
         return node;
      }
      return null;
   }

   public boolean remove(Object o) {
      if(root == null){
         return false;
      }
      if(root.getValue().equals(o)){
         if(root.getLeftChild() != null){
            root.setValue(root.getLeftChild().getValue());
            root.setLeftChild(promote(root.getLeftChild()));
         }
         else if(root.getRightChild() != null){
            root.setValue(root.getRightChild().getValue());
            root.setRightChild(promote(root.getRightChild()));
         }
         else root = null;
         size--;
         return true;
      }
      TreeNode<T> node = root;
      TreeNode<T> parent = node;
      boolean wasLeft = false;
      try{
         while(node != null && !node.getValue().equals(o)){
            int compare = comparator.compare((T)o, node.getValue());
            if(compare < 0){
               parent = node;
               node = node.getLeftChild();
               wasLeft = true;
            }
            else if(compare > 0){
               parent = node;
               node = node.getRightChild();
               wasLeft = false;
            }
         }
         if(node == null){
            return false; // not found
         }
         if(wasLeft){
            parent.setLeftChild(promote(node));
         }
         else{
            parent.setRightChild(promote(node));
         }
```

```
            size--;
            return true;

        }
        catch(Exception e){
            return false;
        }
    }

    public boolean removeAll(Collection<?> c) {
        boolean changed = false;
        for(Object value: c){
            boolean temp = remove(value);
            if(temp){
                changed = true;
            }
        }
        return changed;
    }

    public boolean retainAll(Collection<?> c) {
        boolean changed = false;
        DenseList<T> toRemove = new DenseList<T>();
        for(T value: this){
            if(!c.contains(value)){
                toRemove.add(value);
                changed = true;
            }
        }
        removeAll(toRemove);
        return changed;
    }

    public int size() {
        return size;
    }

    public boolean containsAll(Collection<?> c) {
        for(Object value:c){
            if(!contains(value)){
                return false;
            }
        }
        return true;
    }

    public Object[] toArray() {
        Object[] result = new Object[size];
        int count = 0;
        for(Object value: this){
            result[count] = value;
            count++;
```

```
      } // end for
      return result;
   }

   public <T> T[] toArray(T[] a) {
      throw new UnsupportedOperationException
            ("toArray is beyond the scope of this discussion.");
   }

}
```

4 A Hashed Set Implementation

Here we show a set built as a hash map. It has the same interface as the above, except for the extra constructor of the tree set implementation. Notice that we are illustrating the idea of hashing here, but not the idea of a Map.

```
import java.util.Collection;
import java.util.Iterator;

/** This is something like Java's HashSet, though implemented directly
 * rather than through a HashMap. It is to demonstrate a simple "separate
 * chaining" hash mechanism
 * Important Caveat: This is not adaptable in size. As you add, the
 * performance gets worse.
 * For the best performance, make "buckets" close to your expected
 * capacity.
 * @author jbergin
 *
 * @param <T> the element type to be held in the set
 */
public class HashTable<T> implements Iterable<T>, Collection<T>{

   private DenseList<DenseList<T>> bucketTable = null;
   private int size = 0;

   public HashTable(int buckets){
      bucketTable = new DenseList<DenseList<T>>(buckets);
      for(int i = 0; i < buckets; ++i){
         bucketTable.add(null); // expand the size
      }
   }

   private int doHash(T element){
      return element.hashCode() % bucketTable.size();
   }
```

```
   public Iterator<T> iterator() {
      return new Iterator<T>(){

         private Iterator<T> currentIterator = null;
         private int count = 0;

         public boolean hasNext() {
            if(currentIterator == null || !currentIterator.hasNext()){
               while(count < bucketTable.size() &&
                     (currentIterator == null
                     || !currentIterator.hasNext())){
                  if(bucketTable.get(count) == null){
                     count++;
                     continue;
                  }
                  currentIterator = bucketTable.get(count).iterator();
                  count++;
               }
            }
            if(count > bucketTable.size()){
               return false;
            }
            if(currentIterator == null || !currentIterator.hasNext()){
               return false;
            }
            return true;
         }

         public T next() {
            return currentIterator.next();
         }

         public void remove() {
            throw new UnsupportedOperationException
                     ("remove not implemented.");
         }
      };
   }

   private int contains(DenseList<T> list, T element){
      int result = -1;
      int count = 0;
      for(T value:list){
         if(value.equals(element)){
            result = count;
            break;
         }
         count++;
      }
      return result;
   }
```

```
public boolean add(T o) {
   int where = doHash(o);
   DenseList<T> list = bucketTable.get(where);
   if (list == null){
      list = new DenseList<T>();
      bucketTable.set(where, list);
   }
   where = contains(list, o);
   if(where >= 0){
      return false; // don't change it
   }
   list.add(o);
   size++;
   return true;
}

public boolean addAll(Collection<? extends T> c) {
   boolean changed = false;
   for(T value:c){
      boolean temp = add(value);
      if(temp){
         changed = true;
      }
   }
   return changed;
}

public void clear() {
   size = 0;
   bucketTable = new DenseList<DenseList<T>>();
}

public boolean contains(Object o) {
   try{
      T to = (T)o; // might fail
      int where = doHash(to);
      DenseList<T> list = bucketTable.get(where);
      if (list == null){
         return false;
      }
      where = contains(list, to);
      return where >= 0;
   }
   catch(Exception e){
      System.out.println(e);
      return false;
   }
}
```

```
   public boolean containsAll(Collection<?> c) {
      for(Object value:c){
         if(!contains(value)){
            return false;
         }
      }
      return true;
   }

   public boolean isEmpty() {
      return size == 0;
   }

   public boolean remove(Object o) {
      try{
         T to = (T)o;
         int where = doHash(to);
         DenseList<T> list = bucketTable.get(where);
         if (list == null){
            return false;
         }
         boolean wasThere = list.remove(to);
         if (wasThere){
            size--;
         }
         return wasThere;
      }
      catch(Exception e){
         System.out.println(e);
         return false;
      }
   }

   public boolean removeAll(Collection<?> c) {
      boolean changed = false;
      for(Object value: c){
         boolean temp = remove(value);
         if(temp){
            changed = true;
         }
      }
      return changed;
   }

   public boolean retainAll(Collection<?> c) {
      boolean changed = false;
      DenseList<T> toRemove = new DenseList<T>();
      for(T value: this){
         if(!c.contains(value)){
            toRemove.add(value);
            changed = true;
         }
```

```
      } // end for
      removeAll(toRemove);
      return changed;
   }

   public int size() {
      return size;
   }

   public Object[] toArray() {
      Object[] result = new Object[size];
      int count = 0;
      for(Object value: this){
         result[count] = value;
         count++;
      }
      return result;
   }

   public <T> T[] toArray(T[] a) {
      throw new UnsupportedOperationException
         ("toArray is beyond the scope of this discussion.");
   }

}
```

Index of Terms

Classes Discussed In This Book

Made in the USA
Middletown, DE
15 January 2018